MICROSOFT® OFFICE ACCESS™ 2007

QuickSteps

JOHN CRONAN

BOBBI SANDBERG

New York Chicago San Francisco
Lisbon London Madrid Mexico City
Milan New Delhi San Juan
Seoul Singapore Sydney Toronto

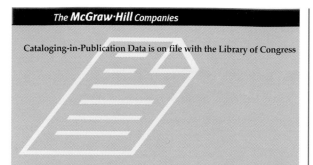

The McGraw·Hill Companies

Cataloging-in-Publication Data is on file with the Library of Congress

McGraw-Hill books are available at special quantity discounts to use as premiums and sales promotions, or for use in corporate training programs. For more information, please write to the Director of Special Sales, Professional Publishing, McGraw-Hill, Two Penn Plaza, New York, NY 10121-2298. Or contact your local bookstore.

Information has been obtained by McGraw-Hill from sources believed to be reliable. However, because of the possibility of human or mechanical error by our sources, McGraw-Hill, or others, McGraw-Hill does not guarantee the accuracy, adequacy, or completeness of any information and is not responsible for any errors or omissions or the results obtained from the use of such information.

MICROSOFT® OFFICE ACCESS™ 2007 QUICKSTEPS

1234567890 CCI CCI 01987

ISBN-13: 978-0-07-226371-8
ISBN-10:   0-07-226371-7

SPONSORING EDITOR / Roger Stewart

EDITORIAL SUPERVISOR / Patty Mon

PROJECT MANAGER / Vasundhara Sawhney

ACQUISITIONS COORDINATOR / Carly Stapleton

SERIES CREATORS AND EDITORS / Marty and Carole Matthews

TECHNICAL EDITOR / Marty Matthews

COPY EDITOR / Lisa McCoy

PROOFREADER / Raina Trivedi

INDEXER / Robert Swanson

PRODUCTION SUPERVISOR / Jim Kussow

COMPOSITION / International Typesetting and Composition

ILLUSTRATION / International Typesetting and Composition

ART DIRECTOR, COVER / Jeff Weeks

COVER DESIGN / Pattie Lee

SERIES DESIGN / Bailey Cunningham

To Aunt Georgie and Aunt Pat…

…you've been super aunts, substitute grandmothers, and
have been there for me for as long as I can remember.
What can I say—you're the greatest!

—John Cronan

To Sam, Royce, Joseph, Helene, Carissa, Gabriel, and Colette…

…remember to follow your dreams and they will take you anywhere!
Thank you for growing and sharing your lives with me.

—Bobbie Sandberg (Grandma Bobbi)

About the Authors

John Cronan was introduced to computers in college over 30 years ago, and has maintained a close relationship with them in personal and professional endeavors ever since. Over the years John has worked on dozens of books and software product manuals, performed several technical reviews of other author's works, runs his own technical services business, and reclaims furniture for his wife's antiques business.

Recent books he has worked on and published by McGraw-Hill include *Microsoft Office Excel 2007 QuickSteps*, *Build an eBay Business QuickSteps*, and *Adobe Acrobat 7 QuickSteps*.

John and his wife, Faye, (and cat, Little Buddy) live in the historic mill town of Everett, WA.

Bobbi Sandberg has been working (and playing) with computers for more than 40 years. As a retired CPA and small business consultant, she teaches, writes about, and discusses computers with anyone who will listen. She has written dozens of software "how-to" worksheets, runs her own small business advisory company, and teaches at a local community college as well as a senior center. Her recent books for McGraw-Hill include *Quicken 2006 QuickSteps* and *Quicken 2007 Personal Finance Software QuickSteps* written with Marty Matthews.

Bobbi lives on an island in the Pacific Northwest surround by trees and a host of inquisitive deer.

Contents at a Glance

Chapter 1 **Stepping into Access** 1
Start Access, learn about the Navigation Pane and the Office 2007
ribbon, find and open databases, customize Access

1

Chapter 2 **Creating Databases and Tables** 25
Plan a database, use templates to create a database, create a table,
add a primary key, define relationships, enforce referential integrity

2

Chapter 3 **Modifying Tables and Fields** 45
Rename databases and tables, change field names, choose data types,
add input masks, add a multivalued field

3

Chapter 4 **Working in the Table** 65
Enter data, move through records, delete records, find and replace
data, check spelling, import data, use Outlook to collect data

4

Chapter 5 **Retrieving Information** 95
Sort records in tables and forms, filter data, use operators, create
a simple query, use the Expression Builder

5

Chapter 6 **Creating Forms and Using Controls** 115
Create forms using several methods, add fields to a form, add bound
and unbound controls, modify the form design

6

Chapter 7 **Working with Reports** 143
Create reports using several methods; group data; calculate values
in report; create a summary report and create labels

7

Chapter 8 **Preparing Your Data for Presentation** 161
Modify images, add charts and graphics, modify forms and reports,
apply themes and rich text, preview data before printing

8

Chapter 9 **Securing and Administrating Access** 183
Learn about security, create certificates and a trusted location,
create passwords, compact and repair a database, back up data

9

Chapter 10 **Extending Access** 201
Analyze data using Crosstab queries and PivotTables, create
a PivotChart, export and link data, learn about SharePoint

10

Index 221

Contents

Acknowledgments..xii

Introduction xiii

Chapter 1 **Stepping into Access** 1
   ✐ Understanding an Access Database 2
   Start Access 2
       Open Access...2
       ✐ Understanding the Ribbon 5
       Open a Database 6
       Use the Navigation Pane 9
       ✐ Understanding Access Objects 10
       Open Older Databases 11
       ✐ Understanding Access File Compatibility 12
       Change the Default File Format in Access 14
       Find a Database...14
   Personalize Access 15
       Customize the Quick Access Toolbar...15
       ✪ Using the Keyboard in Access 18
       Display and Use Ribbon Shortcut Keys..18
       Change How You View Objects..18
   Get Help 21
       Open Help...22
       Use the Access Help Window 22
   End Your Access Session 24
       Close a Database 24
       Exit Access 24

Chapter 2 **Creating Databases and Tables** 25
   ✪ Planning a Database 26
   Design a Database 26
       Use Database Templates 26
       Build a Database on Your Own...32
       Close a Database After Creating It 32
       ✐ Using Datasheet and Design Views 33
   Build the Framework with Tables 33
       Create a Table by Entering Data 33
       Define Field Names in Your Table...34
       Create a New Empty Table..35
       Construct a Table in Design View..35
       Create a Table from a Table Template 38
       Assign a Primary Key...38
       ✐ Understanding the Primary Key 40
       Add Identifying Information to Your Database 40

Identify Relationships..41
  Define Relationships 42
  Relate Tables in the Relationships Tab.............................42
  🏵 Understanding Referential Integrity..............................43
  Enforce Referential Integrity 43

Chapter 3 **Modifying Tables and Fields**............................... 45

Make Basic Changes to Tables and Fields................................45
  Delete a Table...46
  🌐 Renaming an Access Database.......................................47
  Rename a Table..47
  🌐 Switching Views...48
  Change Field Names 48
Fine-Tune the Fields 48
  Change a Data Type in Datasheet View 49
  Change a Data Type in Design View.................................50
  🏵 Understanding Restrictions When Changing Data Types.......51
  Change Display of Data Through the Format Property.............51
  🏵 Understanding Input Masks..54
  Create a Pattern for Data Entry with Input Masks 54
  🌐 Creating a Custom Input Mask.......................................55
  Establish a Field's Default Value 55
  Limit Field Values with a Validation Rule 56
  Require Entry but Allow a Zero-Length String...............57
  Use the Caption Field Property 58
  Index a Data Field 59
  Add Smart Tags...59
  Use the Lookup Wizard 60
  🏵 Deciding to Use a Multivalued Field 63

Chapter 4 **Working in the Table**... 65

Enter and Edit Data 67
  Enter Data in an Existing Table...67
  Use Keyboard Shortcuts in a Table...................................68
  🌐 Moving Through Records...70
  Copy and Move Data 70
  🌐 Selecting Records, Fields, and Columns with the Mouse.......72
  Delete Records and Columns...73
  🌐 Calculating Data in a Field...74
  Find and Replace Text 74
  Verify Spelling 76
  Modify Automatic Corrections 78
Acquire Data..78
  Import Data from Outside Sources 79
  Collect Data from Outlook Messages 85
Arrange a Table 89
  Insert Columns..89
  Adjust Column Width...90
  Move and Rename Columns...91
  🌐 Changing How the Current Datasheet Looks 92
  Lock and Unlock Columns...93
  Adjust Row Height..94

Chapter 5 **Retrieving Information**.. 95
  Sort Data..95
    Sort Records in a Table...96
    Sort Records in a Form..97
  Filter Data..98
    ✔ Choosing a Filter..99
    Filter by Selecting..99
    Filter for an Input..101
    Filter by Form..102
    Use Operators and Wildcards in Criteria..............................102
    🕑 Removing, Clearing, or Reapplying a Filter.........................104
    Use Advanced Filters...105
  Work with Queries..107
    Create a Simple Query with a Wizard.....................................107
    Create or Modify a Query in Design View.............................108
    View the Query Results..111
    Save and Close a Query...111
    🕑 Using the Expression Builder...112
    Set Query Properties..113

Chapter 6 **Creating Forms and Using Controls** 115
  Create Forms...115
    Use the Form Tool...116
    Work with the Split Form Tool..116
    🕑 Setting the Location of the Splitter Bar................................119
    Create a Form with Multiple Records.....................................119
    🕑 Creating a Multiple-Table Form...120
    Employ the Form Wizard...120
    ✔ Understanding Form Views..122
    Use the Blank Form Tool..123
    Create a Form in Design View...124
    🕑 Adding Fields with the Field List...125
    Add Elements to a Form..127
    🕑 Selecting a Form Section...130
  Use Controls...130
    Add Bound Controls...130
    Add Unbound Controls..134
    Copy or Delete a Control..136
    Select Controls..137
    Rearrange Controls..138
    ✔ Understanding Control Layouts...139
    Modify Controls..140
    ✔ Navigating in a Data Entry Form...142

Chapter 7 **Working with Reports** 143
  Create Reports..143
    🕑 Viewing Reports..144
    Use the Report Tool to Create a Report.................................145
    Use the Report Wizard to Create a Report.............................145

⊘ Understanding Grouping in Reports..148
Use the Blank Report Tool 149
Create a Report in Design View 149
Modify Reports...151
Format a Report 151
⊗ Working with Data in Reports 153
Use the Group, Sort, And Total Pane 153
Calculate a Value...157
⊗ Accomplishing Common Tasks in Reports..158
Set Group Headers and Footers in a Report 158
Create a Summary Report 158
Create Labels 159

Chapter 8 Preparing Your Data for Presentation 161

Improve the Data's Appearance 161
Modify Images 162
Use Conditional Formatting..163
Add a Chart 164
Use Graphics..168
Modify the Form or Report Design 170
⊘ Understanding Formatting Rules..171
⊗ Using Windows Themes...173
Work with Rich Text Formatting 173
Print Your Data 175
Set Up the Print Job 175
Review Data Before Printing...178
Output the Print Job 180

Chapter 9 Securing and Administrating Access 183

⊘ Understanding Access 2007 Security 184
Apply Security to an Access Database 184
Create a Trusted Location...184
Create and Use Certificates to Trust Databases.................................185
⊘ Creating Passwords 188
Encrypt a Database 188
Remove Database Objects from View 189
⊗ **Keeping Data Safe** 190
Secure the Database with the User-Level Security Wizard....................190
⊘ Understanding the User-Level Security Model....................................192
Administer a Database 196
Document a Database 196
Compact and Repair a Database 198
⊘ Troubleshooting the Compact And Repair Database Utility................199
Back Up a Database 199

Chapter 10 Extending Access 201

Use Advanced Data Analysis Tools..202
Create a Crosstab Query with a Wizard 202
⊗ Sorting and Filtering a Crosstab Query...204
Create a PivotTable..204
Create a PivotChart..206

⬦ Understanding Drop Zones in PivotTables..209
   Analyze Database Performance and Design..209
⬦ Understanding SharePoint 212
Share Data..212
⬰ Merging Data with Microsoft Word...213
   Export Access Data 213
   Link Tables...215
   Add a Hyperlink Field to an Existing Table 216
⬰ Creating a Hyperlink to a File or Web Page...217
   Create a Welcome Form 217

Index 221

Acknowledgments

Thanks to all who contributed to the success of this book!

Lisa McCoy, copy editor, combined the writing styles of two authors into one cohesive and consistent work, and also acted as a "free" technical editor.

Marty Matthews, technical editor, combined with this role to his writing efforts, ensured the technical accuracy of each chapter.

Robert Swanson, indexer, provided tremendous value to the reader by adding to the overall usability of the book.

Carly Stapleton, acquisitions coordinator and **Vasundhara Sawhney**, project manager, provided the behind-the-scenes project management and ensured chapters moved along at the scheduled pace.

Roger Stewart, sponsoring editor, promoted the QuickSteps series from its inception and helped ensure its continued success.

Introduction

QuickSteps books are recipe books for computer users. They answer the question "how do I…" by providing a quick set of steps to accomplish the most common tasks with a particular operating system or application.

The sets of steps are the central focus of the book. QuickSteps sidebars show how to quickly perform many small functions or tasks that support the primary functions. QuickFacts, Notes, Tips, and Cautions augment the steps, and are presented in a separate column to not interrupt the flow of the steps. The introductions are minimal and other narrative is kept brief. Numerous full-color illustrations and figures, many with callouts, support the steps.

QuickSteps books are organized by function and the tasks needed to perform that function. Each function is a chapter. Each task, or "How To," contains the steps needed for accomplishing the function along with the relevant Notes, Tips, Cautions, and screenshots. You can easily find the tasks you want to perform through:

- The table of contents, which lists the functional areas (chapters) and tasks in the order they are presented
- A How To list of tasks on the opening page of each chapter
- The index, which provides an alphabetical list of the terms that are used to describe the functions and tasks
- Color-coded tabs for each chapter or functional area with an index to the tabs in the Contents at a Glance (just before the Table of Contents)

Conventions Used in this Book

Microsoft Office Access 2007 QuickSteps uses several conventions designed to make the book easier for you to follow. Among these are

- A 🌎 or a 🪐 in the table of contents or the How To list in each chapter references a QuickSteps or QuickFacts sidebar in a chapter.

- **Bold type** is used for words on the screen that you are to do something with, like "…click the **Office Button** and click **Save As**."

- *Italic type* is used for a word or phrase that is being defined or otherwise deserves special emphasis.

- <u>Underlined type</u> is used for text that you are to type from the keyboard.

- SMALL CAPITAL LETTERS are used for keys on the keyboard such as ENTER and SHIFT.

- When you are expected to enter a command, you are told to press the key(s). If you are to enter text or numbers, you are told to type them.

How to...

- *Understanding an Access Database*
- • *Open Access*
- *Understanding the Ribbon*
- • *Open a Database*
- • *Use the Navigation Pane*
- *Understanding Access Objects*
- • *Open Older Databases*
- *Understanding Access File Compatibility*
- • *Change the Default File Format in Access*
- • *Find a Database*
- • *Customize the Quick Access Toolbar*
- *Using the Keyboard in Access*
- • *Display and Use Ribbon Shortcut Keys*
- • *Change How You View Objects*
- • *Open Help*
- • *Use the Access Help Window*
- • *Close a Database*
- • *Exit Access*

Chapter 1

Stepping into Access

Microsoft Office Access 2007 provides a database capability for the Office suite of programs. While maintaining the core features and functionality of Access from years past, this version adds features that support everyone—from the casual user who simply wants to organize and track household assets to the designer who wants easier ways to create custom forms and reports. If you have used earlier versions of Access, one of your first indications that this version is something out of the ordinary is your first look at the new *ribbon* and other user interface items (this collection of screen elements allows you to use and navigate the program). Gone is the familiar menu structure you might have grown accustomed to with Microsoft Office programs, replaced with a new organizational scheme to better connect tools to tasks.

UNDERSTANDING AN ACCESS DATABASE

The container for data and the Access objects that manage the data is a file called a Microsoft Office Access database that includes an .accdb file extension, for example, MyDatabase.accdb (previous versions used an .mdb file extension, which you can convert to the new file format). A *database*, in its simplest form, is just a collection, or list, of data on a related subject—for example, the pertinent information on a publisher's books, such as the title, author, ISBN number, selling price, and the number of books sold and on order.

A database can contain a single collection of data, or it can be divided among sub-collections that are related by common categories. A database can also be utilized in different roles. You can be a database *user*, who adds and/or retrieves data, such as account information in a large corporate system. Or you can be a database *designer*, who creates the structure of the database for others to use. In most cases, you're a bit of both: for example, you might create your own design for keeping track of your music collection and enter the information yourself.

NOTE

This book assumes that you have Access 2007 installed on the Microsoft Windows Vista operating system. Procedures and illustrations used throughout the book reflect this assumption. If you have Windows XP as your operating system, be aware there might be procedural differences in performing certain tasks and some illustrations might not exactly reflect what you see on your screen.

In addition, a new database file format allows for new features, including a new Attachment data type that accommodates multiple files attached to a single record (for example, you can add several photos of a house for sale).

This chapter explains how to open Access and a database file, use the ribbon and the new user interface, and then personalize settings to meet your needs. You will learn how to get help—online and offline—and see how to end an Access session.

Start Access

You can start Access as you would any other program—using the Start menu, using the keyboard, and using shortcuts you have created. Existing Access databases can be opened in similar ways, and recently used databases can be quickly opened from within Access.

Many programs, such as Microsoft Office Excel and Word, open with a new, blank file ready for you to start entering text or data. Access does not do this, as you are more likely to use a template to assist you in setting up a new database. You will see how to open existing databases in this chapter and how to create new databases in Chapter 2.

Open Access

You can open Access using standard features that were set up by Windows when you installed the program, or you can use other shortcuts more to your own way of computing.

OPEN ACCESS FROM THE START MENU

Normally, the surest way to start Access is to use the Start menu.

1. Start your computer if it is not running, and log on to Windows if necessary.

2. Click Start. The Start menu opens. If listed, click **Microsoft Office Access 2007** in the lower portion of the Start menu. Programs you've opened recently will be listed here.

   –Or–

   Click **All Programs**, click **Microsoft Office**, and click **Microsoft Office Access 2007**.

3. In either case, the Access window opens with the Getting Started page displayed, as shown in Figure 1-1.

OPEN ACCESS FROM THE KEYBOARD

1. Press the Windows flag key ⊞ (typically, between the **CTRL** and **ALT** keys), or press **CTRL+ESC**.

2. Press **A** in the Start Search box (Microsoft Windows Vista only).

3. Press **DOWN ARROW** until Microsoft Office Access is selected; press **ENTER** to open it.

CREATE A SHORTCUT TO START ACCESS

1. Click **Start**, click **All Programs**, and click **Microsoft Office**.

2. Right-click **Microsoft Office Access 2007** to display a context menu and perform one of the following actions:

   ● Click **Pin To Start Menu** to add a shortcut to the upper-left "permanent" area of the Start menu.

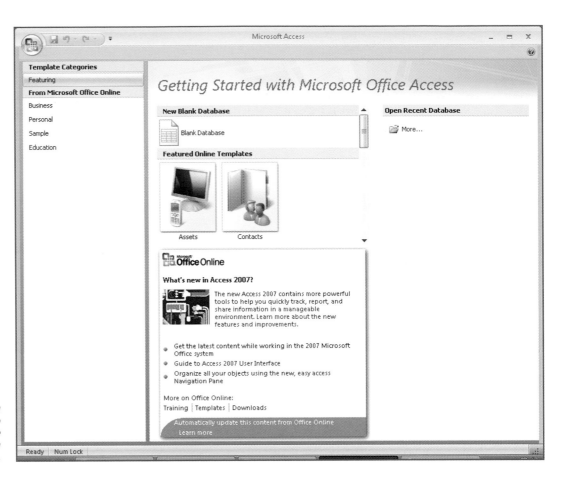

Figure 1-1: When Access opens, you are presented with several ways to open or create a database and with helpful information from Office Online.

- Click **Add To Quick Launch** to add a shortcut to the Quick Launch toolbar on the left end of the taskbar next to Start. (If you don't have a Quick Launch toolbar, right-click a blank area of the taskbar, click **Toolbars**, and click **Quick Launch**.)

- Click **Send To** and click **Desktop (Create Shortcut)** to place an icon on your desktop.

QUICKFACTS

UNDERSTANDING THE RIBBON

The original menu and toolbar structure used in Office products from the late '80s and early '90s (File, Edit, Format, Window, Help, and other menus) was designed in an era of fewer tasks and features that has simply outgrown its usefulness. Microsoft's solution to the increased number of feature enhancements is the *ribbon*, the container at the top of most Office program windows for the tools and features you are most likely to use to accomplish the task at hand (see Figure 1-3). The ribbon collects tools you are likely to use into *groups*. For example, the Font group provides the tools to work with text. Groups are organized into tabs, which bring together the tools to work on broader tasks. For example, the Create tab contains groups that allow you to add objects such as tables, forms, and reports.

Each Office program has a default set of tabs and additional tabs that become available as the context of your work changes. For example, when working on a table, a Table Tools (Datasheet) tab displays. The ribbon provides more screen real estate so that each of the tools (or commands) in the groups has a labeled button you can click. Depending on the tool, you are then presented with additional options in the form of a list of commands, a dialog box or task pane, or galleries of choices that reflect what you'll see in your work. Groups that contain more detailed tools than there is room for in the ribbon include a *Dialog Box Launcher* icon that takes you directly to these other choices.

Two new Office 2007 features that are co-located with the ribbon include the Office Button and the Quick Access toolbar. The Office Button menu (similar to the old File menu) lets you work *with* your database (such as saving it), as opposed to the ribbon, which centers on

Continued . . .

NOTE

Databases can contain code that could cause serious harm to your computer. To alert you to this potential problem, a Security Warning will appear on a message bar under the ribbon, altering you that Access has disabled content it cannot determine is from a trusted source. Click **Options** to see what the issue is (shown in Figure 1-2), and, if you trust the source, click **Enable This Content**. If you do not know or trust the source, leave the default option selected. In either case, click **OK** to close the dialog box. If you do not enable the content, the database will open and you can view data, but any executable code will be disabled. See Chapter 9 for more information on database security.

🛡 **Security Warning**   Certain content in the database has been disabled   Options...

Figure 1-2: Only enable content in databases that you know comes from a trusted source.

QUICKFACTS

UNDERSTANDING THE RIBBON *(Continued)*

working *in* your document (such as entering and editing data). The Quick Access toolbar is similar to the Quick Launch toolbar in the Windows taskbar, providing an always-available location for your favorite tools. It starts out with a default set of tools, but you can add to it. See the accompanying sections and figures for more information on the ribbon and the other elements of the Access window.

TIP

The ribbon adapts to the size of your Access window and your screen resolution, changing the size and shape of buttons and labels. See for yourself by opening a database, maximizing the Access window, and noticing how the ribbon appears. Drag the right border of the Access window toward the left, and see how the ribbon changes to reflect its decreasing real estate.

Open a Database

You open an Access database by locating the database file. You can manually find the database file using a dialog box, Getting Started page, shortcut, or Windows Explorer. (If you do not know the location of the file, you can do a search on your drives, as described in "Find a Database" later in the chapter) For files you have previously opened, Windows and Access provide a number of aids you can use to reopen them quickly.

BROWSE TO AN EXISTING DATABASE

1. Open Access (see "Open Access" earlier in the chapter).

2. Click the **Office Button** in the upper-left corner of the Access window, and click **Open**.

   –Or–

   In the Getting Started page, under Open Recent Database, click **More** (see Figure 1-1).

   –Or–

   Press **CTRL+O**.

   In all cases, the Open dialog box appears, shown in Figure 1-4.

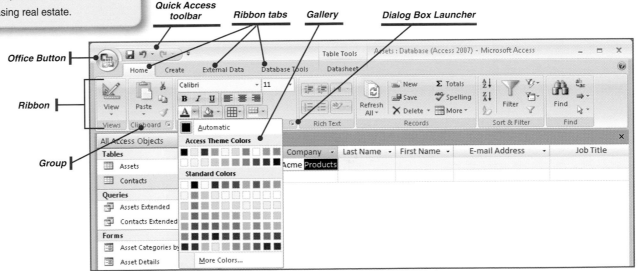

Figure 1-3: The ribbon, containing groups of the most common tools, replaces the familiar Office menu and toolbar structure.

TIP

A handy feature in the Open dialog box (and other browse-type dialog boxes) is that you can create links to often-used folders where you store databases and add them to the Favorite Links area in the left pane of the dialog box (see the first Favorite Links entry in Figure 1-4). Open Windows Explorer and display an often-used folder in the right pane. Right-click the folder and click **Create Shortcut**. In the left pane of Windows Explorer, open your Windows Vista *username* folder (for example "John") to display the subfolders under it. Do not click the folder to open it; instead, use the open and close arrows to the left of the folder name. When you have your Links folder visible in the Windows Explorer left pane and the shortcut to your often-used folder displayed in the right pane, drag the shortcut to the Links folder. The next time you use the Open dialog box, you can open the folder with one click.

NOTE

Access 2007 can open data from other database file formats, such as Paradox, and files that organize data in a database structure, such as an Excel worksheet or text file. In most cases, a wizard will lead you through the steps to accurately organize the data into an Access format. Chapter 5 describes how to work with external data.

Figure 1-4: The Open dialog box provides several ways to browse for a database file.

2. Use the address bar or the left pane containing your favorite links and folders to browse to the folder that contains the database you want.

3. To narrow the list of files displayed, click the file types button to the right of the File Name box, and click a file type if different from the type displayed on the button. Click the file type you want from the list (see the accompanying Note).

4. When you have located it, double-click the database.

   –Or–

   Click the database to select it, and click **Open**.

   In either case, the database opens in Access, similar to that shown in Figure 1-5.

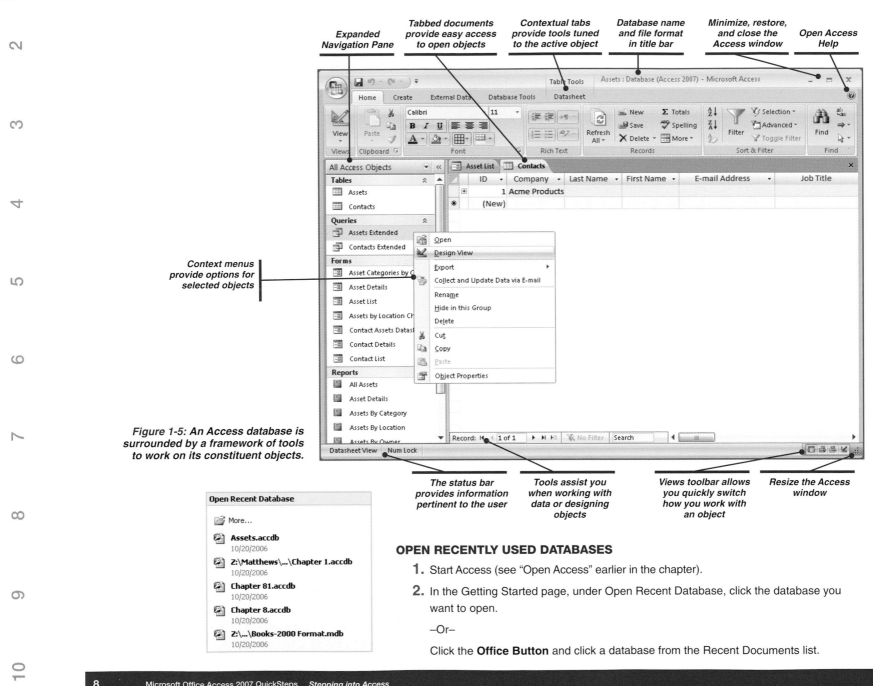

Figure 1-5: An Access database is surrounded by a framework of tools to work on its constituent objects.

Expanded Navigation Pane

Tabbed documents provide easy access to open objects

Contextual tabs provide tools tuned to the active object

Database name and file format in title bar

Minimize, restore, and close the Access window

Open Access Help

Context menus provide options for selected objects

The status bar provides information pertinent to the user

Tools assist you when working with data or designing objects

Views toolbar allows you quickly switch how you work with an object

Resize the Access window

Open Recent Database

📁 More...

📁 **Assets.accdb**
10/20/2006

📁 **Z:\Matthews\...\Chapter 1.accdb**
10/20/2006

📁 **Chapter 81.accdb**
10/20/2006

📁 **Chapter 8.accdb**
10/20/2006

📁 **Z:\...\Books-2000 Format.mdb**
10/20/2006

OPEN RECENTLY USED DATABASES

1. Start Access (see "Open Access" earlier in the chapter).

2. In the Getting Started page, under Open Recent Database, click the database you want to open.

   –Or–

   Click the **Office Button** and click a database from the Recent Documents list.

–Or–

Display the Open dialog box (see "Browse to an Existing Database" earlier in this chapter), and click **Recently Changed** in the Favorite Links area of the dialog box. Click the database you want to open from the list in the right pane.

USE WINDOWS EXPLORER TO OPEN A DATABASE

1. Click **Start** and click **Computer**. If necessary, click **Folders** in the left pane to display the Folders list.

2. Under Computer, open the drive and folder(s) that contain the database you want to open. When you open the folder that contains the database in the left pane, the database file will be displayed in the right pane.

3. Double-click the file name to open the database in Access.

CREATE SHORTCUTS TO OPEN A DATABASE

Just as you can create a shortcut to start Access, you can create a shortcut to a database file. Opening the file will open the database in Access, starting Access if it isn't already open.

1. Locate the database file, as described in the previous section, "Use Windows Explorer to Open a Database."

2. Click the file using the right mouse button, and holding the button down, drag it to the desktop. (This is called right-dragging.)

   –Or–

   Drag the file to the Quick Launch toolbar.

   –Or–

   Drag the file to another folder.

3. Release the mouse button, and click **Create Shortcuts Here** from the context menu if it is displayed.

| Copy Here |
| Move Here |
| Create Shortcuts Here |
| Cancel |

Use the Navigation Pane

The Navigation Pane (see Figure 1-5), provides the functions that used to be performed with the Database window in earlier versions of Access, and then some. From within this framework, you can open, design, organize, import and export data, and delete the objects that comprise a database (see the "Understanding Access Objects" QuickFacts).

TIP

You can change the number of recently opened databases that are displayed in the Getting Started page and from the Office Button menu. Click the **Office Button**, click the **Access Options** button, and click the **Advanced** option. Under Display, click the **Show This Number Of Recent Documents** spinner to change the number of recent databases displayed (nine is the maximum).

Display

Show this number of Recent Documents: 9

TIP

If you are familiar with earlier versions of Access, you are probably wondering what happened to the Database window, the "Grand Central Station" for working with database objects, when you opened a database. The window has been recast into the Navigation Pane.

UNDERSTANDING ACCESS OBJECTS

*O*bjects comprise a database. Objects let you store, find, enter, present, and manipulate your data:

- **Tables** contain data, organized by categories called *fields,* into unique sets of data called *records.*

- **Queries** are requests you make of your data to extract just the information you want or to perform maintenance actions, such as inserting or deleting records.

- **Forms** provide a user-friendly interface for entering or displaying data.

- **Reports** allow you to take mundane collections of data, organize them in a creative package, and print the result.

- **Macros** provide a means to automate actions in Access without in-depth programming skills.

- **Modules** package Visual Basic code into a single container, providing a convenient interface for coupling Access to the possibilities offered by a programming language.

The remaining chapters in this book describe the first four objects in more detail. Macros and modules involve advanced techniques and are beyond the scope of this book.

EXPAND AND COLLAPSE THE NAVIGATION PANE

When a database is first opened, you see the Navigation Pane displayed as a *shutter* bar on the left side of the Access window, shown in Figure 1-6:

- To view the objects contained within the database and access the Navigation Pane's many features, click the bar or the right-pointing open button on top of the bar to expand the pane.

- To collapse the Navigation Pane to its *docked* location on the left side of the Access window, click the left-pointing close button on the right side of its title bar.

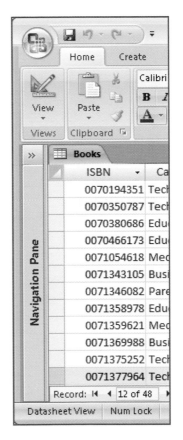

Figure 1-6: The Navigation Pane stands by innocuously until you are ready to use it.

DISPLAY ONLY THE OBJECTS YOU WANT

Expand the Navigation Pane, and click its title bar to display its menu. There are two sections on the menu that let you display the objects in your database as you want to see them:

- Under **Navigate To Category**, click the category that most closely matches how you want to view the objects.

- Under **Filter By Group**, click the group whose objects you want displayed; other groups and their objects will be hidden (the grouping options that are available to you will change according to the category you selected at the top of the menu).

COLLAPSE AND EXPAND GROUPS

Click the upward- and downward-pointing arrows on the right-end of a group's name.

PERFORM ACTIONS ON OBJECTS

Right-click the object you want to work with, and select the action you want to perform from its context menu (see Figure 1-5).

Open Older Databases

You can open earlier versions of Access databases, though what you can do with them and whether Access offers to convert them to a more recent version depends on how old they are.

OPEN ACCESS 95 AND ACCESS 97 DATABASES

If you try to open a database created in Access 95 or Access 97 in Access 2007, you will be presented with the option of *converting* (updating) the database to the default file format you currently have chosen or opening it using its native format (see the "Understanding Access File Compatibility" QuickFacts for more information on Access file formats).

QUICK**FACTS**

UNDERSTANDING ACCESS FILE COMPATIBILITY

The Access database file format changes somewhat in each newly released version to accommodate new features and provide better security. However, Access is not generally *forward-compatible*, meaning that older versions of Access cannot recognize newer file formats without converting them to the older file format (if that's even possible). Access 2007 can open database files created in versions since Access 95; however, Access 2007 can only provide the same level of functionality as the original Access program with database files saved in Access 2000 and later file formats.

By default, Access uses the 2007 file format (using the new .accdb file extension). You can change that to either of two earlier formats (using the .mdb file extension common to earlier versions), ensuring that your database files can be opened by users who have Access 2000 and later. The more prominent advantages to using the new file format include:

- A new Attachment data type to store multiple pictures or files in a single record

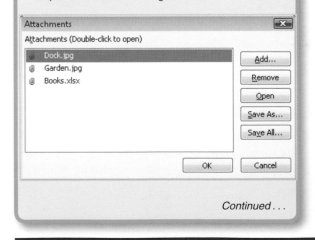

Continued . . .

Figure 1-7: You can choose to convert an earlier Access database to a recent version or open it without conversion but with very limited capabilities.

1. Open the database using the techniques described in "Open a Database." The Database Enhancement dialog box appears, shown in Figure 1-7.

2. Click **Yes** if you want to convert the file to your default Access file format. Doing so will prevent the database from being opened by earlier Access versions. (See the next section, "Change the Default File Format in Access" for information on changing the default format from Access 2007 to an earlier format.)

3. The Save As dialog box appears, shown in Figure 1-8. Locate the folder where you want the database stored, change the file name if needed, and click **Save**. After the conversion, you are notified that the database has been upgraded and are advised of limitations on opening the database by earlier versions.

4. Click **No** if you want to open the database in its original file format. Doing so limits your ability to use many newer Access features. Most notably, you won't be able to change the structure (design) of the database.

QUICKFACTS

UNDERSTANDING ACCESS FILE COMPATIBILITY *(Continued)*

- Multivalued lookup fields that let you store more than one value in a field (by creating a list, or *lookup*, from which you can select one or more values)

- Integration with Microsoft Windows SharePoint Services that allows collaboration and document sharing among a workgroup (setting up a SharePoint site and integrating with Access 2007 is beyond the scope of this book)

- Data collection from forms you send to others in Microsoft Outlook 2007 e-mail messages

When deciding which database format to use, you will have to weigh the features offered by Access 2007 against the ability to share your work with users of earlier versions of Access.

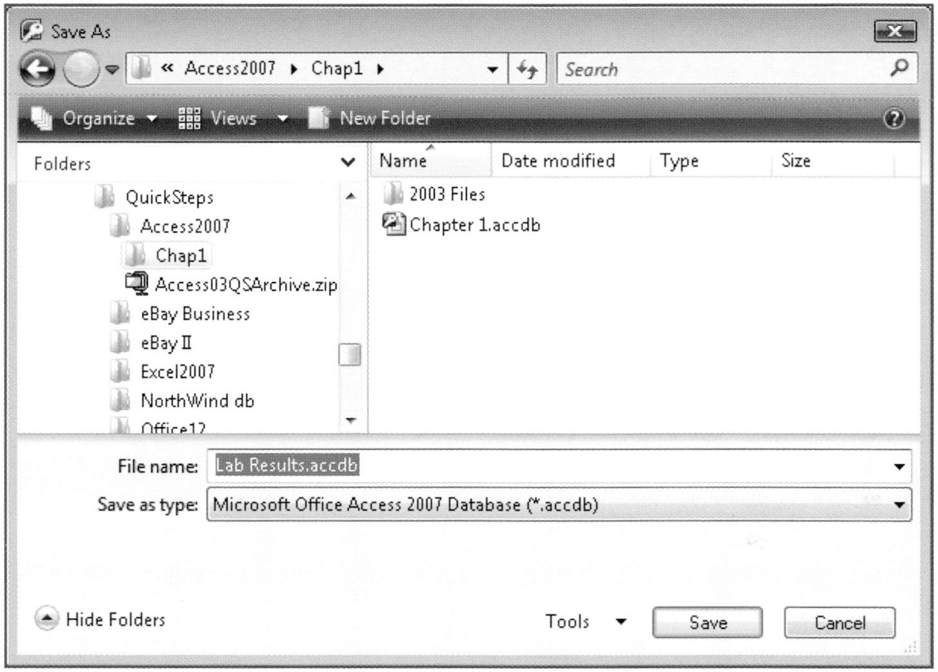

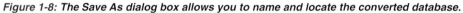

Figure 1-8: The Save As dialog box allows you to name and locate the converted database.

NOTE

Many databases encounter errors during the conversion process. The errors are listed in a Conversion Errors table that's added to the database. See Chapter 2 for information on working with tables.

Microsoft Office Access encountered one or more errors during conversion. To view a summary of these errors, open the 'Conversion Errors' table.

OK   Help

OPEN ACCESS 2000 THROUGH ACCESS 2003 DATABASES

Open the database using the techniques described in "Open a Database." The database opens without needing to convert it to a more recent database format.

You can work on the database as you did in earlier version of Access, but features provided by the Access 2007 file format will not be available to you.

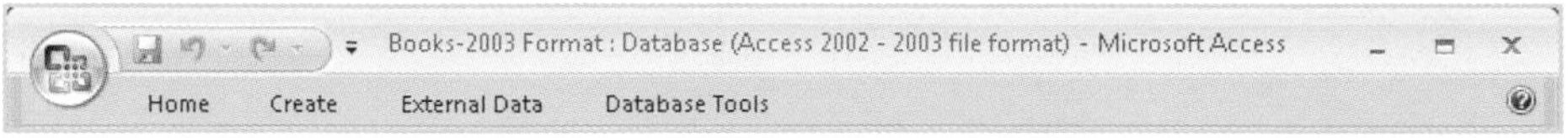

NOTE

Access will not be able to determine that the content in most conversions came from a trustworthy source and will provide you with an opportunity to not open the file. Click **Open** in the Security Notice dialog box if you trust the source of the database.

CONVERT AN OLDER DATABASE AFTER OPENING IT

If you open an older Access database in its native file format without converting and later decide to convert it to the default file format, you can do so within Access 2007 without having to reopen the database.

1. Click the **Office Button**, and click **Convert**. The Save As dialog box appears (see Figure 1-8).
2. Locate the folder where you want the database stored, change the file name if needed, and click **Save**. After the conversion, you are notified that the database has been upgraded and are advised of limitations on opening the database by earlier versions.

Change the Default File Format in Access

New databases and converted databases can be created in the three latest Access file formats. (See "Understanding Access File Compatibility" for information on the pros and cons of using older file formats.) Unless changed, Access uses the 2007 (.accdb) file format. To change to an earlier file format:

1. Open Access (see "Open Access" earlier in the chapter).
2. Click the **Office Button**, click the **Access Options** button, and click the **Popular** option.
3. Under Creating Databases, click the **Default File Format** down arrow, and click **Access 2000** or **Access 2002-2003**.
4. Click **OK** when finished.

Find a Database

To find a database whose name and location you have forgotten, provided you remember other information about it:

1. Click the **Office Button**, and click **Open**. The Open dialog box appears (see Figure 1-4).
2. Use the Folders list or Favorite Links in the left pane or the address bar to narrow your search to the drive and/or folder where you think the database is located.
3. In the **Search** box, type words you know are contained in the database or keywords (words or phrases associated with the database). As you start typing, possible matches are found and displayed. (See Chapter 2 for ways to add identifying information to a database file.)

![Open dialog box showing search results in Z:\Matthews with Books-2000 Format.mdb, Books-97 Format.mdb, Books-2000 Format.accdb, and Books-2003 Format.mdb files listed]

4. To open the database you've found, select the file and click **Open**.

Personalize Access

You can personalize how you work with Access by choosing to display task panes, customizing toolbars and menus, and rearranging windows.

Customize the Quick Access Toolbar

You can provide one-click access to your favorite Access tools by adding them to the Quick Access toolbar, which, by default, is to the right of the Office Button. The starter kit of tools includes Save, Undo, and Redo.

ADD OR REMOVE TOOLS FROM A LIST

1. Click the down arrow 🔻 to the right of the Quick Access toolbar, and click **More Commands**.

–Or–

Click the **Office Button**, click **Access Options**, and click **Customize**.

In either case, the Access Options dialog box appears with the Customize options displayed, as shown in Figure 1-9.

2. Click the **Choose Commands From** down arrow, and click the tab or other option from the drop-down list to find the tool you are looking for.

TIP

Several popular tools can be quickly added to the Quick Access toolbar by clicking the down arrow to the right of the Quick Access toolbar and clicking the tool you want.

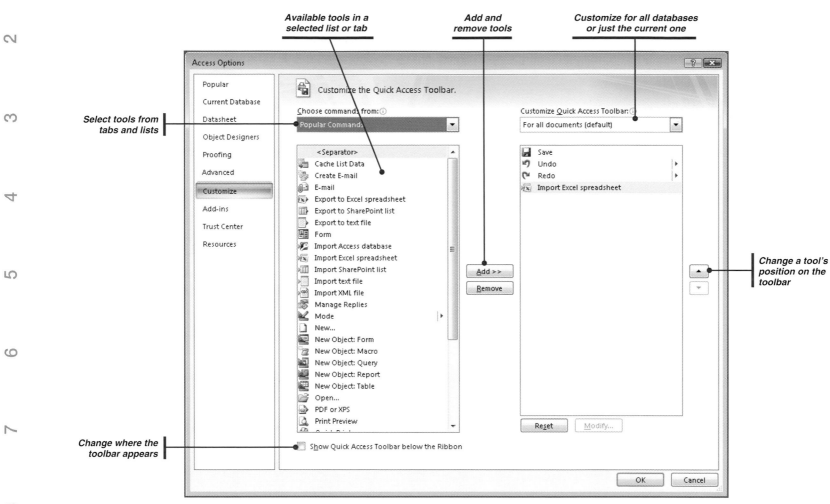

Available tools in a
selected list or tab

Add and
remove tools

Customize for all databases
or just the current one

Select tools from
tabs and lists

Change a tool's
position on the
toolbar

Change where the
toolbar appears

Figure 1-9: Any command or tool in Access can be placed on the Quick Access toolbar for one-click access.

3. Click the tool to select it, and click **Add** in the middle of the right pane. The tool appears in the list of current toolbar tools to the right.

4. To remove a tool from the toolbar, select it from the list on the right, and click **Remove**.

5. Click **OK** when finished.

Though not specifically designed as a site map for all the tools and commands in Access, the list of tools and commands in the Customize pane in the Access Options dialog box performs as a substitute. You can select each tab and see what tools and/or commands are contained therein. See how in the section "Customize the Quick Access Toolbar."

You can hide the tools on the ribbon and show only the list of tabs, thereby providing more "real estate" within the Access window for the object you are working with. Right-click a tool on the Quick Access toolbar or on the ribbon, and click **Minimize The Ribbon**. Click the command a second time to restore the ribbon to its full height. Alternatively, double-click a tab name to minimize the ribbon; double-click a second time to restore it.

ADD OR REMOVE TOOLS DIRECTLY ON THE TOOLBAR

- To add a tool to the Quick Access toolbar, right-click a tool on the ribbon, and click **Add To Quick Access Toolbar**.

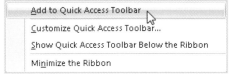

- To remove a tool from the Quick Access toolbar, right-click the tool and click **Remove From Quick Access Toolbar**.

RELOCATE THE QUICK ACCESS TOOLBAR

You can display the Quick Access toolbar at its default position (above the ribbon) or directly below the ribbon using one of the following methods:

- Right-click a tool on the Quick Access toolbar or on the ribbon, and click **Place Quick Access Toolbar Below The Ribbon** (once located below the ribbon, you can move it above the ribbon in the same manner).

  –Or–

- In the Customize pane (click **Customize** in the Access Options dialog box), click the **Show Quick Access Toolbar Below The Ribbon** check box, and click **OK** (to return the toolbar above the ribbon, open the pane and clear the check box).

CUSTOMIZE THE QUICK ACCESS TOOLBAR FOR A DATABASE

By default, changes made to the Quick Access toolbar are applicable to all databases. You can create a toolbar that only applies to the database you currently have open.

1. In the Customize pane (see Figure 1-9), click the **Customize Quick Access Toolbar** down arrow.

2. Click the option that identifies the database to which the toolbar will apply.

3. Click **OK** when finished.

⏰ QUICKSTEPS

USING THE KEYBOARD IN ACCESS

Though most of us live and die by our mouse while using our computers, there isn't much in Access that can't also be done from the keyboard.

USE THE START MENU

1. Press the Windows flag key 🪟 on the bottom row of your keyboard, or press **CTRL+ESC**.

2. Use the arrow keys to move to the item you want.

3. Press **ENTER**.

OPEN A DATABASE

1. Press **CTRL+O**.

2. Press **TAB** to move between the various controls in the window, and use the arrow keys to select drives and folders.

3. Press **ENTER** to open folders, and use the arrow keys to select the database file.

4. Press **ENTER** to open the database in Access.

CLOSE AN OBJECT

Select the object's window or tab (see "Change How You View Objects"), and press **CTRL+F4**. Hold down **CTRL** and continue pressing **F4** to close any other open objects.

CLOSE ACCESS

Press **ALT+F4**.

REARRANGE TOOLS ON THE QUICK ACCESS TOOLBAR

You can change the order in which tools appear on the Quick Access toolbar.

1. In the Customize pane (see Figure 1-9), select the tool in the list on the right whose position you want to change.

2. Click the up or down arrows to the right of the list to move the tool. Moving the tool up moves it to the left in the on-screen toolbar; moving it down the list moves it to the right in the on-screen toolbar.

3. Click **OK** when finished.

Display and Use Ribbon Shortcut Keys

Though ScreenTips display many shortcut keys (for example, **CTRL+C** is shown when you point to the Copy icon in the Home tab Clipboard group), you can view shortcut keys for commands on the ribbon, the Office Button, and Quick Access toolbar commands more readily.

> **Copy (Ctrl+C)**
> Copy the selection and put it on the Clipboard.

1. Press **ALT**, and shortcut icons displaying shortcut letters and numbers will appear on top-level screen elements (the Office Button, Quick Access toolbar, and ribbon tabs).

2. Press the corresponding key(s) to open the next level of detail and display those shortcut icons (see Figure 1-10). Continue working through groups and lists until you reach the tool or command to perform the action you want.

3. Press **ALT** a second time to remove the shortcut icons from the window.

Change How You View Objects

Although you can only work with one database at a time, you can have several Access objects open as tabbed documents or as overlapping windows.

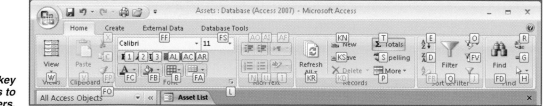

Figure 1-10: Shortcut key icons provide access to tools for keyboard users.

NOTE

By default, databases created in Access 2007 use tabbed documents and databases created in earlier versions use overlapping windows. You can switch to either format after the database is opened.

NOTE

The Window group is only available on the Home tab when using overlapping windows to display objects.

Each style provides unique features for working with multiple open objects. Figures 1-11 and 1-12 show some of the features of each.

SELECT TABBED DOCUMENTS OR OVERLAPPING OBJECT WINDOWS

1. Open the database.

2. Click the **Office Button**, click **Access Options**, and click the **Current Database** option.

3. Under Application Options, click **Overlapping Windows** or **Tabbed Documents**.

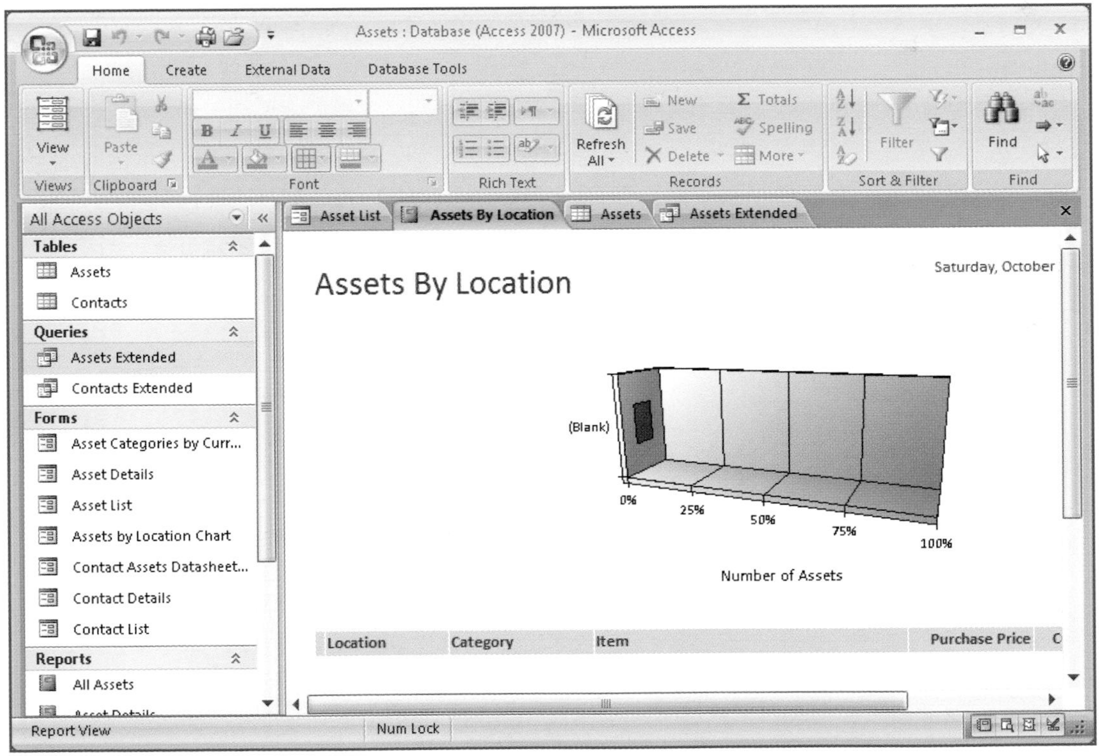

Figure 1-11: Displaying open objects as tabbed documents allows you to quickly view any one with a single click.

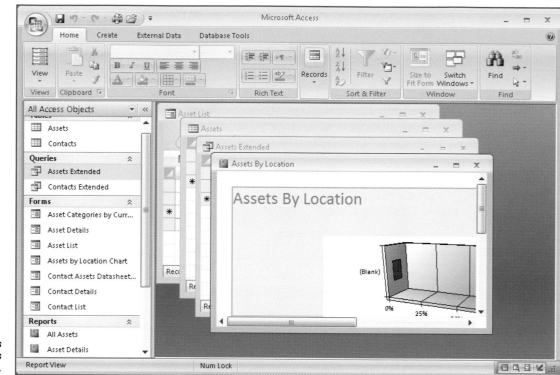

Figure 1-12: Overlapping windows offers several configurations to view open objects.

4. Click **OK** when finished. Click **OK** a second time after reading the message informing you that you must close and reopen the database for the change to take effect.

> **Microsoft Office Access**
>
> You must close and reopen the current database for the specified option to take effect.
>
> OK

ARRANGE MULTIPLE OVERLAPPED WINDOWS

1. Open two or more object windows.

2. In the Home tab Window group, click **Switch Windows**. Select one of these options from the menu that opens:

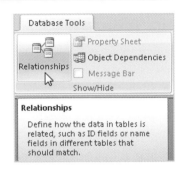

You can check for new updates for Office, activate your copy of Office, attempt to repair problems, and contact Microsoft technical support from one handy location (see Figure 1-13). Click the **Office Button**, click **Access Options**, click the **Resources** option, and click the button next to the service you want.

- Click **Tile Vertically** to align open object windows side-by-side in vertical panes (four or more open windows are *tiled* to fit the available space).

- Click **Cascade** to align open object windows in an overlapping stack (as shown in Figure 1-12).

- Click **Tile Horizontally** to align open object windows on top of each other in horizontal panes (four or more open windows are tiled to fit the available space).

Get Help

Microsoft provides a vast amount of assistance to Access users. If you have an Internet connection, you can automatically take advantage of the wealth of information available at the Microsoft Web site. When offline, information is limited to what is stored on your computer. Also, new to Access 2007 are "super" tooltips that provide much more detailed explanatory information about tools when the mouse pointer is hovered over them.

Figure 1-13: You can get assistance from Microsoft technical support on Access and other Office programs.

TIP

The first time you open the Access Help window, it opens to a default position, size, and connection method. You can reposition and resize the window and change the connection method (offline or online). Access will remember your changes the next time you open Help.

Open Help

You are never far from help in Access:

- Click the **Access Help** question mark icon ⓐ above the rightmost end of the ribbon.

  –Or–

- Press **F1**.

  In either case, the Access Help window opens, as shown in Figure 1-14.

Use the Access Help Window

The Access Help window provides a simple, no-nonsense gateway to volumes of topics, demos, and lessons on using Access. The main focus of the window is a Search text box, supported by a collection of handy tools.

SEARCH FOR INFORMATION

1. Open the Access Help window by clicking the **Access Help** icon or pressing **F1**.

2. In the Search text box below the toolbar, type keywords that are relevant to the information you are seeking.

3. Click the **Search** down arrow to view the connection and filtering options for the search:

- **Connection options** allow you to choose between options regarding online (Content From Office Online) or offline (Content From This Computer) information. If you have an active Internet connection, Help automatically assumes that you want online content each time you open the Help window.

- **Filtering options** let you limit your search to categories of information. For example, if you only want a template to create a family budget, under the online content heading, click **Access Templates**. Your search results will display only templates.

4. Click the **Search** button to have Access search for your keywords.

BROWSE FOR HELP

The initial Help window (shown in Figure 1-14) displays a list of Help categories similar to a table of contents. Click any of the headings to display a list of available topics and articles and/or subcategories of information. Continue following the links to drill down to the information you seek.

TIP

You can have the list of top-level Help headings displayed in the initial Help page always available to you in the Help window. Click **Show Table Of Contents** 📖 on the toolbar. A Table of Contents pane displays to the left of the content pane.

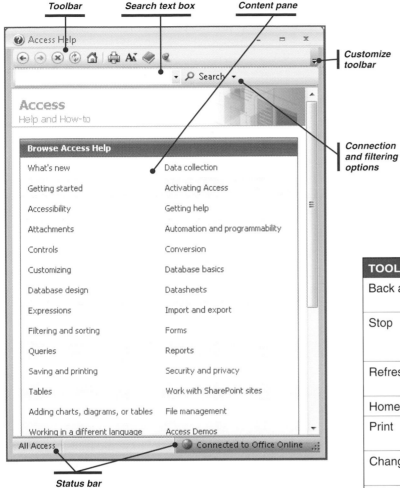

Figure 1-14: The Access Help window allows you to search online and offline articles and topics using tools similar to those in a Web browser.

The Keep On Top tool only works in relationship to Office programs. If you are multitasking with non-Office programs, they will move to the forefront (on top) when active.

USE HELP TOOLS

Several tools are available to assist you in using Access Help. The first collection of buttons contains standard Web browser tools. Table 1-1 describes these and other Access Help tools.

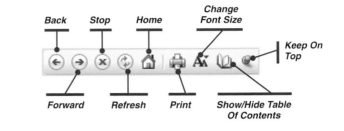

TOOL	DESCRIPTION
Back and Forward	Allows you to move from the current Help page, one page at a time, in the respective direction
Stop	Halts the current attempt at loading a Help page (useful when loading an online demo if you have a slow connection speed)
Refresh	Reloads the current page to provide the most recent information
Home	Displays the Access Help home page
Print	Opens a Print dialog box from which you can choose common printing options
Change Font Size	Opens a menu that lets you increase or decrease the size of text displayed in Help pages
Show/Hide Table Of Contents	Displays or removes a pane showing the list of highest-level Help categories
Keep/Not On Top	Keeps the Help window on top of the Access (and other Office programs) window or allows it to move to the background when switching to the program

Table 1-1: Tools to Enhance Your Search for Access Help

2 3 4 5 6 7 8 9 10

End Your Access Session

Changes that require saving are made as you work in the database object level, such as when you change the design of a table. Therefore, you don't need to "save" a database when you exit, as you would a typical file, such as a Word document.

Close a Database

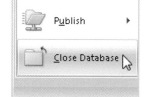

If you want to close a database and keep Access open to work with other databases, use this procedure. Otherwise, to close the database and exit Access in one step, see "Exit Access."

Click the **Office Button**, and click **Close Database**.

Exit Access

- Click **Close** [x] in the upper-right corner of the Access window.

  –Or–

- Click the **Office Button**, and click the **Exit Access** button.

How to...

- ⏣ *Planning a Database*
- *Use Database Templates*
- *Build a Database on Your Own*
- *Close a Database After Creating It*
- 🕸 *Using Datasheet and Design Views*
- *Create a Table by Entering Data*
- *Define Field Names in Your Table*
- *Create a New Empty Table*
- *Construct a Table in Design View*
- *Create a Table from a Table Template*
- *Assign a Primary Key*
- 🕸 *Understanding the Primary Key*
- *Add Identifying Information to Your Database*
- *Define Relationships*
- *Relate Tables in the Relationship Tab*
- 🕸 *Understanding Referential Integrity*
- *Enforce Referential Integrity*

Chapter 2
Creating Databases and Tables

Access 2007 provides some great tools to assist in the creation of a turnkey database solution. In addition to the new user interface discussed in Chapter 1, these tools expedite the building process and help you create a new database with all of its tables, relationships, forms, and reports available at once. While using these templates might rob you of the experience to better understand database structure, if speed is what you want, the database templates will allow you to be up and running quickly. This chapter will show you how to use the featured templates as well as other templates from Office Online to quickly create an Access database. If, however, you choose to obtain a more thorough understanding of databases, you will learn how to step through the process, which includes basic database design, table creation, and table connections through relationships.

QUICKSTEPS

PLANNING A DATABASE

There are several steps you can take to ensure your database efficiently performs the tasks you need, does not contain duplicate information, and that all of the information in the database is complete and correct. To create a successful database:

1. Decide why you are creating the database. What do you want it to accomplish?

2. Think about who will be using the database. Consider not only the reports and forms the database will generate, but also the expertise of the people who will be entering the data.

3. Organize the information that you want in your database, and separate it into major areas. For example, a database used by a manufacturing firm might need information about their customers, their raw materials, the products they manufacture, and so on.

4. Define the information you want included in each major area. These definitions will become fields in your tables.

5. Consider who will see the information produced from the data in the database. Think about how the reports can be designed to best communicate the information.

Continued . . .

Design a Database

Databases are created to provide quick, easy access to information. When you consider creating a database, think clearly about why you need it, what purpose the database will fulfill, and how it will be used. A few minutes of planning before you start creating your new database can pay off in hours saved in re-creating a poorly designed database.

The data, or information, in your database is stored in tables that resemble spreadsheets, as shown in Figure 2-1. They have columns, or *fields*, which span the vertical space of the window; and rows, or *records*, which cover the horizontal area of the window.

After creating the tables, forms can be made to ease the task of data entry. You can ask questions, or create *queries*, about the data stored in the database and generate reports to attractively display the information from your tables or queries. Forms, queries, and reports are covered in subsequent chapters.

Use Database Templates

There are many ways to create an Access database. The first and easiest way is to use one of the templates featured in Access 2007. You will need an Internet connection to download the templates to your computer. The database templates are ready to use and include all you need to get started. Some even contain a few sample records to help you understand how to use the database. Once created, you can modify the database to meet your requirements.

USE TEMPLATES FROM THE GETTING STARTED PAGE

With an Internet connection, commonly used templates are featured on the Getting Started With Microsoft Access (or simply *Getting Started*) page. These are a sampling of pre-structured templates obtainable from Microsoft. To use a featured template:

1. Open Access 2007 using one of the procedures described in Chapter 1.

2. If a database is open, click the **Office Button**, and click **Close Database**. The current database closes and the Getting Started page opens.

UICKSTEPS

PLANNING A DATABASE *(Continued)*

6. Take into account the underlying table data that will be necessary to produce the reports.

7. Reflect on how the tables will interrelate. What primary keys will be used in each table? (See the "Understanding the Primary Key" QuickFacts later in this chapter.) For example, if you want your database to generate purchase orders for a company, you will need tables for product information, purchase order information, vendor information, and so forth.

8. After you have thoroughly planned your database, you can start actually building it.

Columns, or fields, contain different kinds of information about the subject

Minimize the ribbon to provide more viewing room

Rows, or records, contain all the information about one person, thing, or place

Collapse the Navigation Pane to see more of your data

Easy navigation buttons help you reach specific records quickly

ID	TITLE	CATEGORY	FIRST	ISBN
144	Hide or See	Self Esteem	James	0-8007-1
145	What wives	Women	James	0-8423-7
146	The Parents	Family	Bill	0-671-68
147	The Parents	Family	Bill	0-671-68
148	Give your ch	Family	Fitzhugh	0-671-43
149	Give your ch	Family	Fitzhugh	0-671-43
150	Your Money	Money	Joe	0-14-016
151	The Hiberna	Health	Jan	0-93163
152	The Commu	Health	Cresent	SBN671-
153	The Greates	Wisdom	Henry	∅
154	Heaven Clos	Wisdom	Jesse	0-89274
155	Raising Pure	Family	Richard	0-7642-2
156	Raising Pure	Family	Richard	0-7642-2
157	The 30-Day I	Health	Michael	0-471-43
158	Anger Mana	Health	Leona	1-87963
159	The Secret c	Health	Albert	0-97989
160	The Courage	Family	Sheila	0-06-251
161	Loneliness I	Relationships	Sheila	0-06-251
162	The Saint's (	Wisdom	Robert	0-374-25
163	Healing Vist	Health	Gerald	
164	Women Wh	Wisdom	Clarissa	0-345-37
165	Love is an Ev	Health	Colleen	0-89129
166	Lighten Up	Health	Katie	0-7872-4
167	The Verbal A	Relationships	Patricia	1-55850
168	Receipt for a	Health	Ellen	0-345-32
169	F-Plan Diet	Health	Audrey	0-553-23

Record: 14 ◀ 4 of 513 ▶ ▶I ▶* 🔍 No Filter Search

Datasheet View   Num Lock

Figure 2-1: Access tables resemble spreadsheets and are the core containers of information for your database.

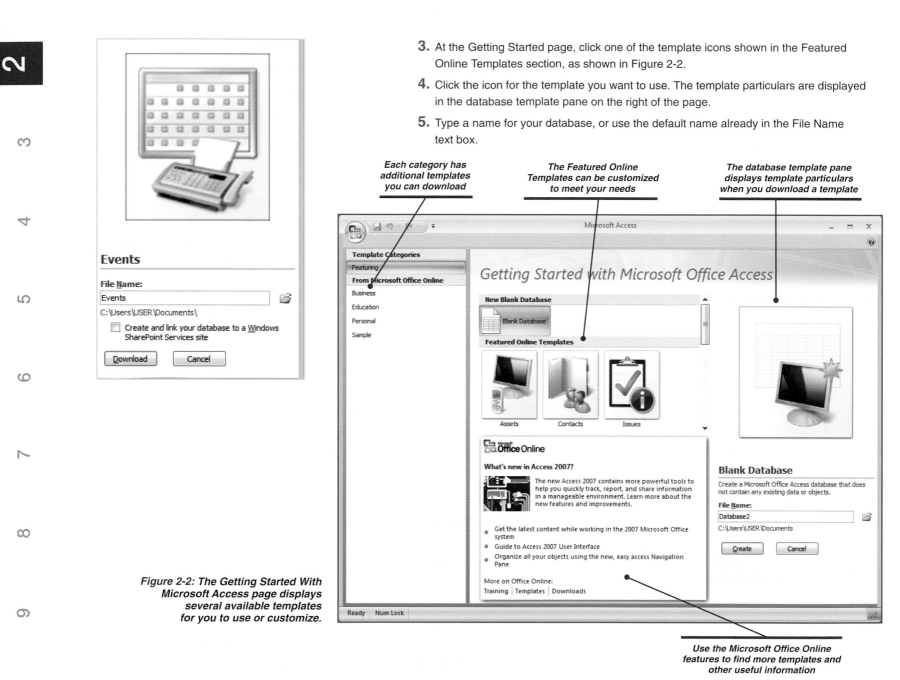

3. At the Getting Started page, click one of the template icons shown in the Featured Online Templates section, as shown in Figure 2-2.

4. Click the icon for the template you want to use. The template particulars are displayed in the database template pane on the right of the page.

5. Type a name for your database, or use the default name already in the File Name text box.

Events

File Name:

Events

C:\Users\USER\Documents\

☐ Create and link your database to a Windows SharePoint Services site

[Download] [Cancel]

Each category has additional templates you can download

The Featured Online Templates can be customized to meet your needs

The database template pane displays template particulars when you download a template

Microsoft Access

Template Categories

Featuring
From Microsoft Office Online
Business
Education
Personal
Sample

Getting Started with Microsoft Office Access

New Blank Database

Blank Database

Featured Online Templates

Assets   Contacts   Issues

Office Online

What's new in Access 2007?

The new Access 2007 contains more powerful tools to help you quickly track, report, and share information in a manageable environment. Learn more about the new features and improvements.

• Get the latest content while working in the 2007 Microsoft Office system
• Guide to Access 2007 User Interface
• Organize all your objects using the new, easy access Navigation Pane

More on Office Online:
Training | Templates | Downloads

Ready   Num Lock

Blank Database

Create a Microsoft Office Access database that does not contain any existing data or objects.

File Name:

Database2

C:\Users\USER\Documents

[Create] [Cancel]

Figure 2-2: The Getting Started With Microsoft Access page displays several available templates for you to use or customize.

Use the Microsoft Office Online features to find more templates and other useful information

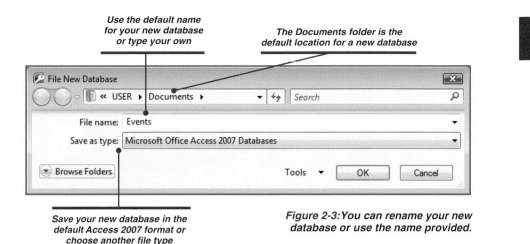

NOTE

The database template pane displays the default location of your new template.

TIP

You can change the location of the default folder. Click the **Office Button**, click **Access Options**, and click **Popular**. Click **Browse** to open the Default Database Path window, and choose a folder to use as the default folder.

TIP

If you use Windows Vista, templates you have downloaded are stored in the c:\Users*user name*\ Documents folder. If you use Windows XP, they are stored in the c:\Documents and Settings*user name*\My Documents folder.

NOTE

If the featured database templates shown on the Getting Started page do not meet your requirements, more are available under the Template Categories area to the left of the Getting Started page.

Use the default name for your new database or type your own

The Documents folder is the default location for a new database

Save your new database in the default Access 2007 format or choose another file type

Figure 2-3: You can rename your new database or use the name provided.

6. If you want to designate a location for your database other than the default folder, click the folder icon 🖼 to display the File New Database dialog box, as seen in Figure 2-3. If you do not want to store your database in the default folder, click **Browse Folders** to locate the folder in which you want your new database stored.

7. Type a name for your database in the File Name text box if you want to use a name other than the one supplied.

8. Click **OK**, and you are returned to the Getting Started page.

9. Click the **Download** button. Access 2007 will download your chosen template and prepare the new database for you to use. Your new database opens in Form View so that you may start entering data at once. To begin, click in the first empty field, and type your first record (see Chapter 6 for more information on working with forms).

DOWNLOAD A TEMPLATE MANUALLY

If the template icons do not appear automatically, or if none of the featured templates on the Getting Started page are exactly what you want, a full library of database examples can be found at Microsoft Office Online.

1. In the More On Office Online area, near the bottom of the Getting Started page, click **Templates**.

2. To find the database examples, click the **Templates** tab at the top of the Web page. A list of templates is displayed, as seen in Figure 2-4.

Use the "Live Search" feature to
find the right database quickly

Microsoft features different
templates each day for your use

Help on
templates
is offered
directly from
Microsoft

Submit a new
database template
or suggest that one
be included in the
template library

Sample database
templates are
categorized to
make your search
more efficient

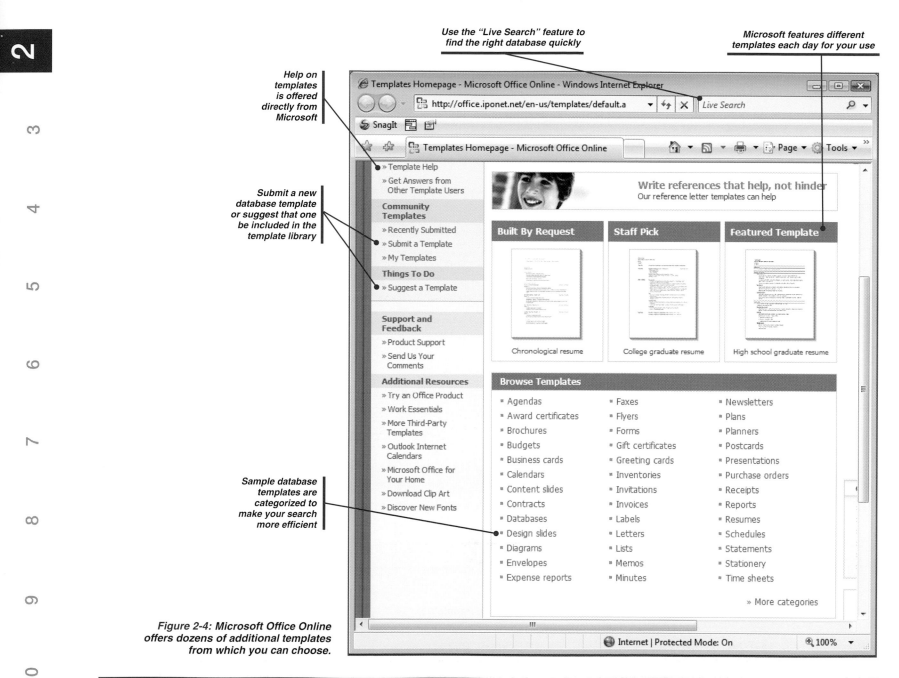

Figure 2-4: Microsoft Office Online
offers dozens of additional templates
from which you can choose.

Save As dialog box (top left):

USER ▸ Documents ▸

Organize ▾ Views ▾ New Folder

Name	Date modified	Type	Size	Tags
SnagIt Catalog			Clients	
Clients - Shortcut			Database1	
Employees			Faculty	
Lending Library			Northwind 2007	
Patrick Mfg. Inc.			Students	

Favorite Links: Documents, Recent Places, Desktop, Computer, Pictures, More »

Folders

File name: Lending library

Save as type:

Hide Folders   Save   Cancel

3. Click **Databases** to open a list of template categories specific to Access. Click a category to see a list of available templates in that category.

4. To download a database for your use, click the database you want from the list. The next screen, as shown in Figure 2-5, will display an example of your chosen database, as well as the download size and earliest version of Access required to run the file. See Chapter 1 for information about opening files created in older versions of Access.

5. Click **Download Now**. [Download Now]

6. A Save As dialog box appears showing the default location of your new template. Use the Folders list to determine another location (if necessary, click **Browse Folders** to view the Folders list). Click **Save** to accept the default location and return to the Getting Started page. The new template is displayed in the pane at the right of your window.

7. Click **Create** to prepare the downloaded template for your use.

Microsoft encourages your feedback

Determine how many similar templates are available

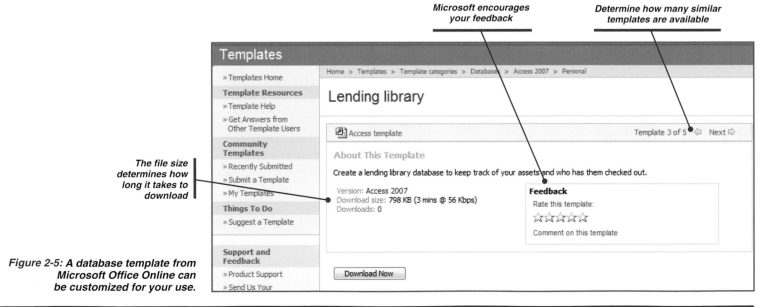

The file size determines how long it takes to download

Figure 2-5: A database template from Microsoft Office Online can be customized for your use.

Templates

» Templates Home

Template Resources
» Template Help
» Get Answers from Other Template Users

Community Templates
» Recently Submitted
» Submit a Template
» My Templates

Things To Do
» Suggest a Template

Support and Feedback
» Product Support
» Send Us Your

Home > Templates > Template categories > Databases > Access 2007 > Personal

Lending library

Access template   Template 3 of 5 ◁ Next ▷

About This Template

Create a lending library database to keep track of your assets and who has them checked out.

Version: Access 2007
Download size: **798 KB** (3 mins @ 56 Kbps)
Downloads: 0

Feedback
Rate this template:
☆☆☆☆☆
Comment on this template

[Download Now]

Build a Database on Your Own

Although the ease of using templates when creating databases is undeniable, there is something to be said for working from your own blueprint. Sometimes, templates don't have the solution you are looking for. Sometimes, you want to create a more simplistic database to better understand the inner workings of Access. Either way, it is at this point that you will start with a blank database.

1. At the Getting Started With Microsoft Office Access page (see Figure 2-2), click **Blank Database**.

2. The Blank Database pane appears at the right side of the Access window. Click the **File Name** text box, and type a file name for your database or use the default name.

3. Click **Create** to create your new database in the default folder (to create it in a different folder, click the folder icon next to the File Name text box. Access creates the new database and opens an empty table, show here. A column headed Add New Field is highlighted and ready to accept text. To start entering information into this new table, see "Create A Table By Entering Data" later in this chapter.

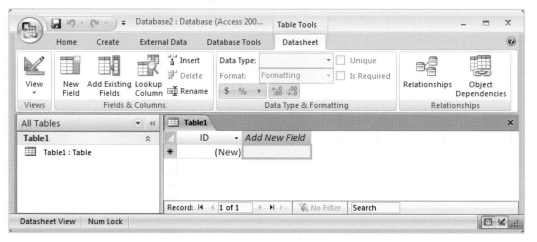

Close a Database After Creating It

When you have finished creating your new database, you may start working with it, as described later in this chapter or you may close it.

When finished, close the database by clicking the **Office Button** and clicking **Close Database**:

- If you only added data, the database will save your changes in the default table and close.
- If you made any changes to the design of the table, such as adding a field, Access will ask you to accept those changes to the table and then close. If you neither added data nor changed the table design, the database will close and you will need to create a new table the next time you open the database (see the next several sections for ways to do this.)

NOTE

There is no space between the word "Table" and the number 1 in a new table's name. This convention is used throughout Access; however, you can rename a table with up to 64 characters, including spaces.

Access 2007 provides several different ways to look at, or "view" objects that facilitate working with them or designing their structure. The two views that we refer to throughout this chapter are:

- **Datasheet View** allows you to see your data presented in a spreadsheet-type format. You can enter and manipulate data in much the same manner. See Chapter 4 for more information on working with data in tables in Datasheet View.

- **Design View** is where you can create a new table by entering fields, data types, and so on. You can modify and format each field to meet your needs. See "Construct a Table in Design View" later in this chapter and Chapter 3 for more information on using Design View to set up a table.

In database parlance, the intersection of a column/field and record/row is commonly referred to as a "field." In spreadsheet usage, such as in Microsoft Excel, that same location would be called a "cell." As Microsoft continues to blur the distinction between tables in its Office suite, the terminology used within each program will eventually have to be reconciled. In the meantime, this book will use both terms interchangeably.

Build the Framework with Tables

Although Access is comprised of many objects, the basic database framework revolves around tables. Each table usually holds information about a single topic and is connected or related to other tables through similar pieces of information (or fields). Each row of a table contains information about a specific item. For example, in a table that contains information about your friends, you might have fields such as first name, last name, address, and so on. Each row is called a *record*. If you are building your own database and have just created a blank database, you will need to enter data into the table that was created with the new database. You can create a new table by entering data from a table template, or you can create a new table in Design View. You can also create tables from imported or linked information, as explained in Chapter 4.

Create a Table by Entering Data

If you are an active spreadsheet user, it may be more comfortable for you to create a table simply by entering data into the datasheet when you open Access. When you create a blank database, the database opens in Datasheet View with a new, blank table named Table1.

The first field is highlighted, so you can immediately start entering information into this table cell as you would in a spreadsheet.

Unlike earlier versions of Access, you can press either **TAB** or **ENTER** to move from one field to the next. As you move from one row to the next, Access saves that row, or record. As shown in Figure 2-6, the column headings become Field1, Field2, Field3, and so forth.

OPEN AN EXISTING TABLE

To open a table in an existing database:

1. Open the database as described in Chapter 1.

2. If necessary, display the Navigation Pane to the left of the Access window.

3. Double-click any of the available tables listed. If you see only groups, click the downward-pointing arrows in the group title to display all the objects in each group. The table will open in Datasheet View.

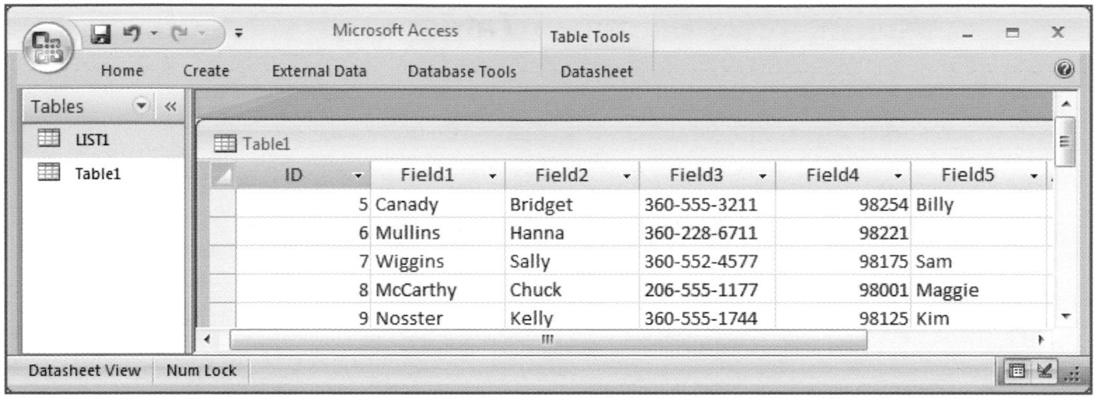

Microsoft Access — Table Tools

Home | Create | External Data | Database Tools | Datasheet

Tables

▦ LIST1
▦ Table1

▦ Table1

	ID ▾	Field1 ▾	Field2 ▾	Field3 ▾	Field4 ▾	Field5 ▾
	5	Canady	Bridget	360-555-3211	98254	Billy
	6	Mullins	Hanna	360-228-6711	98221	
	7	Wiggins	Sally	360-552-4577	98175	Sam
	8	McCarthy	Chuck	206-555-1177	98001	Maggie
	9	Nosster	Kelly	360-555-1744	98125	Kim

Datasheet View | Num Lock

Figure 2-6: At first glance, your new table looks like a spreadsheet.

NOTE

You can check your table for duplications. See "Check Tables For Duplicate Data" in Chapter 10.

Add New Field

📋	Copy
📋	Paste
↔	Column Width...
	Hide Columns
	Unhide Columns...
▦	Freeze Columns
	Unfreeze All Columns
🔍	Find...
	Insert Column
	Lookup Column...
	Delete Column
	Rename Column

CLOSE A TABLE

You can easily close an open table.

1. If the table in which you are working is displayed as a window, click **Close**, either in its title bar or next to the Access Help icon. (The location of Close depends on whether the object window is maximized.)

–Or–

Right-click the **Name** tab of any table. From the resulting context menu, click **Close**.

2. To close all open tables, right-click the **Name** tab of any open table. Click **Close All** on the context menu.

Define Field Names in Your Table

After you have entered several records into a table, you may want to identify your field names. To do so:

1. Click anywhere in the column for the field you want to define. In many cases, the first field you select will be Field1.

2. In the Datasheet tab (Table Tools) Fields & Columns group, click **Rename**.

New Field | Add Existing Fields | Lookup Column | Insert | Delete | Rename

Fields & Columns

–Or–

Right-click the field name/column header for the field you want to name. Click **Rename Column** on the context menu that appears.

–Or–

Double-click the field name/column header.

In any case, the field name is highlighted, indicating that you can type the new name.

3. Type the new field name, and press **ENTER** or **TAB**.

4. Follow the same steps for each field you want to rename.

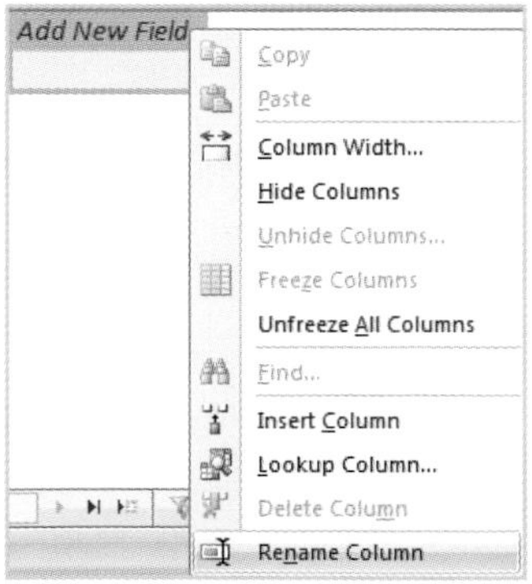

Create a New Empty Table

1. Open Access 2007 using one of the procedures described in Chapter 1.

2. Open an existing database or create a new database as described in "Build a Database on Your Own" earlier in this chapter.

3. In the Create tab Tables group, click **Table** to create a new table. A new table named Table1 (or Table2 and so forth) is created. It opens in Datasheet View with the Add New Field highlighted for text entry.

4. Enter your data and follow the steps as described in "Create a Table by Entering Data" earlier in this chapter.

5. To save the table, right-click the **Name** tab (if you're working with tabbed documents) or title bar (if you're working in the object window), and click **Save**.

   –Or–

   Press **CTRL+S**.

   In the Save As dialog box that appears, type a name for your new table.

6. Click **OK** to close the Save As dialog box.

Construct a Table in Design View

Tables can be created manually, adding fields one at a time. To use this method, you must start in Design View, as shown in Figure 2-7.

OPEN A TABLE IN DESIGN VIEW

1. Open a blank or existing Access database. See Chapter 1 for ways to open an existing database, or see "Build a Database on Your Own" earlier in this chapter to see how to create a new database.

2. In the Create tab Tables group, click **Table Design**. A new blank table opens in Design View with the insertion point blinking in the first Field Name field or cell.

CREATE THE FIELD STRUCTURE

The upper section of the table design window has columns that hold the basic definitions for each field included in your table. The field name, data type, and description for each individual field are entered into the rows. There are several

Create new tables using the Field Name, Data Type, and Description fields

A description can help users understand the type of data to be entered in a field

You can set the data type for each field; "Text" is the default

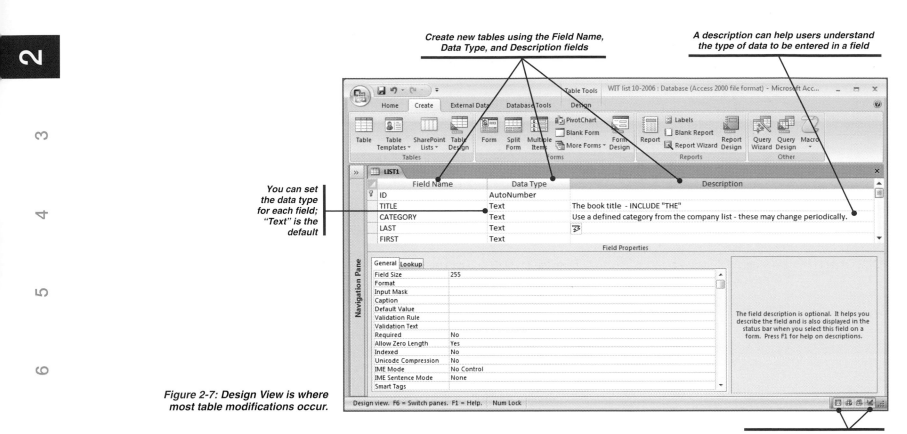

Figure 2-7: Design View is where most table modifications occur.

Use the buttons on the status bar to switch between views

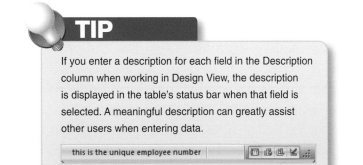

TIP

If you enter a description for each field in the Description column when working in Design View, the description is displayed in the table's status bar when that field is selected. A meaningful description can greatly assist other users when entering data.

data types from which to choose. The lower portion of this window is where you set more specific field properties, which is discussed in more detail in Chapter 3. This section changes as you select different fields:

● **Data Type** defines the type of data the field will contain. See Table 2-1 for the different data types and their usage. Text is the default data type, as it provides the most flexibility with data entry.

● The optional **Description** field is used to provide other information that may be required, such as the type of information that is expected in this field.

DATA TYPE	DESCRIPTION	COMMENTS
Text	Numbers or letters	Stores up to 255 characters
Memo	Text that is too long to be stored in text fields	Up to 65,535 characters if you enter them manually. Up to 2 GB if you enter them from the program
Number	Digits only	You set the field size, up to 16 bytes of information
Date/Time	A valid date or time	
Currency	Same as number, but with decimal places and currency symbol added	Can be up to four decimal places. Used to store financial data
AutoNumber	A unique sequential number	
Yes/No	Accepts yes/no; true/false; on/off	
OLE Object	Any object that can be linked or embedded in a table	Limited to 2 GB and can make your program run slowly. Using an attachment field is a better option in most cases
Hyperlink	A path to an object, file or Web site	
Attachment	Any supported type of file, including pictures, charts, text files, and so on	This is a new type in Access 2007, and works only with the .accdb file format. It is more flexible than the OLE Object data type
Lookup Wizard	Creates a drop-down list from existing data or data you enter	A special usage of the Text data type

Table: 2-1: Data Types That Can Be Assigned to Table Fields

Design View opens with an insertion point in the first field name. To complete your table in Design View:

1. Type a field name.
2. Press ENTER. This will move your insertion point to the Data Type column and display the default data type, which is Text.
3. Click the **Data Type** down arrow to open the Data Type menu, as shown in Figure 2-8. Data types are discussed in more detail in Chapter 3.
4. Select a data type. Press TAB to move to the Description column. Enter a description for your field if you choose.
5. Press TAB or ENTER, or use your mouse to move to the next field or row.
6. Repeat steps 1–5 until you have entered all of the field descriptions for the table.

SAVE THE TABLE

After you have changed or added fields to a table, you should save the new design. While records within your database are saved automatically, new designs are not. To save your table:

- Click the **Office Button**, and click **Save**.
  –Or–
- Right-click the table's **Name** tab, and click **Save** in the context menu.

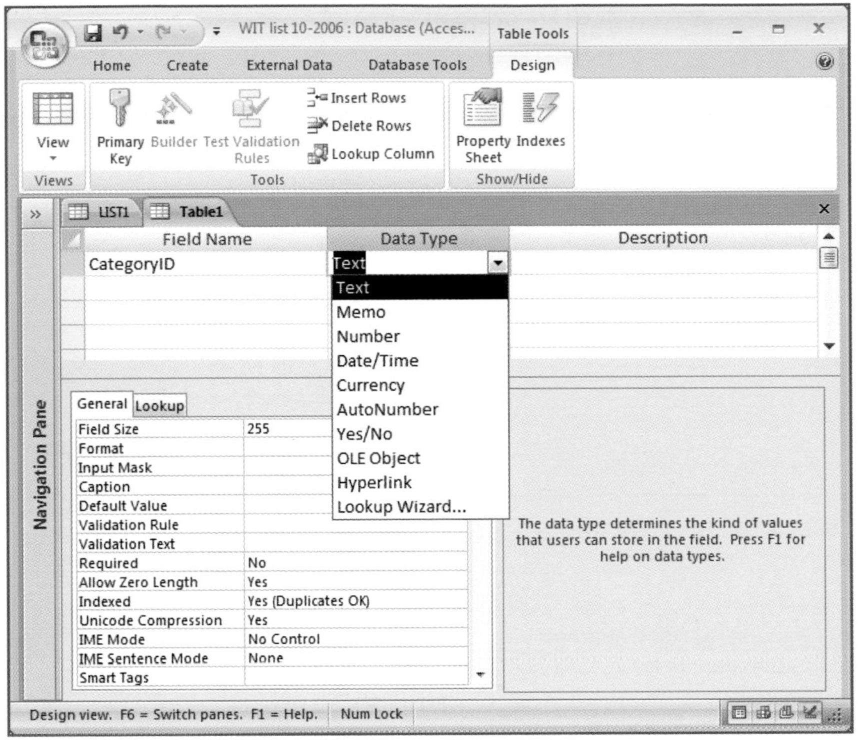

Create a Table from a Table Template

Access supplies several table templates for use in many types of databases. The table templates come with preset field names and are ready for you to enter data or paste information from an external source. To use one of these templates:

1. Open a new or existing database.

2. In the Create tab Tables group, click **Table Templates**.

3. Click one of the available templates from the displayed list. A new table opens in Datasheet View. It contains preset fields you can use or modify.

4. Click in the first empty cell to start entering data. See Chapter 4 for other ways to add data into a table.

5. Close the table when finished, and save any changes to its design.

Figure 2-8: While "Text" is the default data type, there are several data types from which to choose.

Assign a Primary Key

It is important to assign at least one field in each table as a primary key to ensure that each record is unique. For information on using primary keys, see the "Understanding the Primary Key" Quickfacts later in the chapter.

ADD A PRIMARY KEY TO A NEW TABLE

1. Open a new or existing database.

2. In the Create tab Tables group, click **Table**. This opens a new table in Datasheet View.

3. The first field is labeled "ID," as shown in Figure 2-9. Type some data in the field labeled Add New Field.

4. Continue to add new information, as described in "Create a Table by Entering Data" earlier in this chapter. After you have completed entering data, click **Close**. You are asked if you want to save the changes to the design of this table. Click **Yes**, and the Save As dialog box appears. Type a name for your new table. Click **OK**, and the table closes.

[Screenshot of Access window - Table Tools Datasheet ribbon with "Clinic Data : Database (Access 2007)" title]

Tables list: cashreceipts_aug_2006, cashreceipts_sep_2006, Clinic Patients, Employees, Procedures, Table1, Vendors

Table1 — ID — Add New Field — (New)

Record: 1 of 1 — No Filter — Search

Datasheet View   Num Lock

Figure 2-9: A new table opens with two fields, one for the "ID" and the second field available for you to add.

[Screenshot of Design tab ribbon: Home, Create, External Data, Database Tools, Design — Primary Key, Builder, Test Validation Rules, Insert Rows, Delete Rows, Lookup Column, Property Sheet, Indexes — Tools, Show/Hide]

NOTE

If you want to use more than one field as a primary key, hold down the **CTRL** key, and click the row selector for each field you want to use.

5. In the Navigation Pane, right-click the new table. Click **Design View** in the context menu to open the table. Note that the ID field has been set as the primary key, as seen in Figure 2-10.

USE AN EXISTING FIELD AS THE PRIMARY KEY

In some tables, you may already have a unique identifier. This could be a serial number or some other combination of numbers and letters that is unique to a specific record. Any such symbol makes a good primary key. To use this unique code as a primary key:

1. Open an existing database.

2. In the Navigation Pane, right-click the table in which you want to create the primary key. Click **Design View** in the context menu to open the table.

3. Click the row selector for the field you want to set as the primary key.

4. In the Design tab (Table Tools) Tools group, click **Primary Key**. The key indicator appears in the row selector for each field you have chosen.

REMOVE AND CHANGE A PRIMARY KEY

If you need to change a primary key within a table:

1. Open the database you want to use.

2. In the Navigation Pane, right-click the table in which you want to remove the primary key, and click **Design View**.

3. Click the row selector for the current primary key field.

4. In the Design tab Tools group, click **Primary Key**. The key indicator disappears from each of the selected fields.

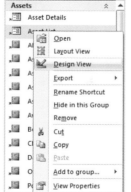

[Lending Library / Assets navigation pane with context menu: Open, Layout View, Design View, Export, Rename Shortcut, Hide in this Group, Remove, Cut, Copy, Paste, Add to group..., View Properties]

UNDERSTANDING THE PRIMARY KEY

It is important to assign at least one field in each table as a primary key. Primary keys are fields that identify records as unique. They ensure that duplicate records are not entered and expedite locating records in the database. It is also through primary keys that databases are connected, or related.

Once a primary key is established in a table, you can use it to connect tables. For example, in a Vendors table, the primary key might be a vendor identification number. This number might also appear in a Products table so that you can establish a relationship between products that you sell and the vendors that supply the products. In the Products table, the vendor key would be known as a *foreign key*, or simply another table's primary key.

There are several attributes for a primary key:

- A primary key is unique and is never repeated in the table.

- A primary key is never empty.

- A primary key never changes.

Access 2007 automatically assigns a primary key for you when you create a new table in Datasheet View, with ID as its field name and the data type of AutoNumber (tables created in Design View are not automatically provided a primary key). AutoNumber is the best choice for a primary key, since using an automatic number will ensure that no two IDs are the same, no matter how many records are entered into the table.

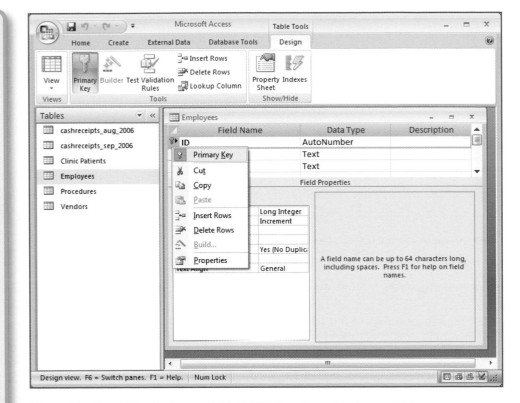

Figure 2-10: A small key indicates which field is the primary key in your table.

5. Set a new primary key by creating a field and assigning it the AutoNumber data type, and then assigning it as a primary key.

–Or–

Assign an existing field to be the primary key.

See the two previous sections for procedures on how to assign a primary key.

Add Identifying Information to Your Database

You can add identifying information to an Access database to make it easier to find when using search tools.

1. Open your database using one of the methods discussed in Chapter 1.

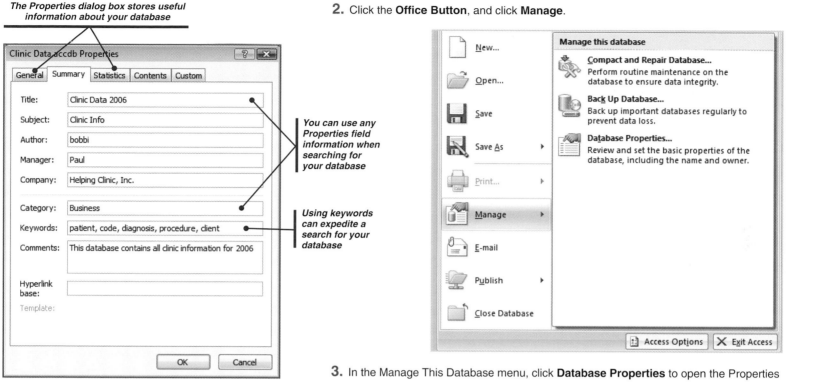

The Properties dialog box stores useful information about your database

You can use any Properties field information when searching for your database

Using keywords can expedite a search for your database

Figure 2-11: The search for a particular database can be eased by entering identifying information.

2. Click the **Office Button**, and click **Manage**.

3. In the Manage This Database menu, click **Database Properties** to open the Properties dialog box.

4. In the Properties dialog box, enter any identifying information, as shown in Figure 2-11. Good descriptors can include a title, subject, and keywords (words or phrases that are associated with the database).

Identify Relationships

Access is a *relational* database: it uses relationships to establish connections between tables. Each table, or group of data, should have a primary key, and that primary key can also be part of another table but viewed as a *foreign key*. Because this same primary key is in both tables, the two tables can relate and mix in multiple settings—such as queries, forms, reports, and data access pages.

Figure 2-12: *Different relationships can be created among the tables in your database.*

Define Relationships

There are three types of table relationships: one-to-many; many-to-many; and, in some cases, one-to-one. This is because some tables hold a single record that relates to multiple records in another database:

- For example, a small manufacturer has a database with three tables. The tables are as shown in Figure 2-12. As an example of a one-to-many relationship, the Orders table can hold many orders from the same customer.

- Each order can have multiple products on it and, reversing the thought, each product can be on multiple orders. This would be a many-to-many relationship. The ideal way to relate the latter relationship is to create a third *junction,* or linking table (shown as Order Details in Figure 2-13).

- A one-to-one relationship exists when each record in the first table can have only one matching record in the second table and each record in the second table can have only one matching record on the first table. Usually, this type of information can be stored in only one table; however, you could establish a one-to-one relationship to isolate part of a table for security reasons, for instance, or to archive part of a large table. For example, if a few of your 705 employees are subject to a miscellaneous deduction every third year, you might store that information in a separate table, because storing the information in the Employee table would result in empty spaces for every employee to whom the deduction does *not* apply.

The OrderDetails table acts as the junction table

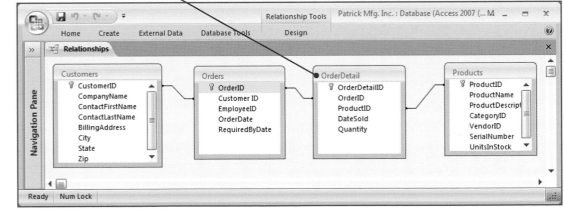

Relate Tables in the Relationships Tab

Access has an easy way to relate tables once you've defined their primary keys.

1. Open Access 2007 using one of the procedures described in Chapter 1. Open an existing database.

Figure 2-13: *Junction tables create the connection between tables having a many-to-many relationship.*

Earlier versions of Access referred to the container where relationships are diagrammed as the **Relationships window**. You can view relationships in a window if you change how you view open objects from the default for Access 2007—tabbed documents—to overlapping windows. Chapter 1 describes how to change the way you view open objects.

UNDERSTANDING REFERENTIAL INTEGRITY

As you work with tables and relationships, the very nature of data is that it changes. The relationships you so carefully create can be damaged if only one facet is removed. For example, if you have established a one-to-many relationship between your Employee table and your Customer table to identify sales representatives and their clients and an employee leaves your company, the employee ID in the Customer table is no longer valid because the record that particular employee ID references is no longer available. The customer records that contain those references are called "orphans" after the Employee record is deleted.

Access 2007 has a method, called *referential integrity* that prevents these situations and ensures that all references are synchronized. See "Enforce Referential Integrity" for instructions on how to ensure your relationships are not damaged when one part of a relationship is changed.

2. In the Database Tools tab Show/Hide group, click **Relationships**. The Show Table dialog box will appear if you have not yet established any relationships. (If it does not appear, in the Design tab Relationships group, click **Show Table**.) The Show Table dialog box displays both the tables (and queries) in your database (queries are described in Chapter 5).

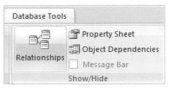

3. Select a table and click **Add**. Repeat to add all the tables needed to create relationships.

4. Click **Close**. The Relationships tab will be displayed. The primary key fields are indicated by the small key by the field name within each table list.

5. Drag the primary key field from one table to the equivalent foreign key field in another table. Continue dragging the primary key fields until all chosen tables are related.

6. Close the Relationships tab.

Enforce Referential Integrity

Referential integrity allows Access to check the validity of relationships between records. It also ensures that changes, such as deleting or altering related data, don't impair the relationships.

1. Open the database whose referential integrity you want to enforce.

2. In the Database Tools tab Show/Hide group, click **Relationships**.

3. In the Design tab Relationships group, click **All Relationships** to ensure that all relationships are displayed.

4. Double-click the line representing the relationship to which you want to apply referential integrity.

5. At the bottom of the Edit Relationships dialog box, select **Enforce Referential Integrity**, as shown in Figure 2-14:

- Click **Cascade Update Related Fields** to ensure that changing a primary key value in the primary table automatically updates the foreign key field.

- Click **Cascade Delete Related Records** to ensure that when records are deleted in the primary table, corresponding records in a related table will also be deleted.

6. Click **OK** to return to the Relationships tab.

7. If prompted, select **Yes** to save changes to the relationships layout.

"1" represents the one member of the one-to-many relationship

" " represents the many member of the one-to-many relationship

Bold connectors display enforced referential integrity

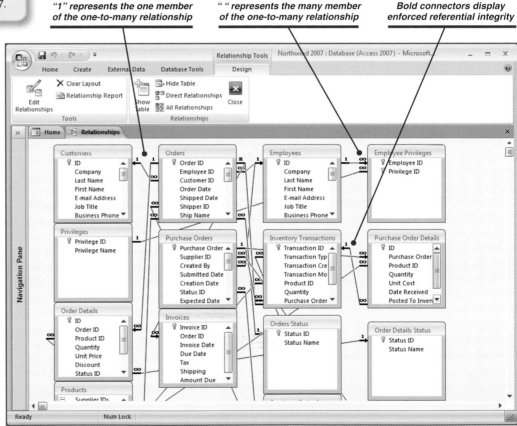

Figure 2-14: Enforcing referential integrity assures that changes will not impair the established relationships in your tables.

How to...

- • Delete a Table
- Renaming an Access Database
- • Rename a Table
- Switching Views
- • Change Field Names
- • Change a Data Type in Datasheet View
- • Change a Data Type in Design View
- Understanding Restrictions When Changing Data Types
- • Change Display of Data Through the Format Property
- Understanding Input Masks
- • Create a Pattern for Data Entry with Input Masks
- Creating a Custom Input Mask
- • Establish a Field's Default Value
- • Limit Field Values with a Validation Rule
- • Require Entry but Allow a Zero-Length String
- • Use the Caption Field Property
- • Index a Data Field
- • Add Smart Tags
- • Use the Lookup Wizard
- Deciding to Use a Multivalued Field

Chapter 3

Modifying Tables and Fields

As with any powerful machine, an Access database requires some fine-tuning to optimize its purpose and performance. The modifications covered in this chapter involve making changes to tables and adjustments to the field properties. Basic table changes can occur within the Navigation Pane, as shown in Figure 3-1. You make field adjustments in the field properties area of the table in Design View.

Make Basic Changes to Tables and Fields

You will sometimes need to make basic changes to the objects in your database. This is an easy task within Microsoft Access.

Navigation Pane

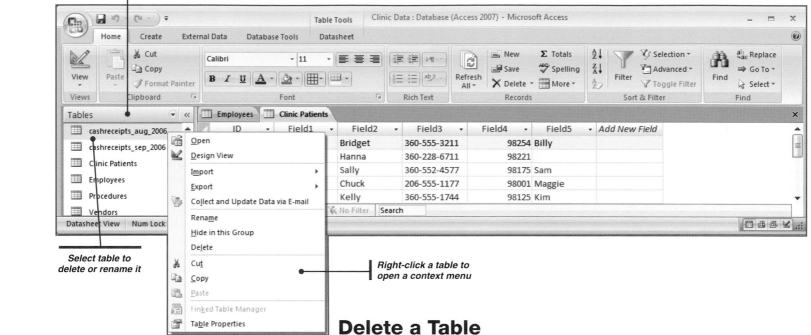

Figure 3-1: Basic edits to tables can be made from the Navigation Pane.

Select table to delete or rename it

Right-click a table to open a context menu

CAUTION

If the table is open, a dialog box will appear, saying that you cannot delete the database object while it is open. Click **OK** and close the table. Chapter 2 describes how to close tabbed and windowed objects.

Delete a Table

When a table is no longer necessary, you can easily delete it.

1. Within the Access window, display the Navigation Pane. If you do not see the list of tables, click the **Navigation Pane** down arrow, and click **All Tables**, as shown in Figure 3-2.

2. Right-click the table you want deleted, and click **Delete**. A dialog box will appear, stating that deleting this table will remove it from all groups. Click **Yes** to confirm the deletion. This will bring you back to the Access window. (If you have established relationships between tables, continue to step 3.)

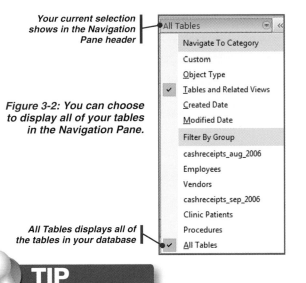

Your current selection shows in the Navigation Pane header

Figure 3-2: You can choose to display all of your tables in the Navigation Pane.

All Tables displays all of the tables in your database

TIP

Don't panic if you mistakenly delete a table. Click **Undo** on the Quick Access toolbar, and the table will be restored.

QUICKSTEPS

RENAMING AN ACCESS DATABASE

To rename an Access database:

1. Click the **Office Button**, and click **Open.**

2. Locate the folder in which you store your database, and open the folder so that its contents appear in the right pane.

3. In the right pane, right-click the database whose name you want to change, and click **Rename,** as seen in Figure 3-3.

4. Type the new name for the database, and press **ENTER.**

3. If you have established relationships between the table you want deleted and other tables, you will see another alert dialog box. (See Chapter 2 for information regarding table relationships.) The alert informs you of the need to delete the relationships with this table prior to its deletion. It also offers to delete the relationships for you. Click **Yes** if you would like to delete both the relationships and the table. This will bring you back to the Access window.

Rename a Table

Changing the name of a table is a simple task, if you are at the right location.

1. In order to rename a table, you must have the table closed and be in the Access window.

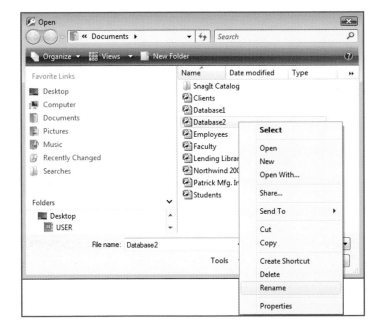

Figure 3-3: You can quickly rename a database using the Office Button.

TIP

Unlike earlier versions of Access, you do not have to perform a separate procedure to save a table after you have changed its name or the name of a field. Access 2007 saves these changes automatically.

QUICKSTEPS

SWITCHING VIEWS

When editing tables, and the fields within those tables, you will be switching between Datasheet View and Design View frequently. There are several ways to switch views. Find the way that is quickest for you.

USE THE RIBBON WITH A MOUSE

In the Home, Design, or Datasheet tab Views group, click the **View** button down arrow to display a list of the available views. Click the view that you want to use. (See Chapter 10 for information regarding PivotTable and PivotChart Views.)

–Or–

Click the upper half of the **View** button to switch to the last view that was displayed.

Continued . . .

2. Expand the Navigation Pane, if necessary. Right-click the table whose name you want to change, and click **Rename**. The name field will be highlighted. Type the new name, and press **ENTER**.

–Or–

Click the table name, and press the **F2** key to highlight the name field. Type the new name, and press **ENTER**. The new table name is displayed within the Navigation Pane.

Change Field Names

Later in this chapter, we will go into table Design View and change field properties. To change a field name, however, you may follow a similar path, as explained in "Rename a Table."

1. Open the table that contains the field name(s) you want to change. From the Navigation Pane, double-click a table.

–Or–

If there are no other open objects, drag the table from the Navigation Pane to the Access work area.

In either case, the table will open.

2. Double-click the field name you want to change. The current name is highlighted.

–Or–

In the Datasheet tab Fields & Columns group, click **Rename** to highlight the current name.

3. Type a new name, and press **ENTER**.

Fine-Tune the Fields

The fine-tuning that can take place within fields and their properties is quite extensive. The first part of this fine-tuning revolves around the field's data type. As discussed in Chapter 2, there are several data types to choose from when first defining a field. This section takes you a step deeper into not only the data types, but also the properties that further define those data types. You can fine-tune your fields in either Datasheet or Design View. Access 2007 automatically assigns a data type based on the data that's entered in a field.

Figure 3-4: The KeyTips displayed when you press the ALT key can make moving around your database much faster.

Change a Data Type in Datasheet View

Data types can restrict certain information from being entered incorrectly into the database. For example, if a number is supposed to be entered into a field and a user tries to enter text, a warning dialog box will appear saying that Access will not accept the entry until a number is supplied. To change a data type in Datasheet View:

1. From the Navigation Pane, open the table to be customized.

2. Click anywhere in the column corresponding to the field you want to change.

3. In the Datasheet tab (Table Tools) Data Type & Formatting group, click the **Data Type** down arrow to display the list of available data types.

4. Select the data type you want, as shown in Figure 3-5.

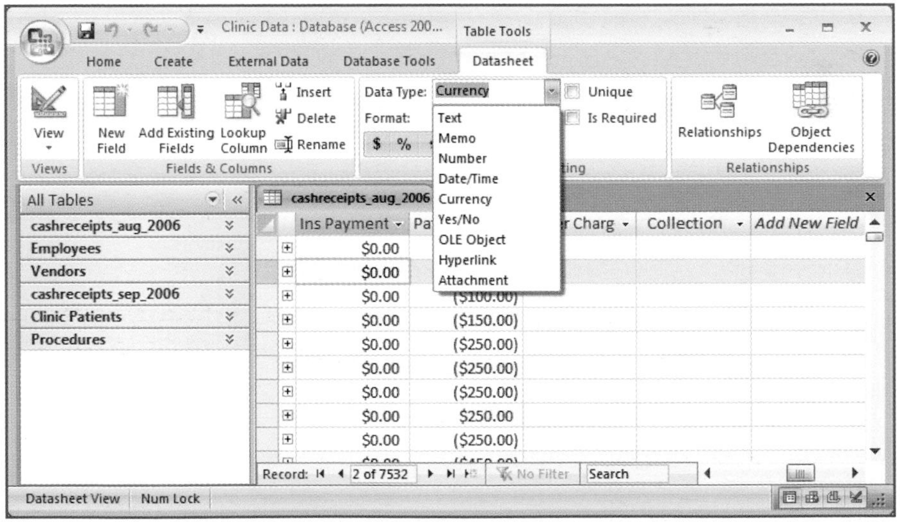

QUICKSTEPS

SWITCHING VIEWS (Continued)

USE THE RIBBON FROM THE KEYBOARD

1. In any view, press **ALT** to display the keyboard shortcuts in the ribbon, as seen in Figure 3-4.

2. In Datasheet View, press **W** twice and press **D** to go to Design View.

3. In Design View, press **D**, press **W**, and then press **H** to go to Datasheet View.

USE THE STATUS BAR

Click the **View** button for the view you want at the right end of the status bar.

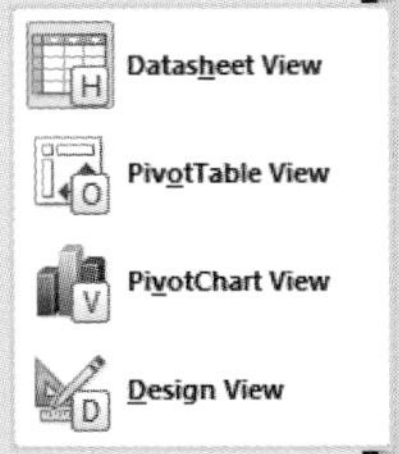

Datasheet View

PivotTable View

PivotChart View

Design View

USE A TABLE'S CONTEXT MENU

Right-click a table in the Navigation Pane.

–Or–

Right-click the tab of an open table.

In either case, click **Design View** or **Datasheet View**.

Figure 3-5: Use Datasheet View to quickly change a data type.

TIP

To quickly enter a data type in the data type field in Design View, just type the first letter.

Change a Data Type in Design View

If you are going to make several changes, or want to work with formatting, (see "Change Display of Data Through the Format Property" later in this chapter), it is often easier to work in Design View.

1. From the Navigation Pane, right-click the table with which you want to work.

2. Click **Design View** from the context menu to open the table.

3. Click the **Data Type** field you want to change. Click the down arrow that appears to display the list of data types, as seen in Figure 3-6.

4. Click the data type you want.

5. Press **CTRL+S** to save the change.

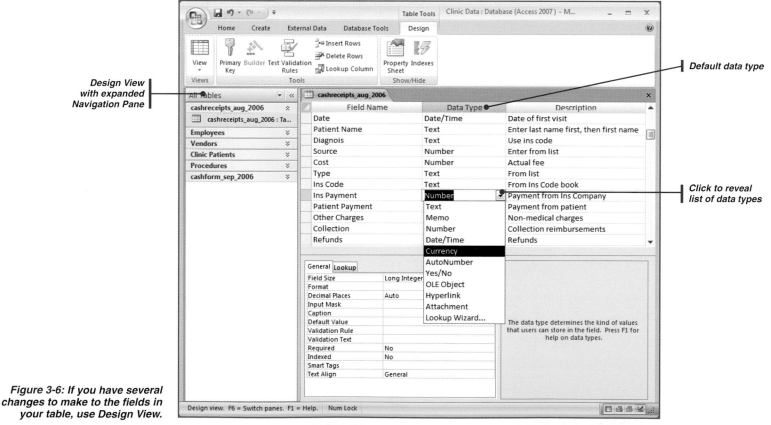

Figure 3-6: If you have several changes to make to the fields in your table, use Design View.

UNDERSTANDING RESTRICTIONS WHEN CHANGING DATA TYPES

When you change a data type, the information you have already entered into your table may be affected. For example, if you change a data type from Memo to Text, since Text allows only 255 characters, all of the other information in that field will be deleted. The following data types cannot be changed:

- Attachment fields

- Number fields when you have chosen a field size setting of *Replication ID*—a special Microsoft setting that creates a randomly generated 16-byte number

- OLE Object fields

Table 3-1 lists some effects when changing from Text to several other data types.

TIP

To switch between the Field Properties area and the upper section of Design View, press **F6** which will cycle you through the upper section to the Field Properties area to the ribbon shortcut keys.

ORIGINAL DATA TYPE	NEW DATA TYPE	CONCERNS
Text	Memo	None
	Number	The original text must be numbers. Also acceptable are currency symbols and decimals. The size set for the number of text characters must fit with the new number size
	Date/Time	The original text must be recognizable as either a date or a time, such as 11-13-2006 or 13:50:27
	Currency	The original text must be numbers and decimals
	AutoNumber	Allowed *only* when the field is *not* the primary key
	Yes/No	The original text must be Yes/No, On/Off, or True/False
	Hyperlink	Access converts original text to a hyperlink if it is a Web address

Table 3-1: Effects of Changing the Text Data Type

Change Display of Data Through the Format Property

The Field Properties area of the table Design View, as shown in Figure 3-7, presents numerous ways to customize your table and restrict the type of data being entered.

WORK WITH FORMAT SYMBOLS

You can change the way data is displayed (but not stored) in a database by entering specific symbols into the Format text box of the Field Properties area. Several symbols are used within the Format text box, many unique to one or two data types. The symbols used in the Text data type are listed in Table 3-2. See "Display All Characters in Uppercase" for one example on how to use format symbols.

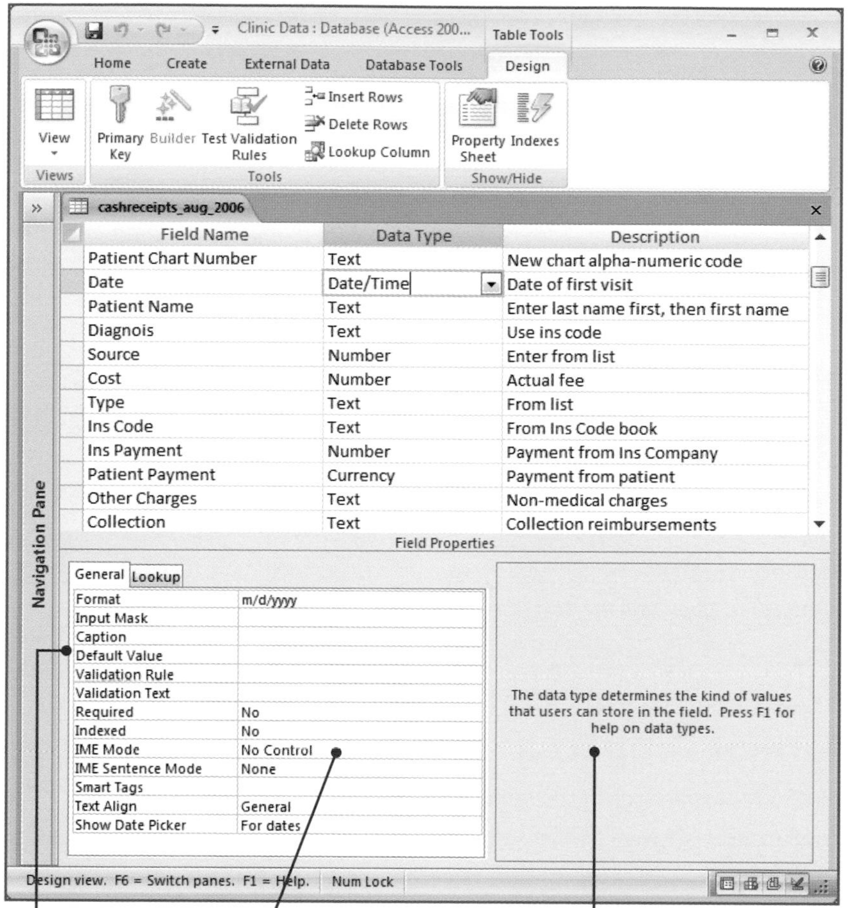

Figure 3-7: The Field Properties area within the Design View provides several ways to fine-tune the fields.

Lists properties for the data type for the selected field

Field properties change depending on the selected data type

Displays description of the selected field or property

SYMBOL	DISPLAY PURPOSE
>	Uppercase characters.
<	Lowercase characters.
@	Placeholder for character or space. (Placeholders fill underlying data from right to left.)
&	Placeholder for character or optional space.
!	Left-aligns data and forces placeholders to fill from left to right; must be the first character in format string.
"Text"	Displays the item in quotation marks exactly as typed, in addition to data.
\	Displays a character immediately following data.
*	Fills all blank spaces with character following *.
[color]	Formats data text in black, blue, green, cyan, red, magenta, yellow, or white; must be used with other symbols.

Table 3-2: Formatting Symbols for Text Data Types

DISPLAY ALL CHARACTERS IN UPPERCASE

You can format a field to display its contents in uppercase letters. For example, if you have a State field, you could ensure that all two-letter abbreviations, such as WA, are uppercased.

1. Open the table in Design View.

2. Click the field you want formatted. The field you chose will be outlined to confirm the field is active, and a color will appear in the record selector field at the left of the row, as shown in Figure 3-8.

3. Click the **General** tab in the Field Properties area.

4. Click the **Format** text box, and type ≥ (or to accomplish another formatting task, choose the appropriate symbol, as shown in Table 3-2). If you have additional objects within the database that use the field name, the Property Update Options Smart Tag will display to the left of the text box.

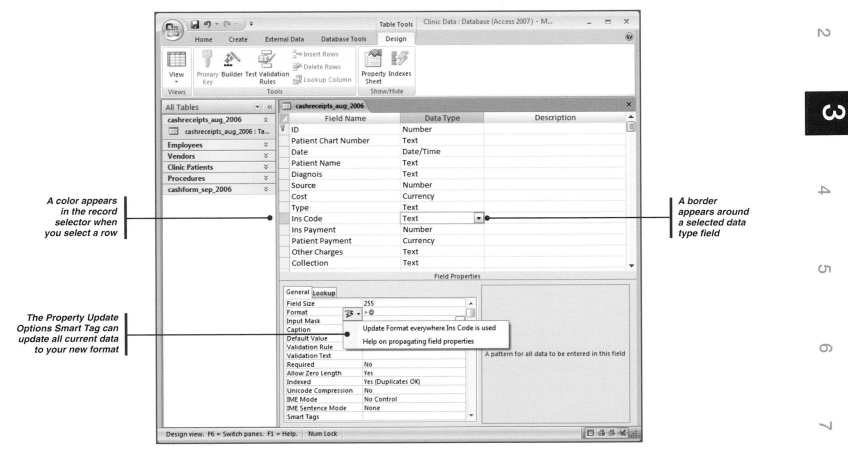

*A color appears
in the record
selector when
you select a row*

*A border
appears around
a selected data
type field*

*The Property Update
Options Smart Tag can
update all current data
to your new format*

**Figure 3-8: Design View allows you to change the
format of a field.**

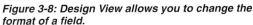

Microsoft Office Access

No objects needed to be updated.

OK

5. Click the **Property Update Options** Smart Tag down arrow, and click **Update Format
Everywhere** *Fieldname* **Is Used**. By doing so, the format you have chosen will be
propagated across all objects with the selected field name. For example, if you formatted
the state field to uppercase, all state fields—whether in forms, queries, reports, or
other tables—will be changed to uppercase. If no objects contain the same field name
as your newly formatted field, a dialog box will display a message stating that no
objects needed to be updated. Click **OK**.

6. In order to view your changes, you must save the table. If you try to switch views prior
to saving, a dialog box will appear asking if you want to save the table now. Click **Yes**
to save changes, and the display will switch to Datasheet View.

QUICKFACTS

UNDERSTANDING INPUT MASKS

Input masks provide a pattern for formatting data within a field by using characters or symbols to control how data will be displayed. There are actually three parts to an input mask. The first part includes the mask characters or mask *string* (series of characters) along with embedded literal data—such as parentheses, periods, and hyphens. The second part is optional and refers to the embedded literal characters and their storage within the field. If the second part is set at "0," it will store the characters; "1" means the characters will only be displayed, not stored. The third part of the string indicates the single character used as a placeholder. An example of a telephone number input mask would be: **!\(999")"000\-0000;0;_**:

- Exclamation point (!) indicates the mask should fill data from right to left.

- Backslash (\) causes characters immediately following to be displayed as a literal character. In this case, the parenthesis is the literal character.

- "9" means optional digits can be entered into these spaces.

- Double quotation ("") is like the backslash, in that anything enclosed in this will be taken literally.

- "0" means a single digit is mandatory.

An example of the displayed phone number would be (555)555-1212. Table 3-3 provides more detailed descriptions of mask characters. However, Access provides an easier way to enter input masks than to create one from scratch. See "Create a Pattern for Data Entry with Input Masks" for information on using the Input Mask Wizard.

SYMBOL	EXPLANATION
0	Required single digit (0 to 9)
9	Optional digit (0 to 9)
#	A digit, a space, the plus sign, and the minus sign can be entered
L	Required letter
?	Optional letter
>	Converts all letters that follow to uppercase
<	Converts all letters that follow to lowercase
A	Required digit or letter
a	Optional digit or letter
&	Required character or space
C	Optional character or space
!	Mask will fill from right to left
\	Characters immediately following will be displayed literally
""	Characters enclosed in double quotation marks will be displayed literally

Table 3-3: Input Mask Definition Characters

Create a Pattern for Data Entry with Input Masks

The Input Mask Wizard is a simple tool to use.

1. Open a table in Design View.

2. Click the field for which you want to have an input mask.

3. Click the **General** tab in the Field Properties area.

4. Click anywhere inside the Input Mask property text box. Click the **Builder** button [...] at the right side of the text box to display the Input Mask Wizard.

5. In the Input Mask list, click the mask you want to use, as shown in Figure 3-9. (Click **Try It** to enter data and see how it will be displayed.) If no changes are needed, click **Next**.

Try It: (__) ___-____

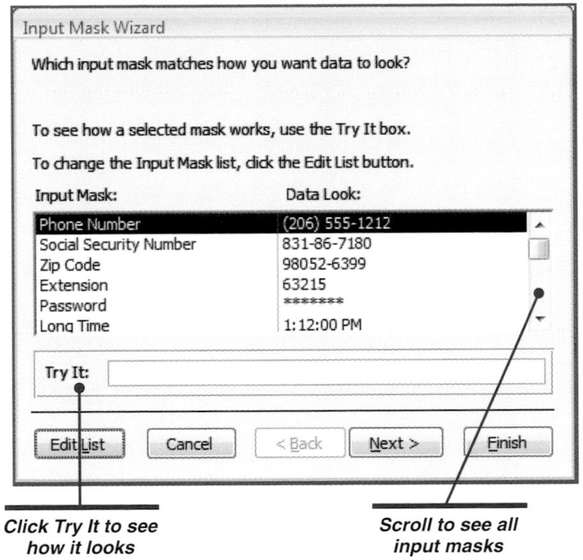

Figure 3-9: Input masks assist in formatting common data types.

Click Try It to see how it looks

Scroll to see all input masks

Edit to meet your specifications

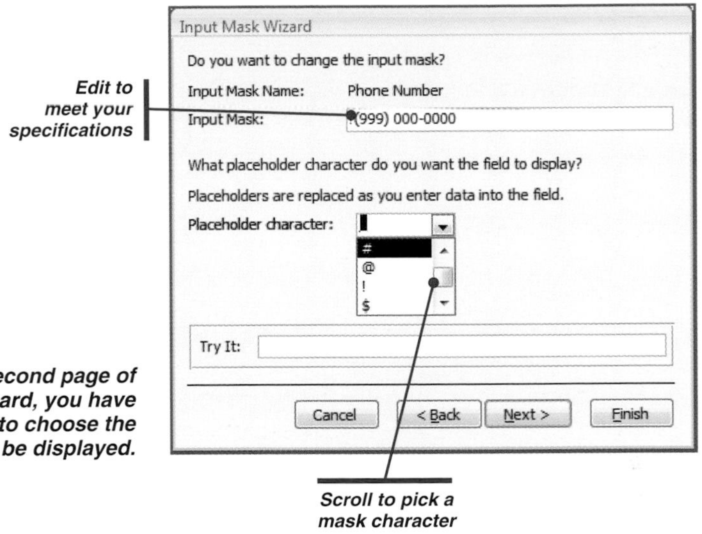

Figure 3-10: In the second page of the Input Mask Wizard, you have the opportunity to choose the placeholder that will be displayed.

Scroll to pick a mask character

QUICKSTEPS

CREATING A CUSTOM INPUT MASK

The Input Mask Wizard provides great sample patterns for some of the most common formatting situations. However, you may want to customize one of the patterns to use a format specific to your circumstances. There are two methods for doing this. The first is within the Input Mask Wizard itself, and the second is directly in the Input Mask text box.

1. Open your database in Design View, and click the field you would like to format with an input mask.

2. Click the **Builder** button (at the right of the Input Mask text box in the General tab of the Field Properties area) to start the Input Mask Wizard.

Continued . . .

6. If changes in the input mask are needed, type them in the Input Mask text box. You will see in Figure 3-10 an area that allows you to change the default placeholder. Either keep the default or click the **Placeholder Character** down arrow and select another. Click **Next**.

7. Choose **With The Symbols In The Mask** or **Without The Symbols In The Mask** to establish how to store your data. (Although choosing to store data with symbols allows them to be displayed in all objects, this method makes the size of your database slightly larger.) Click **Next** and then click **Finish** to return to Table Design view.

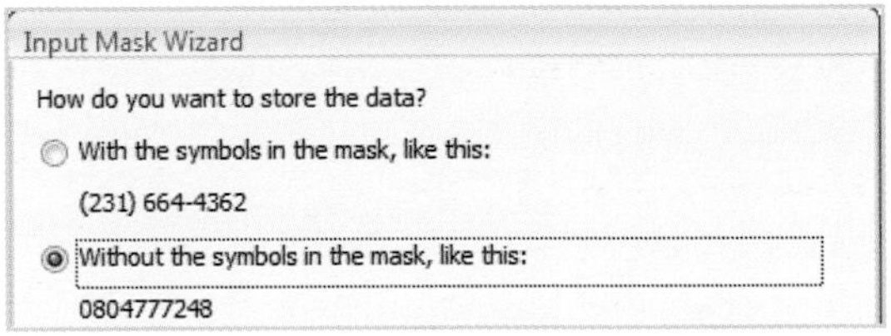

Establish a Field's Default Value

In many cases, a field contained in multiple records will include the same data. For example, employees of a small company may all reside in the same state.

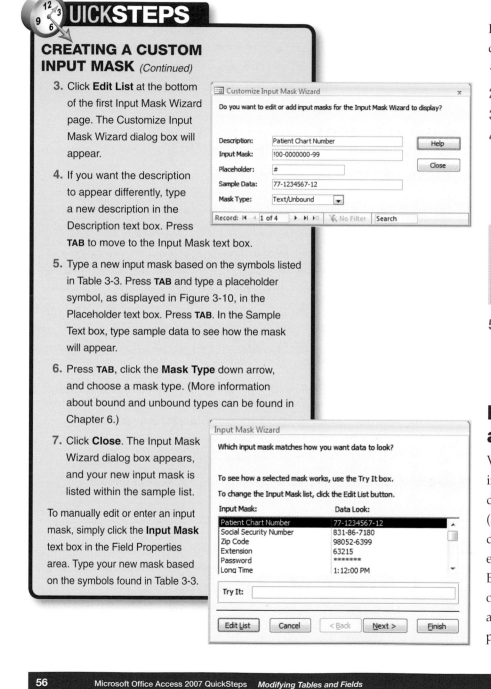

3. Click **Edit List** at the bottom of the first Input Mask Wizard page. The Customize Input Mask Wizard dialog box will appear.

4. If you want the description to appear differently, type a new description in the Description text box. Press **TAB** to move to the Input Mask text box.

5. Type a new input mask based on the symbols listed in Table 3-3. Press **TAB** and type a placeholder symbol, as displayed in Figure 3-10, in the Placeholder text box. Press **TAB**. In the Sample Text box, type sample data to see how the mask will appear.

6. Press **TAB**, click the **Mask Type** down arrow, and choose a mask type. (More information about bound and unbound types can be found in Chapter 6.)

7. Click **Close**. The Input Mask Wizard dialog box appears, and your new input mask is listed within the sample list.

To manually edit or enter an input mask, simply click the **Input Mask** text box in the Field Properties area. Type your new mask based on the symbols found in Table 3-3.

Rather than entering that state several times, place a default value for the state name in field properties.

1. Open a table in Design View.

2. Click the field you want to have a default value.

3. Click the **General** tab in the Field Properties area.

4. Type a value in the Default Value text box, and press **ENTER**. The typed value will automatically become enclosed in double quotes (the Caption property displayed in the illustration is described in "Use the Caption Field Property" later in the chapter).

5. Press **CTRL+S** to save your table, and switch to Datasheet View to see how the default value has affected your table. You will notice that the new record row displays your new default value.

Limit Field Values with a Validation Rule

Validation rules set parameters around the values inputted. Access applies these validity checks during data entry. A validation rule is made up of an *expression* (a group of functions, characters, and field values) that defines the acceptable values. The expression may be entered manually, or you can use a tool called Expression Builder. Not a wizard, Expression Builder is more of an organizational tool that helps you see the fields you can use and the operators or functions that are available. Chapter 5 provides more detail on using Expression Builder. You can,

NOTE

Access saves new records and changes in current records as you move through the object or close a database, form, or other object. You have to manually save changes to your table design, but Access will prompt you to do so before you can continue.

CAUTION

Changing the default value of a field will affect only future entries, not records you have already entered into your database.

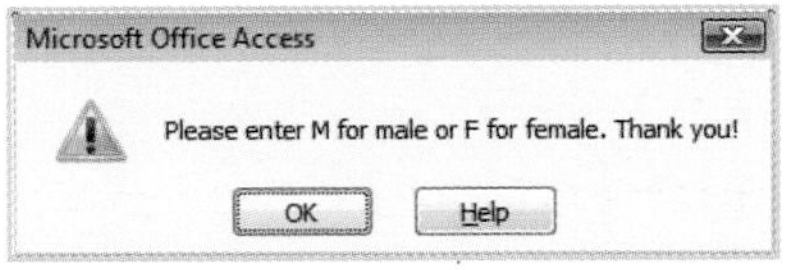

TIP

You can also require data input by using the Validation Rule property. The benefit to using this property is that you can then use your own validation text to display a customized message when the appropriate data is not entered.

and should, include some validation text with your validation rule. This text will be displayed in a dialog box if the rule is violated. For example, let's say you have an employee table that holds a "gender" field. It is designed to have either "M" for male or "F" for female. If a character other than "M" or "F" is entered into the field, the validation text will pop up in a dialog box.

1. Open a table in Design View.

2. Click the field you want to receive a validation rule and validation text.

3. Click the **General** tab in the Field Properties area.

4. Type your rule or expression in the Validation Rule text box, as shown in Figure 3-11. Press **TAB** or **ENTER**. The insertion point will move to the Validation Text text box.

5. Type your validation text, and press **ENTER**.

6. Press **CTRL+S** to save your table, and select **Datasheet View** to experiment with data entry in the field with validation rules and text. If you don't adhere to the rule you established, Access will alert you with a dialog box and prevent you from making the illegal entry.

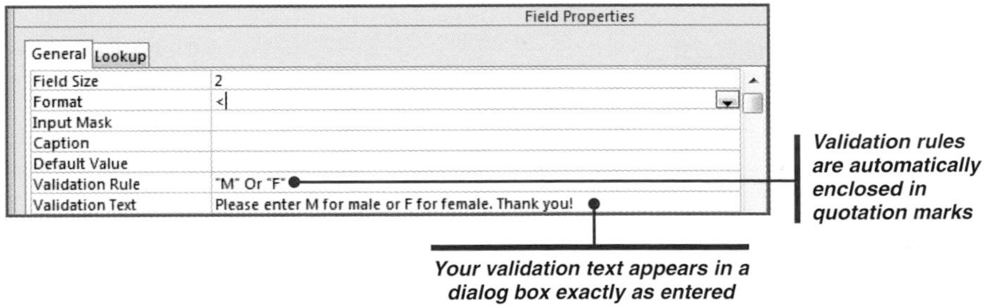

Your validation text appears in a dialog box exactly as entered

Validation rules are automatically enclosed in quotation marks

Figure 3-11: Validation rules should include validation text to aid in data entry.

Require Entry but Allow a Zero-Length String

For certain fields within your database, you may want to require data entry in order to maintain integrity within your database structure. There are situations where an entry is important, but there is no data to place in the field(s). For example, in a customer table, you may choose to require entry of the customers' fax numbers in order to send reservation confirmations. Some customers,

Figure 3-12: *Access will remind you to enter data into a required field.*

General	Lookup	
Field Size	25
Format	
Input Mask	
Caption	
Default Value	
Validation Rule	
Validation Text	
Required	Yes
Allow Zero Length	Yes

NOTE

You can establish a different caption for the same field in each database object. For example, your company's internal database table may use the field name and caption "Category ID." Your company's report, which is seen by those outside the company, may use the caption "Product Line" for the "Category ID" field.

General	Lookup	
Field Size	25
Format	
Input Mask	!\(999") "000\-0000;;#
Caption	Home Phone

however, may not have a fax machine. You would want to require the entry but allow a *zero-length string*. This way, a blank space or double quotation marks (" ") could be entered into the fax number field, confirming the customer has no fax number.

1. Open a table in Design View.
2. Click the field you would like to make required. Click the **General** tab in the Field Properties area. In the Required text box, type <u>Y</u> for yes or <u>N</u> for no.

   –Or–

   Click the **Required** down arrow at the right of the text box, and click **Yes** or **No**.
3. Press **TAB** to move to the Allow Zero Length text box. Type <u>Yes</u> or <u>No</u> in the text box using the same techniques as in the Required field text box.
4. Right-click the table's tab, and click **Save**. Switch to Datasheet View to experiment with required fields. If you don't type data in the required field, Access will alert you with a dialog box and prevent you from entering the record, as seen in Figure 3-12.

Use the Caption Field Property

You may have noticed many of the wizard-based data fields have names with no embedded spaces. For example, rather than "Home Phone," the field name is "HomePhone." If you foresee growth in your database and the potential for upsizing it to a SQL-based database, it is a good idea to follow this practice. SQL databases, such as Oracle or Microsoft SQL Server, do not support spaces within names. To ensure that "friendly" names are displayed within your database, however, use the Caption Field property. This will display your field names with embedded spaces.

1. Open a table in Design View.
2. Click the field name you would like to provide with a "friendly" name.
3. Click the **General** tab in the Field Properties area.
4. Enter your "friendly" name for the field in the Caption text box. As with other field property changes, you must save your table prior to switching to Datasheet View.

Index a Data Field

An *index* is an internal table that contains two columns. One holds the value in the field or fields being indexed, and the other holds the physical location of each record in the table containing that value. Access uses an index in a manner similar to how you use a book index: it finds the value desired and jumps directly to the page, or place, where that value is held. Each time a record is added to or updated in the database, Access updates all of its indexes. This may sometimes slow down the process of data entry, however, so overuse of indexes is not recommended.

1. Open a table in Design View.
2. Click the field you want to have indexed.
3. Click the **General** tab in the Field Properties area.
4. Click the **Indexed** down arrow, located to the right of the text box.
5. "No" is the default choice within the Indexed field. Click **Yes (Duplicates OK)** if the field will have multiple entries with the same value.

   –Or–

   Click **Yes (No Duplicates)** if you do not allow duplicate values in this field.
6. Save your table.

General	Lookup
Format	@
Input Mask	
Caption	
Default Value	
Validation Rule	
Validation Text	
Required	Yes
Allow Zero Length	Yes
Indexed	Yes (Duplicates OK)

Add Smart Tags

Smart Tags are like hyperlinks on steroids. They are little applications you can hook into fields to recognize items—such as names, addresses, or stock symbols—and provide options, or actions, for those recognized items. Smart Tags are limited in the number available within the standard Access application. There is, however, a button within the Smart Tags dialog box, as shown in Figure 3-13, that can connect you to the Microsoft Office Online Web site and let you check out current offerings within the Smart Tag product line. The current Smart Tags included with Access are:

- **Date** is used to schedule a meeting or check your calendar within Microsoft Outlook.
- **Telephone Number** adds a telephone number to your Contacts list in Microsoft Outlook.

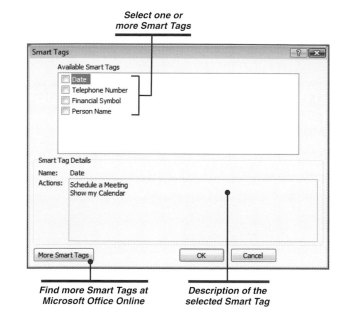

Select one or
more Smart Tags

Find more Smart Tags at
Microsoft Office Online

Description of the
selected Smart Tag

Figure 3-13: Accomplish common tasks using Smart Tags.

- **Financial Symbol** is used to obtain a stock quote, company reports, or news surrounding an accepted NYSE or NASDAQ company—all from the MSN MoneyCentral Web site.

- **Person Name** is used to accept a person's name or e-mail address and, assuming you are using Microsoft Outlook, send an e-mail, schedule a meeting, open your Contacts list, or add the name to your Contacts list.

When a Smart Tag is added to your field, a drop-down menu will be displayed as your mouse pointer hovers over the field within the record. This menu will provide the above-listed Smart Tag options.

1. Open a table in Design View.

2. Click the field in which you would like to include a Smart Tag.

3. Click the **General** tab in the Field Properties area.

4. Click the **Builder** button to the right of the Smart Tags text box. The Smart Tags dialog box will appear, as shown in Figure 3-13.

5. Click any of the Smart Tags that apply to your field, and the available actions (menu choices) will be displayed in the Smart Tag Details area of the dialog box.

6. Click **OK** to return to Design View. Save the table and switch to
Datasheet View to experiment with Smart Tags.

(206) 555-1212 ⓘ

Use the Lookup Wizard

There are times when the data to be entered in a field can be found in another table, and/or the data is a series of data points that would benefit from being provided only once to eliminate data entry errors. Rather than selecting a data type for your field, it may be helpful to call upon the Lookup Wizard to create a drop-down list of values from which you can choose.

START THE LOOKUP WIZARD

1. Open a table in Design View.

2. Type a field name, and press **TAB** to move to the Data Type column.

    –Or–

    Click the **Data Type** field next to a preexisting field name.

3. Click the **Data Type** down arrow, scroll to the bottom of the list, and click **Lookup Wizard**. The Lookup Wizard dialog box will appear.

This wizard creates a lookup column, which displays a list of values you can choose from. How do you want your lookup column to get its values?

○ I want the lookup column to look up the values in a table or query.

○ I will type in the values that I want.

TIP

To use a lookup column, click the down arrow at the right of its text box. Scroll through the list, and click the value you want to use.

4. Click **I Want The Lookup Column To Look Up The Values In A Table Or Query** to pull data from an existing table or query. Click **Next** and continue through the next page.

–Or–

Click **I Will Type In The Values That I Want** if you would like to create your own data list. Click **Next** and skip to "Create Your Own Value List with the Lookup Wizard."

FIND YOUR LOOKUP VALUES IN A TABLE OR QUERY

1. Use steps 1–3 of "Start the Lookup Wizard," and select the first option in step 4.

2. Click **Tables**, **Queries**, or **Both** to display their contents.

Which table or query should provide the values for your lookup column?

Table: cashform_sep_2006
Table: Clinic Patients
Table: Employees
Table: Procedures
Table: Vendors

View
○ Tables   ○ Queries   ○ Both

3. Select a specific table or query, and click **Next**. A dialog box with the available fields will appear.

4. Select the field you would like to include in the lookup column, and click the single right arrow to add the field to the Selected Fields box, as shown in Figure 3-14. Continue this process until you have chosen all the desired fields. If you would like to remove any of the fields from the selected field box, simply select the field, and click the single left arrow. (Click a double arrow to move all fields at once.) Click **Next**.

5. Choose to sort field(s) by ascending or descending order, as shown in Figure 3-15 (Chapter 5 describes sorting in more detail). Click **Next**.

6. Adjust the column width for your lookup fields in the next page of the wizard. Do this by placing the mouse pointer near the right edge of the column header. When a double-headed arrow appears, drag the column to the desired width.

–Or–

Move selected field to
the Selected Fields box

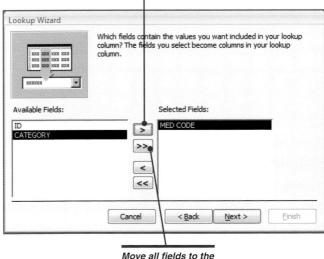

Move all fields to the
Selected Fields box

Figure 3-14: You can choose multiple fields in the third page of the Lookup Wizard.

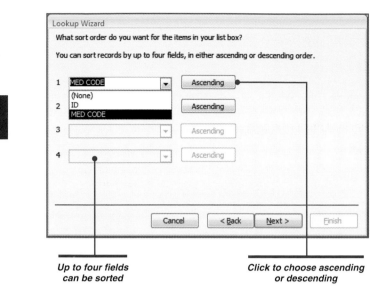

**Up to four fields
can be sorted**

**Click to choose ascending
or descending**

*Figure 3-15: The sort order of the lookup column will affect
the order in which fields are displayed.*

Double-click the right edge of the column header to have Access fit the column to the widest entry.

Click **Next** when satisfied with the results. The last page of the wizard will appear.

7. Clear the **Hide Key Column** check box if you want to include the primary key in your list of options. Access 2007 recommends that you hide this column. Click **Next**.

8. Accept the default label for the lookup column, or type a new name.

9. Click **Allow Multiple Values** if you want Access 2007 to store the values you just entered so that you can choose more than one value for each record. These values will display as a drop-down list of check boxes when the table is in Datasheet View. Click **Finish**.

10. Save your table and switch to Datasheet View to enter data using the lookup column.

CREATE YOUR OWN VALUE LIST WITH THE LOOKUP WIZARD

This option allows you to have a set group of values from which you can choose when entering data.

1. Display the Lookup Wizard (see steps 1–3 of "Use the Lookup Wizard").

2. Select **I Will Type In The Values That I Want**, and click **Next**.

3. Type your first value in the empty field, and press **TAB**. Continue entering values until your list is complete. If multiple columns of data are desired, enter the appropriate number in the **Number Of Columns** text box.

4. Adjust the column width by placing the mouse pointer near the right edge of the column header. When a double-headed arrow appears, drag the column to the desired width.

   –Or–

   Double-click the right edge of the column header to have Access fit the column to the widest entry.

   Click **Next** when satisfied with the results. The last page of the wizard will be displayed.

5. Accept the default label for the lookup column, or type a new name. Click **Allow Multiple Values** to store your field choices. Click **Finish**.

6. Save your table and switch to Datasheet View to enter data using the lookup column.

TIP

You can edit your own value list directly in the Row Source text box; however, lists generated from another table or query need to be edited in their source object.

QUICK**FACTS**

DECIDING TO USE A MULTIVALUED FIELD

While the ability to use more than one value in a field is useful, as with all parts of your database, think it through carefully before making the decision. In some cases, having more than one value in a field can reduce the functionality of your database should you ever need to move it to another, larger database system, such as Oracle or Microsoft SQL Server. However, if any of the following apply to your database, multiple values may be just what you need. Consider using multiple values in a field when:

- You have a current list of values that are used repeatedly.

- There are a small number of choices a user could make when entering data.

- You work with a database that often accesses a SharePoint site.

- You need to link your database with a SharePoint site.

EDIT THE LOOKUP LIST

After entering your data in a lookup list, you may find you need to add an additional item to this list.

1. Open a table in Design View.

2. Click the field with the lookup column.

3. Click the **Lookup** tab in the Field Properties area.

4. In the Row Source text box:

- Add additional values to the end of your list by typing the values enclosed in double quotation marks ("value") and separated with semicolons ("value1";"value2").

General	Lookup	
Display Control	Combo Box
Row Source Type	Value List
Row Source	"Medical";"Surgical";"Obstetrics";"Oncology";"Addiction";"Emotional"

- Delete any values in your list by selecting the entire value, including quotation marks and semicolon, and pressing **DELETE**.

5. Save your table and switch to Datasheet view to enter data using the lookup column.

WORK WITH MULTIPLE VALUES IN THE LOOKUP WIZARD

New in Access 2007 is the ability to use multiple values in a lookup box. For example, you may have a sales area that has several sales representatives assigned to it. With the ability to enter multiple values in the list, you can easily check the appropriate sales rep for each record you enter. You can create your own value list or use an existing table or query.

If you want your field value to be based on data that you enter:

1. Follow the steps described in "Create Your Own Value List with the Lookup Wizard" earlier in the chapter.

2. The default label is the name you entered as a field name, as seen in Figure 3-16.

3. Click **Allow Multiple Values** if you want Access 2007 to store the values you just entered so that you can choose more than one value for each record. These values will display as a drop-down list of check boxes when the table is in Datasheet View.

4. Click **Finish**. Save the table and switch to Datasheet View to enter data.

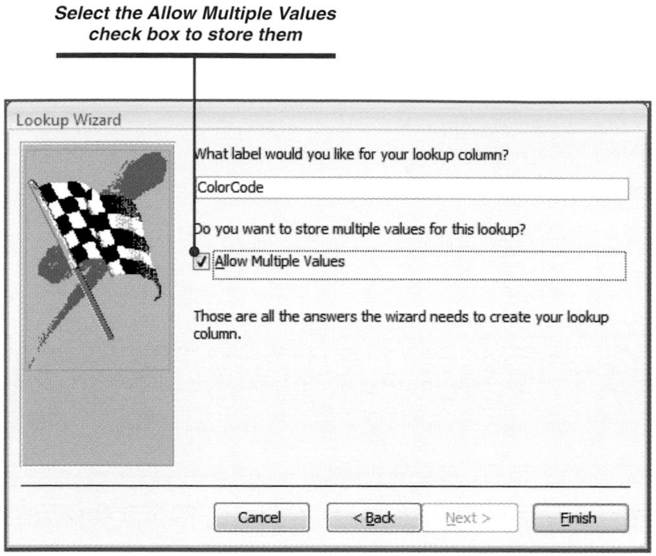

Select the Allow Multiple Values check box to store them

Lookup Wizard

What label would you like for your lookup column?

ColorCode

Do you want to store multiple values for this lookup?

☑ Allow Multiple Values

Those are all the answers the wizard needs to create your lookup column.

| Cancel | < Back | Next > | Finish |

Figure 3-16: In Access 2007, you can create lookups with multiple values.

CAUTION

Once you have created a multivalue lookup field from an existing table or query, you cannot change either the data type or the field size of your lookup field without deleting the relationships.

To create a multivalue field when your values will come from an existing table or query:

1. Follow the steps in "Find Your Lookup Values in a Table or Query" earlier in this chapter.

2. Click **Allow Multiple Values** to store your field choices.

3. Click **Finish**. You are prompted to save the table. Click **Yes**. After the table is saved, a relationship is created between your table and the objects from which you selected your fields.

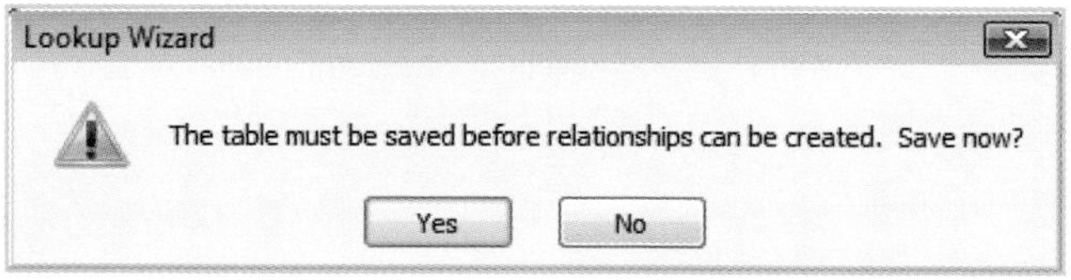

Lookup Wizard

⚠ The table must be saved before relationships can be created. Save now?

| Yes | No |

USE DATASHEET VIEW TO CREATE A MULTIVALUE LOOKUP FIELD

You can use Datasheet View to quickly create a multivalue lookup field.

1. From the Navigation Pane of an open database, double-click the table you want to modify to open it.

2. From the Datasheet tab (Table Tools) Fields & Columns group, click **Lookup Column**. This launches the Lookup Wizard.

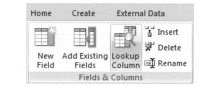

3. Continue through the pages of the wizard, following the steps in "Work with Multiple Values in the Lookup Wizard."

How to...

- Enter Data in an Existing Table
- Use Keyboard Shortcuts in a Table
- Moving Through Records
- Copy and Move Data
- Selecting Records, Fields, and Columns with the Mouse
- Delete Records and Columns
- Calculating Data in a Field
- Find and Replace Text
- Verify Spelling
- Modify Automatic Corrections
- Import Data from Outside Sources
- Collect Data from Outlook Messages
- Insert Columns
- Adjust Column Width
- Move and Rename Columns
- Changing How the Current Datasheet Looks
- Lock and Unlock Columns
- Adjust Row Height

Chapter 4

Working in the Table

Data is Access's *raison d'etre* (or reason to be), yet before we can organize the data, retrieve it, present it, or otherwise *use* it, we have to get it into a table. Chapters 2 and 3 described how to create a database, set up a table design, and change the properties of the table fields so that data entered into the table will conform to formatting, input masks, and other rules you establish.

In this chapter you will learn how to add data to a table in Datasheet View, as shown in Figure 4-1, which includes acquiring data from external sources. In addition, you will learn how to format the table to better present the data or emphasize just the data you want to see.

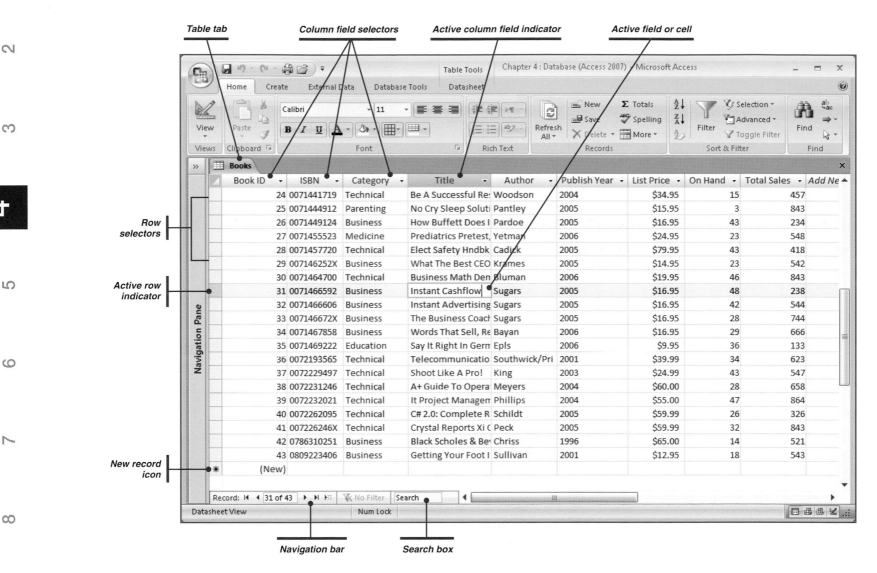

Figure 4-1: Datasheet View lets you enter and edit data in a table's row-and-column matrix.

NOTE

The terms *datasheet* and *table* are often confused, and no wonder, because they can refer to the same Access component. Strictly speaking, a datasheet can be one of several matrix-based containers for storing data, for example, a table, the result set of a query, and a data sheet in a form. Most of the techniques described in this chapter for use in tables are also applicable to other forms of datasheets. The same goes for *fields* and *columns*. Fields are the design elements and columns are the structural elements in a datasheet/table. The confusion usually arises when field names appear in column headers.

TIP

When you start entering or editing a value in a field, a pencil icon displays in the row selector column, indicating that the current record is in editing/entering text mode. Several keyboard shortcuts work differently when in this mode than when in navigation mode. See "Use Keyboard Shortcuts in a Table," later in this chapter, for information on switching between the two modes and tables that list the shortcuts.

𝒫				
	16	0071418695	Medicin	Pha
	17	0071418717	Business	Hoj

Enter and Edit Data

This section will show you ways to populate a designed table with new data you enter. You will also see how to modify data you add to the datasheet by using editing techniques that include moving and copying, locating and replacing data, using a dictionary to flag spelling mistakes, and automatically correcting data as you type. Since data entry is keyboard-intensive, you will learn several shortcuts to move around a datasheet and edit the information you enter without using a mouse.

Enter Data in an Existing Table

You use the keyboard to type new data into the table. You will start adding data in the new record at the end of the datasheet (see Chapter 2 for information on creating a table and adding data to it; Chapter 3 describes how to design a table). The last blank row in the datasheet, identified with a large asterisk in its row selector, is the new record row into which you add new data.

1. Do one of the following:

- Click a field in the new record row (see Figure 4-1).

- Click the new record button 🔤 on the navigation bar.

- In the Home tab Find group, click **Go To** and click **New**.

- In the Home tab Records group, click **New**.

  In each case, the first field in the new record row is selected.

2. Type the value you want in the first field, and press **TAB** or **ENTER**. If you do not have a value to add to a field (you do not have to type a value in a field unless it has a field property requiring you to do so), press **TAB** or **ENTER** until the insertion point is in the field you want, or click the next field you want to enter a value into.

   As soon as you start typing in the new record row, a new row is added to the bottom of the table.

NOTE

Many shortcut key combinations work differently, depending on whether Access considers you to be navigating through or editing data. For example, when an entire field's value is selected (or the insertion point is at the end of the value), pressing **RIGHT ARROW** moves the selection to the next field to the right. If you click a field's value, placing the insertion point in the value, pressing **RIGHT ARROW** moves the insertion point one character to the right. Press **F2** to toggle from one mode to the other. Table 4-1 lists the navigation mode options.

TIP

Windows computers come with a built-in *Extend* mode that makes selecting fields and records even easier than the standard shortcuts. Press **F8** to enable Extend mode. You will see "Extended Selection" displayed toward the right end of the status bar. Now when a field or record is selected, you can extend that selection by using the arrow keys. (If the behavior doesn't work, press **F2**.) Press **ESC** to stop using Extend mode.

Extended Selection

Use Keyboard Shortcuts in a Table

Data entry is largely done using the keyboard. Becoming familiar with using the keyboard for other related tasks can be quite a time-saver.

USE THE KEYBOARD TO NAVIGATE

Table 4-1 lists several of the more commonly used keyboard shortcuts for navigating within a table.

TO MOVE...	PRESS...
To the next (to the right) field	**TAB, RIGHT ARROW**, or **ENTER** (see the Tip on changing the behavior of using **ENTER** in the datasheet)
To the previous (to the left) field	**SHIFT+TAB** or **LEFT ARROW**
To the last field in the active record	**END**
To the first field in the active record	**HOME**
Up one record at a time in the same field	**UP ARROW**
Up to the first record in the same field	**CTRL+UP ARROW**
Up one screen	**PAGE UP**
Down one record at a time in the same field	**DOWN ARROW**
Down to the last record in the same field	**CTRL+DOWN ARROW**
Down one screen	**PAGE DOWN**
The first field in the first record	**CTRL+HOME**
The last field in the last record	**CTRL+END**
Right one screen	**CTRL+PAGE DOWN**
Left one screen	**CTRL+PAGE UP**

Table 4-1: Shortcuts for Navigating in a Datasheet

USE THE KEYBOARD TO INSERT DATA

Table 4-2 lists several shortcuts for inserting commonly used information and performing other tasks.

TO...	PRESS...
Add a new record	**CTRL++**
Delete the current record	**CTRL+-**
Insert the current time	**CTRL+SHIFT+:**
Insert the current date	**CTRL+;**
Insert the same value from the same field in the previous record	**CTRL+'**

Table 4-2: Shortcuts for Inserting Commonly Used Information

USE THE KEYBOARD TO EDIT DATA

Table 4-3 lists shortcuts for editing data.

TO...	PRESS...
Undo a typing action	**CTRL+Z**
Cancel typing actions in a record	**ESC** (pressing once cancels actions in the current field; pressing a second time cancels actions for the record)
Delete the character to the left of the insertion point	**BACKSPACE**
Delete the character to the right of the insertion point	**DELETE**
Delete all characters in a word to the right of the insertion point	**CTRL+DELETE**
Move one character to the right (if this takes you one field to the right, press **F2**)	**RIGHT ARROW**
Move one character to the left (if this takes you one field to the left, press **F2**)	**LEFT ARROW**
Move to the beginning of the next word to the right	**CTRL+RIGHT ARROW**
Move to the beginning of the previous word to the left	**CTRL+LEFT ARROW**
Move to the end of the field	**END**
Move to the beginning of the field	**HOME**

Table 4-3: Shortcuts for Editing Data

MOVING THROUGH RECORDS

The navigation bar at the bottom of table (see Figure 4-2) and the Go To tool in the Find group provide several options for quickly getting to the record you want in a datasheet.

◄	First
◄	Previous
►	Next
►►	Last
⬚	New

MOVE TO THE FIRST RECORD

- Click the **First Record** button on the navigation bar.

  –Or–

- In the Home tab Find group, click **Go To** and click **First**.

MOVE TO THE LAST RECORD

- Click the **Last Record** button on the navigation bar.

  –Or–

- In the Home tab Find group, click **Go To** and click **Last**.

MOVE TO THE NEXT RECORD

- Click the **Next Record** button on the navigation bar.

  –Or–

- In the Home tab Find group, click **Go To** and click **Next**.

MOVE TO THE PREVIOUS RECORD

- Click the **Previous Record** button on the navigation bar.

  –Or–

- In the Home tab Find group, click **Go To** and click **Previous**.

MOVE TO A SPECIFIC RECORD

Type the record number in the Current Record text box, and press **ENTER**.

USE THE KEYBOARD TO SELECT DATA

Table 4-4 lists shortcuts for selecting data.

TO...	PRESS...
Select a character to the right	**SHIFT+RIGHT ARROW**
Select a character to the left	**SHIFT+LEFT ARROW**
Select remaining characters in a word to the right	**CTRL+SHIFT+RIGHT ARROW**
Select remaining characters in a word to the left	**CTRL+SHIFT+LEFT ARROW**
Select the next field	**TAB**
Extend the selection above a selected record	**SHIFT+UP ARROW**
Select a record below a selected record	**SHIFT+DOWN ARROW**
Select all records	**CTRL+A**

Table 4-4: Shortcuts for Selecting Data

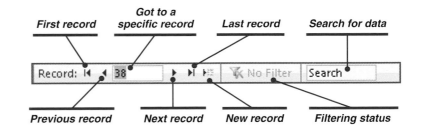

Figure 4-2: The navigation bar provides several ways to quickly locate records.

Copy and Move Data

You can duplicate or remove data within a table by using the standard copy, cut, and paste techniques. (See "Use Keyboard Shortcuts in a Table" and the "Selecting Records, Fields, and Columns with the Mouse" QuickSteps for ways to select fields and records.)

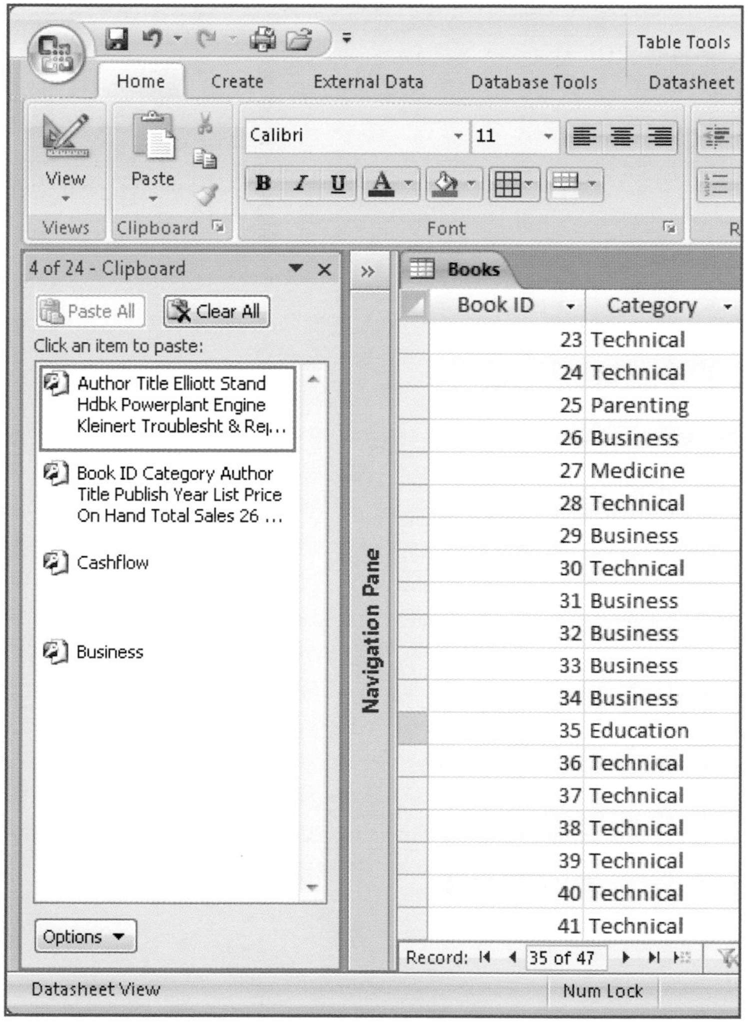

TIP

The last 24 items you copy or cut in Access are listed in the Office Clipboard, where you can select which ones you want to paste to another location, either within an Office or other Windows program (only the most recent copy or cut is available to paste in non-Office programs). In the Home tab Clipboard group, click the **Dialog Box Launcher** in the lower-right corner of the group. The Clipboard task pane displays along the left edge of the Access window, as shown in Figure 4-3. Click the item you want pasted into a selected item or where the insertion point is located.

Figure 4-3: The Clipboard task pane allows you to store the last 24 items you copied or cut and paste them at a future time.

UICKSTEPS

SELECTING RECORDS, FIELDS, AND COLUMNS WITH THE MOUSE

Open a table in Datasheet View.

SELECT RECORDS

- To select a single record, click the record selector to the left of the record (see Figure 4-1).

  –Or–

  Place the insertion point in the record. In the Home tab Find group, click **Select** and click **Select** a second time.

  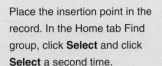

  In either case, the record becomes highlighted.

- To select adjacent records, point at the first/last row in the group you want to select. When the mouse pointer becomes a right-pointing arrow, drag over the selectors of the records. The selected rows are shaded and surrounded by an orange border.

- To select all records, in the Home tab Find group, click **Select** and click **Select All**.

  Continued . . .

CAUTION

Records are usually pasted to the end of the table because most tables have a primary key set to the AutoNumber data type. Any records added to the table are given a unique, sequential number. If you copy or move records within the same table, you may have the same data in two or more records or cause other irregularities in your data.

COPY AND MOVE CHARACTERS

1. In Datasheet View, select the characters you want to copy or move.

2. In the Home tab Clipboard group, click **Copy** , or right-click the selection and click **Copy**. A duplicate of the selected data is placed on the Clipboard, and the original data is retained.

   –Or–

   In the Home tab Clipboard group, click **Cut** , or right-click the selection and click **Cut**. A duplicate of the selected data is placed on the Clipboard, and the original data is removed.

3. In the destination field, either place your insertion point where you want the new characters inserted or select characters that will be overwritten by the new characters.

4. In the Home tab Clipboard group, click **Paste** (the upper half of the icon); or right-click where you want to add the characters, and click **Paste**.

COPY AND MOVE FIELDS

In Datasheet View, select the fields you want to copy or move (see the "Selecting Records, Fields, and Columns with the Mouse" QuickSteps).

Books		
Book ID ▾	Category ▾	Author
23	Technical	Huettenmu
24	Technical	Woodson
25	Parenting	Pantley
26	Business	Pardoe
27	Medicine	Yetman
28	Technical	Cadick

1. In the Home tab Clipboard group, click **Copy**, or right-click the selection and click **Copy**. A duplicate of the selected data is placed on the Clipboard, and the original data is retained.

   –Or–

   In the Home tab Clipboard group, click **Cut**, or right-click the selection and click **Cut**. A duplicate of the selected data is placed on the Clipboard, and the original data is removed.

2. Select an equivalent block of fields where you want the new data. For example, if you selected three adjacent fields in a record that you wanted to copy, ensure that you select three adjacent destination fields where you want the data pasted.

3. In the Home tab Clipboard group, click **Paste**; or right-click the selected fields, and click **Paste**. Any existing data in the destination fields will be overwritten by the new data.

SELECTING RECORDS, FIELDS, AND COLUMNS WITH THE MOUSE

(Continued)

SELECT DATA IN A FIELD

● To select partial data in a field, drag over the characters you want.

SELECT FIELDS

● To select a single field, point at the left edge of the field. When the pointer changes to a large cross, click your mouse button.

| Cadick |
| ✛ Krames |
| Bluman |

● To select adjacent fields, point at the left edge of the first field. When the pointer changes to a large cross, drag left or right across the fields you want to select.

SELECT COLUMNS

● To select all fields in a column, click the column selector (the box that contains the field name) at the top of the column.

↓ Author ▾	Title
Huettenmuelle	Pre-Calculu:
Woodson	Be A Succes:

● To select adjacent columns, point at the column selector in the first column to be selected. When the pointer changes to a down arrow, drag left or right across the columns you want selected.

TIP

If you click **Delete Record** without selecting a record, the active record will be deleted.

COPY OR MOVE RECORDS

In Datasheet View, select the records you want to copy or move.

1. In the Home tab Clipboard group, click **Copy**, or right-click the selection and click **Copy**. A duplicate of the selected records is placed on the Clipboard, and the original records are retained.

   –Or–

   In the Home tab Clipboard group, click **Cut**, or right-click the selection and click **Cut**. A duplicate of the selected records is placed on the Clipboard, and the original records are removed.

2. In the Home tab Clipboard group, click the **Paste** down arrow (the lower half of the icon), and click **Paste Append**. The copied or moved records will be added to the end of the table.

Delete Records and Columns

In Access, unlike most Office programs, when you remove data by deleting records and columns, you cannot undo your actions. However, Access will ask you to confirm your deletions before they are irretrievably gone.

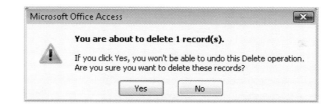

DELETE RECORDS

1. Select the record(s) you want to delete (see "Use the Keyboard to Edit Data" earlier in the chapter and the "Selecting Records, Fields, and Columns with the Mouse" QuickSteps for ways to select records).

2. In the Home tab Records group, click **Delete**.

   –Or–

   Right-click the selection and click **Delete Record**.

3. Click **Yes** to confirm your deletion.

QUICKSTEPS

CALCULATING DATA IN A FIELD

You can add a row that provides options for performing calculations on the data within a field.

ADD THE TOTAL ROW

1. Open a table in Datasheet View.

2. In the Home tab Records group, click **Totals**. A new row labeled "Total" is added to the bottom of the table.

	43	0809223406	Business
*	(New)		
	Total		

CALCULATE DATA

1. Click the field in the Total row whose data you want to calculate, and click the down arrow that appears.

2. Click the calculation method you want to apply to the data in the column. The result is displayed in the Total row.

$65.00
$12.95

▼
None
Sum
Average
Count
Maximum
Minimum
Standard Deviation
Variance

REMOVE THE TOTAL ROW

In the Home tab Records group, click **Totals**.

DELETE COLUMNS

1. Select the column(s) you want to delete (see "Use the Keyboard to Edit Data" and the "Selecting Records, Fields and Columns with the Mouse" QuickSteps for ways to select columns).

2. In the Datasheet (Table Tools) tab Field & Columns group, click **Delete**, or right-click the selection and click **Delete Column**.

3. Click **Yes** to confirm your deletion.

Find and Replace Text

In tables that span thousands of rows and columns, you need the ability to locate data quickly, as well as to find instances of the same data so that consistent replacements can be made.

FIND DATA

1. Open a table in Datasheet View.

2. In the Home tab Find group, click **Find**, or press **CTRL+F** to open the Find And Replace dialog box, shown in Figure 4-4. If it isn't selected, click the **Find** tab.

3. Type the characters you want to find in the Find What text box.

4. Click the **Look In** down arrow, and choose whether to search the entire table or just the field where the insertion point is currently located.

Figure 4-4: The Find tab lets you refine your search based on several criteria.

5. Click the **Match** down arrow, and choose one of the following:

- **Any Part Of Field** to locate fields that contain the searched-for characters embedded in any text within a field (For example, searching for "pen" would find fields that contained "opening.")

- **Whole Field** to locate fields that contain only the searched-for characters (For example, searching for "pen" would find fields that contained only "pen.")

- **Start Of Field** to locate fields that contain the searched-for characters at the beginning of the field (For example, searching for "pen" would find fields that contained "Penn Station.")

6. Click the **Search** down arrow to determine the scope of the search. Choose among the following:

- **All** searches the entire datasheet.

- **Up** searches from the current insertion point location toward the first record.

- **Down** searches from the current insertion point location toward the last record.

7. Select the **Match Case** check box to only find fields that match the case of the characters (For example, searching for "pen" would not find "Penn Station" but would find "pencil.")

8. Click **Find Next**.

REPLACE DATA

The Replace tab of the Find And Replace dialog box looks and behaves similar to the Find tab covered earlier.

1. Open a table in Datasheet View.

2. In the Home tab Find group, click **Find**, or press **CTRL+F** to open the Find And Replace dialog box. Click the **Replace tab**.

3. Type the characters you want to be found and replaced in the Find What text box.

4. Type the replacement characters in the Replace With text box. If specific search criteria are needed, see "Find Data" for the options' descriptions.

5. Click **Find Next** and then click **Replace** to make replacements one at a time.

–Or–

Click Replace All to perform all replacements at once.

> **TIP**
>
> If the correct spelling of a misspelled word is not shown in the Suggestions list box, edit the word in the Not In Dictionary text box, and click **Add** to include it in a custom dictionary that is checked in addition to the main dictionary.

Verify Spelling

You can check the spelling of selected fields, columns, records, or the entire table using Access' main dictionary and a custom dictionary you add words to. (Both are shared with other Office programs).

1. Open a table in Datasheet View.
2. Select the fields, columns, or records to check. If nothing is selected, the entire table will be checked.
3. In the Home tab Records group, click **Spelling**. When the spelling checker doesn't find anything to report, you are told the spelling check is complete. Otherwise, the Spelling dialog box appears, as shown in Figure 4-5.

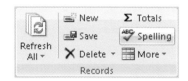

4. With a highlighted word in the Not In Dictionary/Capitalization text box, you may change the characters by picking from the Suggestions list and clicking **Change** or **Change All** to replace the current or all occurrences of the highlighted word. If you have a correct term that is not found in the dictionary, you may:
   - Click **Ignore *'Field'* Name** to discontinue searching in the current column for misspelled or incorrectly capitalized words.
   - Click **Ignore** to disregard the current occurrence of the word shown in the Not In Dictionary/Capitalization text box.
   - Click **Ignore All** to disregard all occurrences of the word shown in the Not In Dictionary/Capitalization text box.
5. Click **AutoCorrect** if you want to automatically replace words in the future. (See the next section, "Modify Automatic Corrections," for more information on using AutoCorrect.)
6. Click **Options** to open the Access Options Proofing page (see Figure 4-6), where you can change languages, create and modify custom dictionaries, and set other spelling criteria.

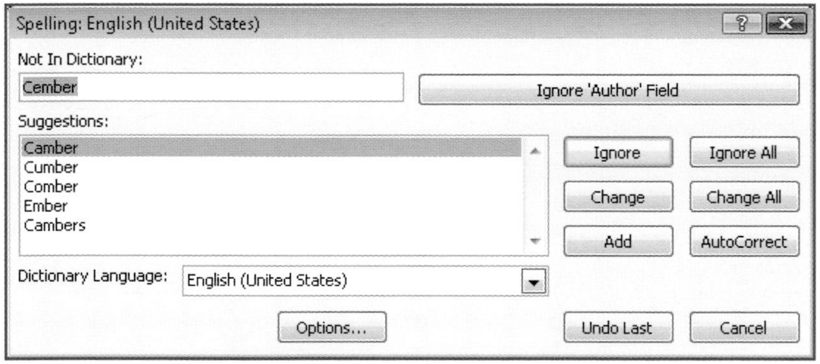

Figure 4-5: The Spelling dialog box provides several options to handle misspelled or uncommon words.

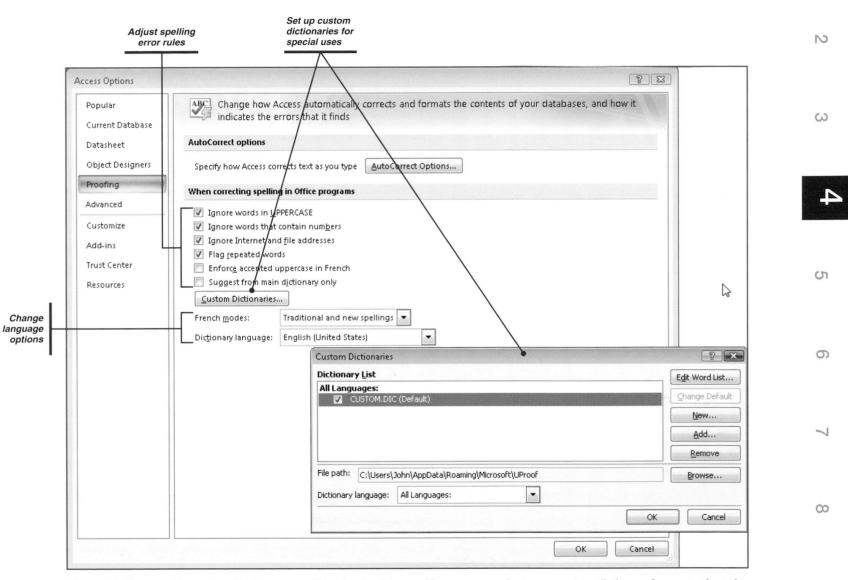

Adjust spelling error rules

Set up custom dictionaries for special uses

Change language options

Figure 4-6: You can change how the Access spelling checker flags spellings errors and set up a custom dictionary for unusual word forms you might use.

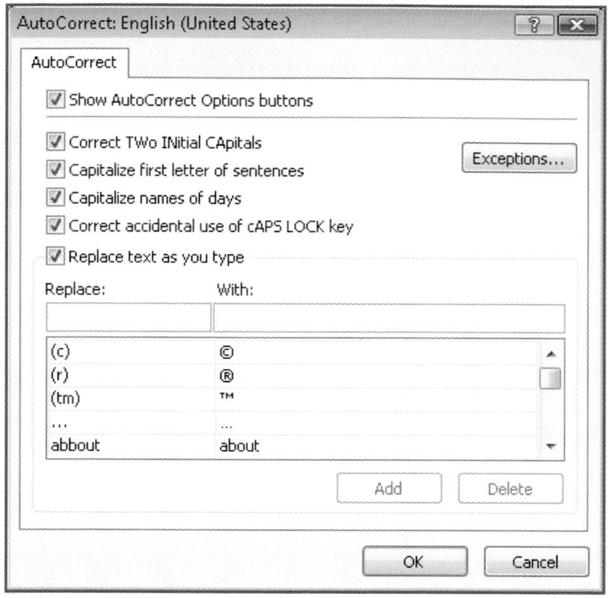

Figure 4-7: AutoCorrect provides several automatic correction settings and lets you add words and characters that are replaced with alternatives.

TIP

Importing data into Access tables is a one-shot process—that is, you get whatever data is in the source at the moment you import. You can maintain a real-time connection to external data if you link it to an Access table. Linking data, and other data-exchange methods, is covered in Chapter 10.

Modify Automatic Corrections

Access automatically corrects common data entry mistakes as you type, replacing characters and words you choose with other choices. You can control how this is done.

1. Open a table in Datasheet View.

2. Click the **Office Button**, click **Access Options**, and click the **Proofing** option. On the Proofing page, click **AutoCorrect Options**. The AutoCorrect dialog box appears, as shown in Figure 4-7. As appropriate, do one or more of the following:

   - Choose the type of automatic corrections you do or do not want from the options at the top of the dialog box.
   - Click **Exceptions** to set capitalization exceptions.
   - Click **Replace Text As You Type** to turn off automatic text replacement (this is turned on by default).
   - Add new words or characters to the Replace and With text boxes, and click **Add**
   - Change a current item by selecting the item in the list, edit the With text box entry, and click **Replace**.
   - Delete replacement text by selecting the item in the Replace and With lists and clicking **Delete**.

3. Click **OK** when you are done.

Acquire Data

In addition to typing data directly into a datasheet, you can enter data by using a form (see Chapter 6) or get existing data into a datasheet by:

- Importing from several different sources into a new or existing Access table
- Copying and pasting
- Collecting data from e-mail replies

Once the data is "safely" in your Access datasheet/table, you have all the tools and features this book describes to format, organize, analyze, retrieve, and otherwise convert the data into the information you want.

Import Data from Outside Sources

Most external data sources use a similar initial Get External dialog box, shown in Figure 4-8, to determine if you want to add the data to a new table or append it to an existing table (You can also create a linked table to maintain an update

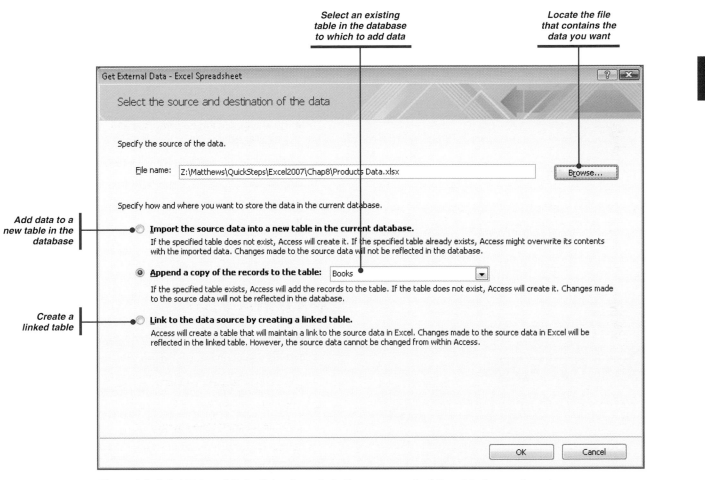

Select an existing table in the database to which to add data

Locate the file that contains the data you want

Add data to a new table in the database

Create a linked table

Figure 4-8: A Get External Data dialog box starts the process of adding data from external sources.

path to the data. Linked tables and linking data are covered in Chapter 10). The data types you can import from are:

• dBASE	• Paradox
• Lotus 1-2-3	• SharePoint
• Microsoft Access	• Text files
• Microsoft Excel	• Web pages
• Microsoft Outlook	• XML files
• ODBC-compliant databases	

IMPORT DATA FROM TEXT FILES

Text files have file extensions such as .txt and .csv (comma-separated values) that can be formatted using commas, spaces, tabs, and other separators to organize their data. Though the data may not appear to be structured, as shown in Figure 4-9, Access can correctly place the data in columns as long as the data is separated in a consistent and recognizable format.

1. Open the database into which you want to add the data from the text file.

2. In the External Data tab Import group, click **Text File**. In the Get External Data dialog box (see Figure 4-8), locate the text file, and select whether to create a new table or to add the data to an existing table in the database.

3. In the first page of the Import Text Wizard, preview the file in the lower half of the dialog box. If all appears to be in order, Access has done a good job so far. If not, try choosing the other format. In any case, click **Next** to continue with other options.

4. The second page lets you fine-tune the delimiter used or set fixed-length widths, depending on your choice in the previous dialog box. Click the **First Row Contains Field Names** check box if your text file is set up that way. Click **Next**.

5. In the third page, you can set up field information about each column. Click the field you want to change. To change more detailed field information, click the **Advanced** button. (If you do not want to bother with field changes now, you can modify the field information in Design View after the data has been imported.) Click **Next** when finished.

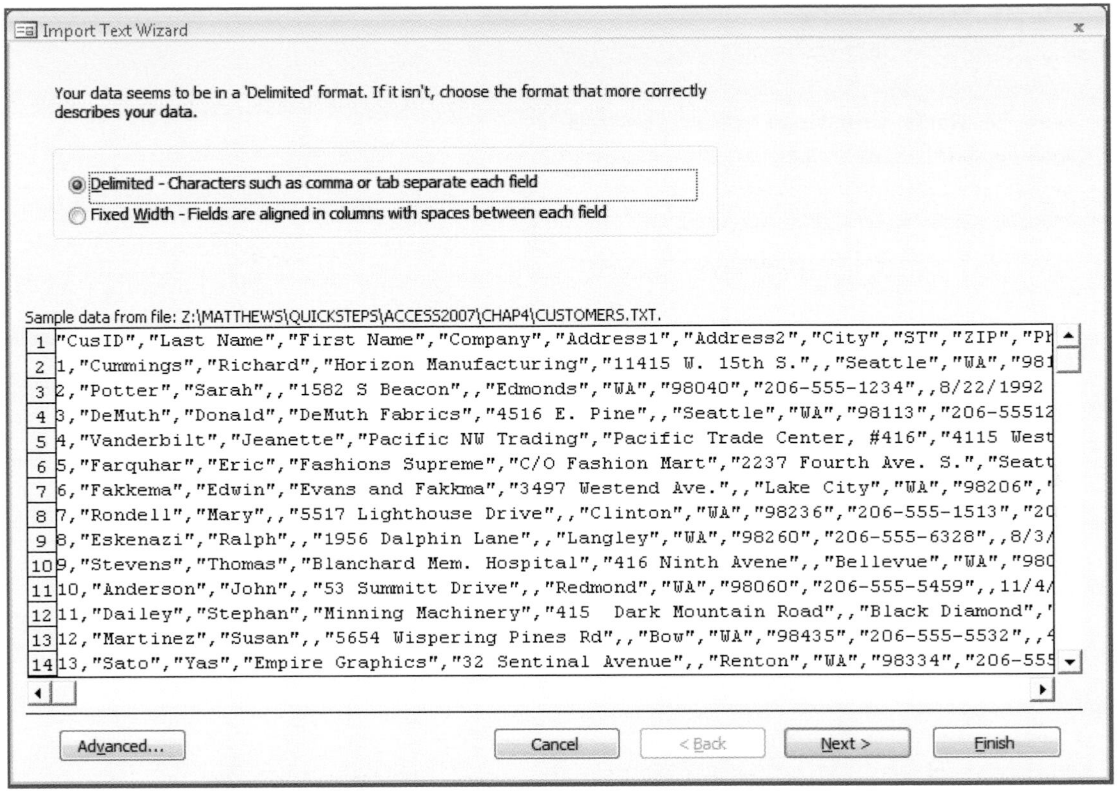

Figure 4-9: The first step to import data from a text file is to tell Access how it's organized.

6. In the fourth page, choose whether and how to assign a primary key to the new table (see Chapter 2 for information on primary keys). This page is omitted if you are appending data. Click **Next**.

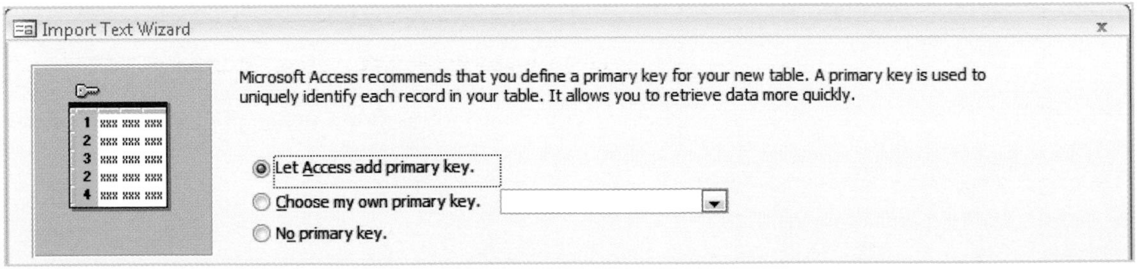

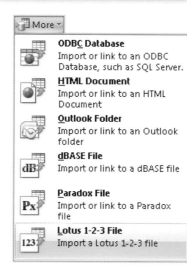

7. In the last page, type a new name for the new table in the **Import To Table** text box.

   –Or–

   Verify the name of the table you want to append data into.

   Click **Finish**.

IMPORT DATA FROM SPREADSHEETS

Data created by spreadsheet programs, such as Microsoft Excel and Lotus 1-2-3, is imported using the Import Spreadsheet Wizard.

1. Open the database into which you want to add the data from the text file.

2. In the External Data tab Import group, click **Excel**.

   –Or–

   Click **More** and click **Lotus 1-2-3 File**.

3. In the Get External Data dialog box (see Figure 4-8), locate the spreadsheet file, and select whether to create a new table or to add the data to an existing table in the database.

4. In the first page of the Import Spreadsheet Wizard, choose whether to get data from worksheets or named ranges. Select the item that contains the data, and preview the item in the lower half of the dialog box. Click **Next** to continue with other options.

5. The second page lets you use column headings for field names in Access. Click the **First Row Contains Column Headings** check box if your data is set up that way. Click **Next**.

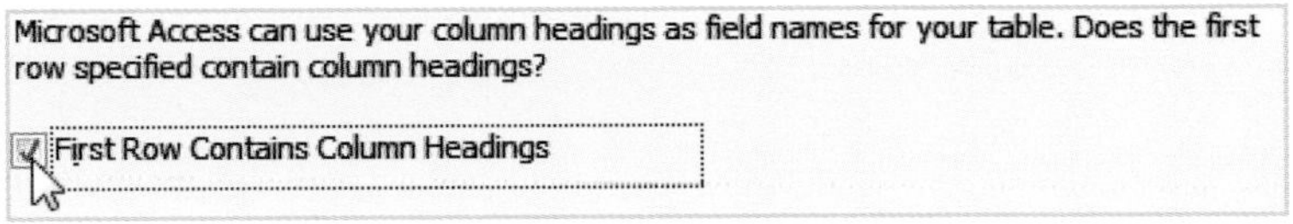

Microsoft Access can use your column headings as field names for your table. Does the first row specified contain column headings?

☑ First Row Contains Column Headings

6. In the third page, you can set up field information about each column. If you do not want to bother with that now, you can modify the field information in Design View after the data has been imported. Click **Next** when finished.

7. In the next page, choose whether and how to assign a primary key to the new table (see Chapter 2 for information on primary keys). This page is omitted if you are appending data. Click **Next**.

8. In the last page, type a name for the new table in the Import To Table text box.

   –Or–

   Verify the name of the table you want to append data into.

   Click **Finish**.

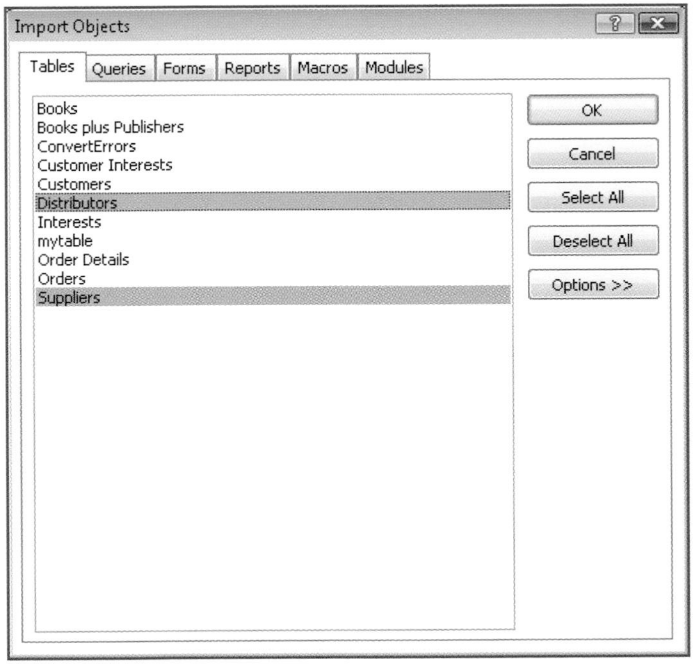

IMPORT ACCESS TABLES

You can import tables (and other Access objects) from other Access databases.

1. Open the database into which you want to add the data from the text file.

2. In the External Data tab Import group, click **Access**. In the Get External Data dialog box (see Figure 4-8), locate the Access database, and select the first option to import Access objects into the database.

3. In the Import Objects dialog box, shown in Figure 4-10, select the table(s) whose data you want. If you need to deselect a choice, either click the table you want deselected or use the **Deselect All** button and start over.

4. Click the **Options** button to display detailed importing options:

Import Objects

Tables | Queries | Forms | Reports | Macros | Modules

Books
Books plus Publishers
ConvertErrors
Customer Interests
Customers
Distributors
Interests
mytable
Order Details
Orders
Suppliers

OK
Cancel
Select All
Deselect All
Options >>

Figure 4-10: You can choose a table, as well as other objects, to import from an Access database.

Import	Import Tables	Import Queries
☑ Relationships	◉ Definition and Data	◉ As Queries
☐ Menus and Toolbars	○ Definition Only	○ As Tables
☐ Import/Export Specs		
☐ Nav Pane Groups		

- Under **Import**, select one or more of the features to include with the imported table(s).

- Under **Import Tables**, choose whether to import the table's definition (design) and data or just its definition.

5. Click **OK**.

6. In the final Save Import Steps dialog box, click the Save Import Steps check box if you want to repeat the importing steps without working through the wizard. Saved imports are available by clicking Saved Imports in the Import group. In any case, click **Close**.

PASTE DATA INTO A TABLE

You can add existing rows (records) or columns of data to your table by pasting them from other data sources.

1. Open the program that contains the data you want.

2. Select the rows or fields you want using the selection techniques of the source program.

3. Copy the data to the Windows Clipboard, either by clicking the **Copy** command from a toolbar or ribbon or by pressing **CTRL+C**.

4. Open the Access table into which you want to place the data in Datasheet View. Do one of the following:

   - To paste the data as new records to the end of the datasheet, in the Home tab Clipboard group, click the **Paste** down arrow, and click **Paste Append**.

- To replace records, select the records to be replaced, and in the Home tab Clipboard group, click **Paste**.

> Microsoft Office Access
>
> ⚠ **You are about to paste 4 record(s).**
>
> Are you sure you want to paste these records?
>
> [Yes]   [No]

- To replace fields, select the fields to be replaced, and in the Home tab Clipboard group, click **Paste**; or right-click the selected fields, and click **Paste**.

NOTE

When pasting data into a table, it's important to ensure that the field structure of the source and destination tables are the same so that data isn't lost. For example, if your source record contains more fields than your destination table, the data in the additional fields is simply not added to the destination table. Also, the data types need to be compatible. If there is a data type mismatch, Access will display an error. Also, data unable to be pasted will be added to a Paste Errors table

⊞ **Paste Errors** .

> Microsoft Office Access
>
> ① **The value you entered isn't valid for this field.**
>
> For example, you may have entered text in a numeric field or a number that is larger than the FieldSize setting permits.
>
> [OK]

Collect Data from Outlook Messages

Office 2007 provides a feature whereby you can send data collection forms to e-mail recipients and then have the data contained in the e-mail responses added to a new or existing Access table.

CREATE AND SEND THE DATA REQUEST

1. Open the database that contains the table where you want to collect data. In the Navigation Pane, select the table that will be used to collect data.

2. In the External Data tab Collect Data group, click **Create E-mail**. The first page of the Collect Data Through E-mail Messages Wizard provides an overview of the process, as shown in Figure 4-11. Click **Next**.

3. In the second page, accept the **HTML Form** option (this is selected by default) as the type of form you want to send, and click **Next**.

4. In the third page, select whether you are collecting new data or updating existing data. Click **Next**.

5. In the fourth page, select the fields from your selected table (see step 1) that you want recipients to provide data for, using the controls as shown in Figure 4-12. Click **Next**.

6. The fifth page lists the Outlook folder where the replies will be stored. Click the **Automatically Process Replies** check box if you want Access to add incoming data directly to your selected table (you can apply this after you receive messages).

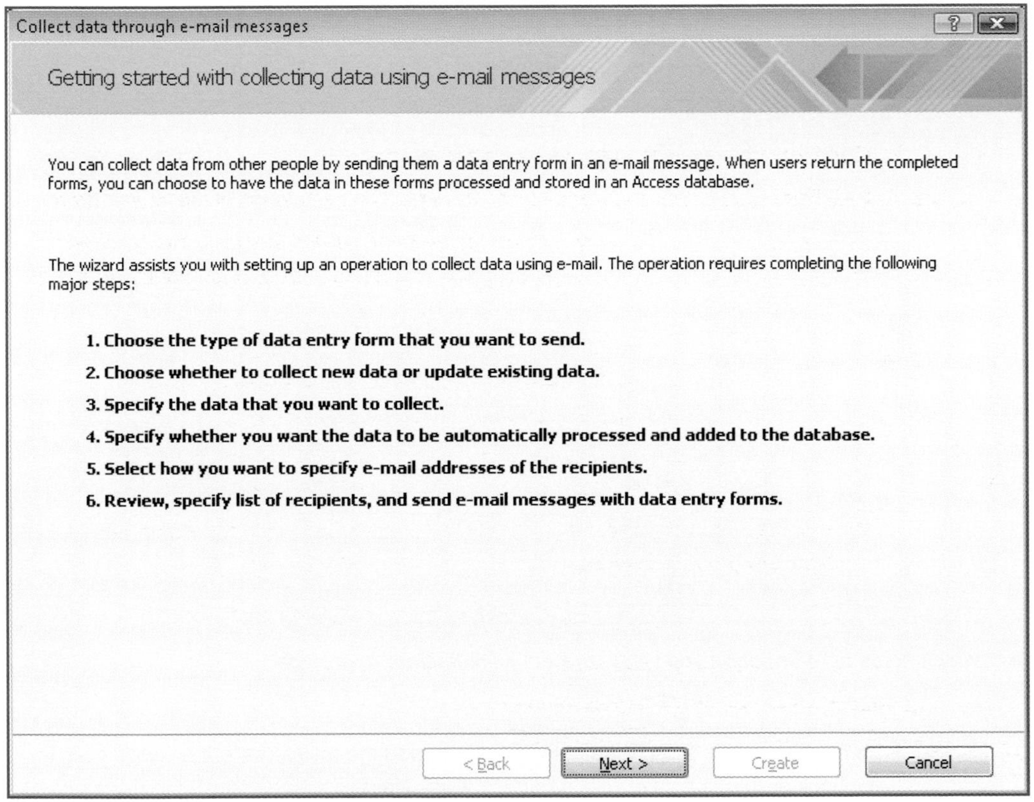

Collect data through e-mail messages

Getting started with collecting data using e-mail messages

You can collect data from other people by sending them a data entry form in an e-mail message. When users return the completed forms, you can choose to have the data in these forms processed and stored in an Access database.

The wizard assists you with setting up an operation to collect data using e-mail. The operation requires completing the following major steps:

1. Choose the type of data entry form that you want to send.
2. Choose whether to collect new data or update existing data.
3. Specify the data that you want to collect.
4. Specify whether you want the data to be automatically processed and added to the database.
5. Select how you want to specify e-mail addresses of the recipients.
6. Review, specify list of recipients, and send e-mail messages with data entry forms.

< Back   Next >   Create   Cancel

Figure 4-11: The several steps to create a form for data collection are straightforward and worth the effort.

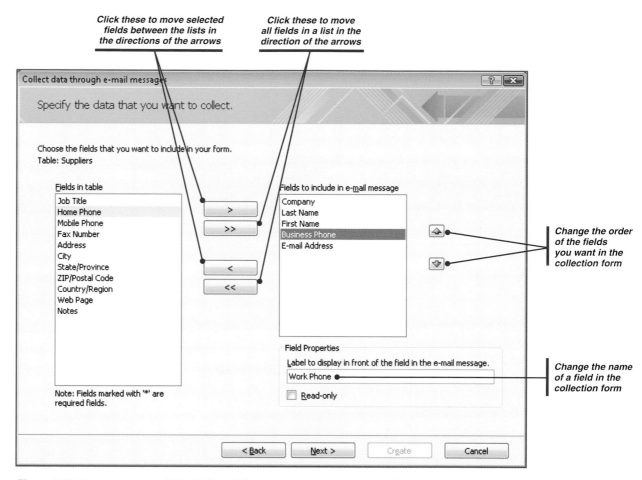

Click these to move selected fields between the lists in the directions of the arrows

Click these to move all fields in a list in the direction of the arrows

Change the order of the fields you want in the collection form

Change the name of a field in the collection form

Collect data through e-mail messages

Specify the data that you want to collect.

Choose the fields that you want to include in your form.
Table: Suppliers

Fields in table
- Job Title
- Home Phone
- Mobile Phone
- Fax Number
- Address
- City
- State/Province
- ZIP/Postal Code
- Country/Region
- Web Page
- Notes

Note: Fields marked with '*' are required fields.

Fields to include in e-mail message
- Company
- Last Name
- First Name
- Business Phone
- E-mail Address

Field Properties
Label to display in front of the field in the e-mail message.
Work Phone
☐ Read-only

< Back   Next >   Create   Cancel

Figure 4-12: You can select which fields of information you want your e-mail recipients to provide with their own data.

7. In the sixth page, select whether you want to add the recipients' e-mail addresses in Outlook or from a field in your database. Click **Next**.

8. In the seventh page, type a subject and message for the recipients, and click **Next**.

9. Click **Create** in the final page to open an Outlook 2007 message form, similar to that shown in Figure 4-13. Review the message, make any changes to the subject or message text, and add recipient addresses, as necessary. Click **Send** when finished.

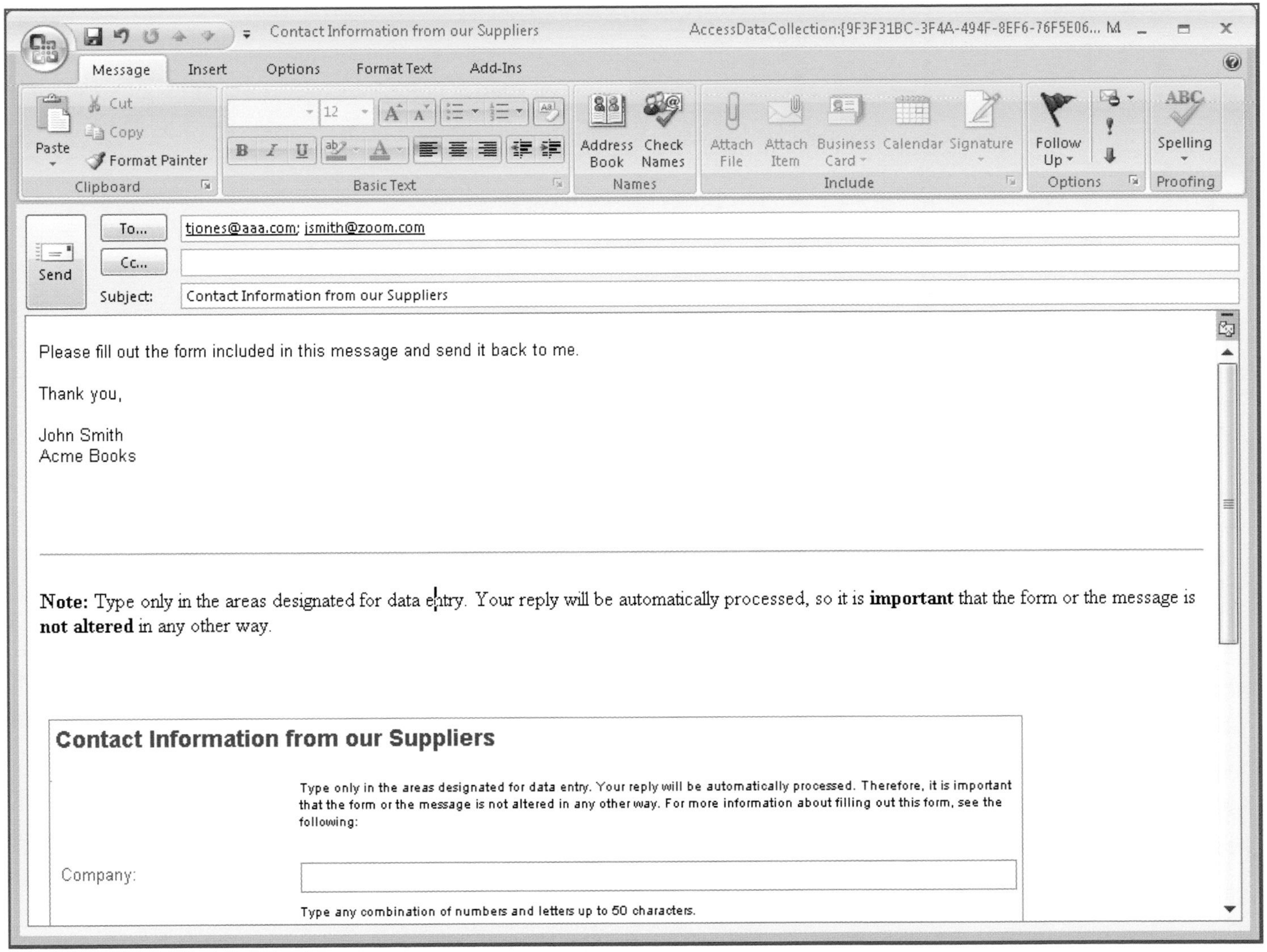
Contact Information from our Suppliers
AccessDataCollection:{9F3F31BC-3F4A-494F-8EF6-76F5E06... M
Message
Insert
Options
Format Text
Add-Ins
Paste
Cut
Copy
Format Painter
Clipboard
Basic Text
Address Book
Check Names
Names
Attach File
Attach Item
Business Card
Calendar
Signature
Include
Follow Up
Options
Spelling
Proofing
Send
To...
Cc...
Subject:
tjones@aaa.com; jsmith@zoom.com
Contact Information from our Suppliers
Please fill out the form included in this message and send it back to me.
Thank you,
John Smith
Acme Books
Note: Type only in the areas designated for data entry. Your reply will be automatically processed, so it is important that the form or the message is not altered in any other way.
Contact Information from our Suppliers
Type only in the areas designated for data entry. Your reply will be automatically processed. Therefore, it is important that the form or the message is not altered in any other way. For more information about filling out this form, see the following:
Company:
Type any combination of numbers and letters up to 50 characters.

Figure 4-13: Access adds a professionally designed form to your outgoing Outlook 2007 message.

MANAGE REPLIES

Replies from your requests for data are automated in one fashion or another, depending on your choice in the Collect Data Through E-mail Messages Wizard. If you chose to automatically add the data to a table, all you really need to do is view the data. If you didn't choose this option, replies are gathered in a common Outlook folder where you can easily manage them.

1. Open the database that contains the table from which you created the data collection message.

2. In the External Data tab Collect Data group, click **Manage Replies**. The Manage Data Collection Messages dialog box appears, shown in Figure 4-14.

   - To automatically add data to the collection table, select a message and click **Message Options**. Click the **Automatically Process Replies And Add Data To The Database** check box, and select any importing options you want. Click **OK** when finished.

   - To resend or delete a message, or to view message details, select a message. Use the applicable controls in the dialog box to perform the action you want.

3. Click **Close** when finished.

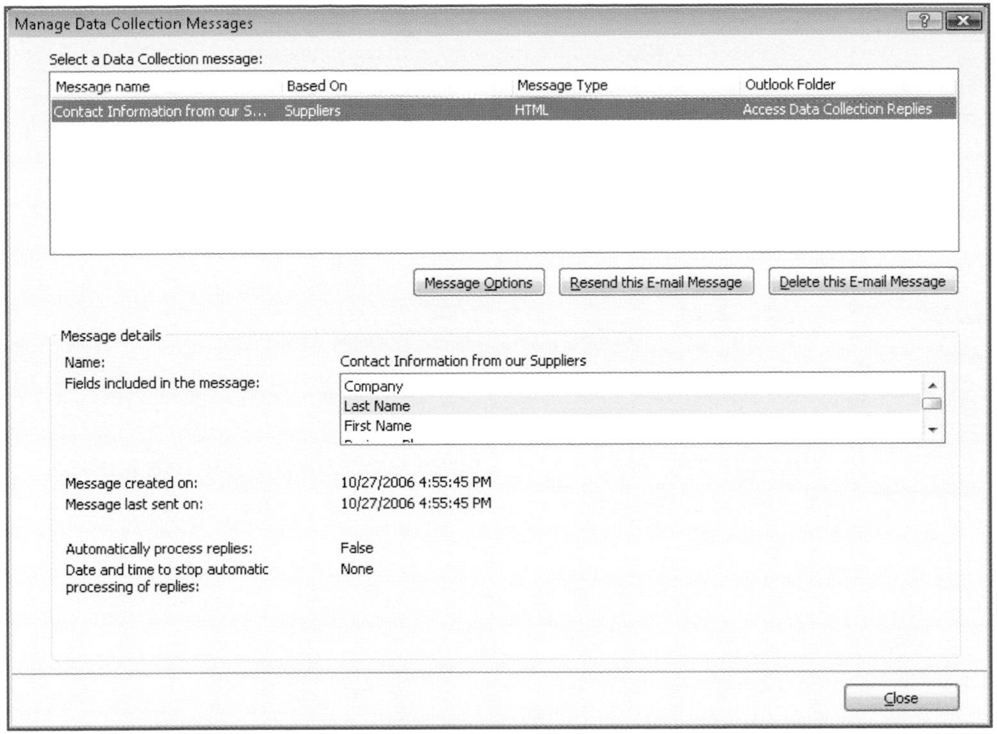

Manage Data Collection Messages

Select a Data Collection message:

Message name	Based On	Message Type	Outlook Folder
Contact Information from our S...	Suppliers	HTML	Access Data Collection Replies

[Message Options] [Resend this E-mail Message] [Delete this E-mail Message]

Message details

Name: Contact Information from our Suppliers
Fields included in the message: Company
                                        Last Name
                                        First Name

Message created on: 10/27/2006 4:55:45 PM
Message last sent on: 10/27/2006 4:55:45 PM

Automatically process replies: False
Date and time to stop automatic   None
processing of replies:

[Close]

Figure 4-14: E-mail replies from a data collection request are listed and managed in a single location.

TIP

To use a lookup column you've created, simply click any field in the lookup column where you want to add a value. Clicking the down arrow that appears on the right side of the field opens a drop-down list of values—either those you entered or those that are pulled from a table or query you selected. Click the value you want entered in the field.

Arrange a Table

There are several actions you can take to customize how you see the data presented in a table (or datasheet). You can resize rows and columns, hide columns, and format the appearance of the table.

Insert Columns

You can insert blank columns or columns that are formatted with lookup or hyperlink data types. (See the "Selecting Records, Fields, and Columns with the Mouse" QuickSteps for information on selecting columns.)

INSERT BLANK COLUMNS

1. Click the column selector for the column to the right of where you want to add a new blank column.

2. In the Datasheet tab (Table Tools) Fields & Columns group, click **Insert**.

   –Or–

   Right-click the selected column, and click **Insert Column**. A new column is added to the left of your selected column.

3. Rename the column name as necessary (see "Rename a Column," later in this chapter).

Field1	Author
	Elliott
	Kleinert
	Pen
	Nash

INSERT A LOOKUP COLUMN

1. Click the column selector for the column to the right of where you want to add a lookup column.

2. In the Datasheet tab (Table Tools) Fields & Columns group, click **Lookup Column**.

   –Or–

   Right-click the selected column, and click **Lookup Column**.

   In either case, the Lookup Wizard opens, as shown in Figure 4-15.

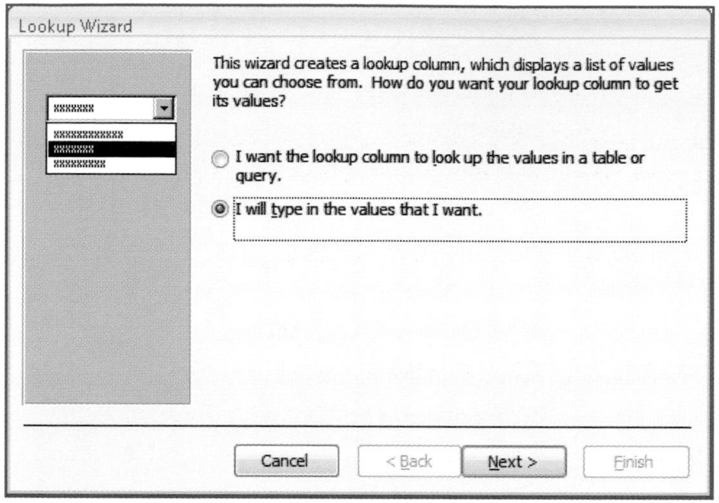

Figure 4-15: The Lookup Wizard helps you add items to a drop-down list from tables (or queries) or by allowing you to type them in.

3. Choose whether to pull lookup items from a table or query or to add your own items. Click **Next** and follow the instructions in the wizard (see Chapter 3 for specifics on using the Lookup Wizard).

4. Click **Finish** in the last wizard page. The lookup column is added to the left of the selected column.

Adjust Column Width

There are several ways to change the width of a column:

- Use the mouse to drag the column to the width you want.

- Type a precise width.

- Let Access choose a default or tailored width.

CHANGE THE WIDTH FOR A SINGLE COLUMN WITH THE MOUSE

1. Point to the right border of the column selector until the pointer changes to a cross.

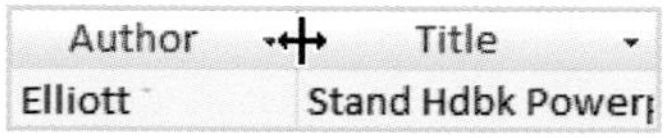

2. Drag the border to the left or right to the width you want.

CHANGE THE WIDTH FOR ADJACENT COLUMNS WITH THE MOUSE

When you change the column width for a group of selected columns, the widths of each column are changed by the same amount.

1. Select the columns whose widths you want to adjust.

2. Drag the right border of any of the selected columns to the left or right to the width you want.

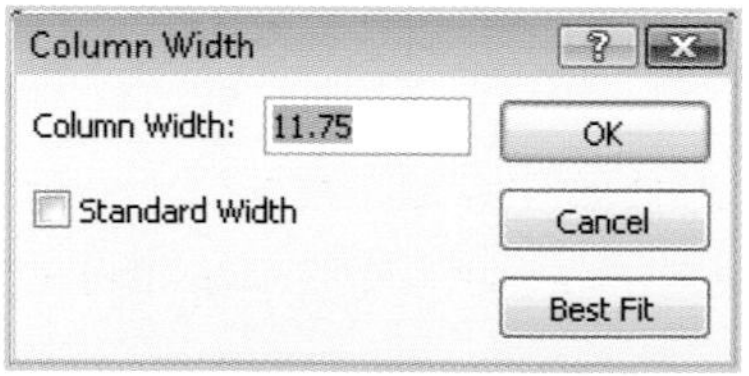

CHANGE THE WIDTH OF COLUMNS PRECISELY

1. Select the column(s) whose width you want to adjust.

2. In the Home tab Records group, click **More** and click **Column Width**.

   –Or–

   Right-click the selection and select **Column Width**.

3. In the Column Width dialog box, type a column width, and click **OK**.

LET ACCESS DETERMINE THE COLUMN WIDTH

1. Select the column(s) whose width you want to adjust.

2. Right-click the selection and select **Column Width**.

3. In the Column Width dialog box, click the **Standard Width** check box to have Access change the width based on the default font (see the associated Tip).

–Or–

Click **Best Fit** to change the column(s) width to be just wider than the widest content in each column.

Move and Rename Columns

You can position and rename columns, as well as hide them from view and freeze them in place.

POSITION A COLUMN

1. Click the column selector for the column whose position you want to change in the table.

2. Drag the column selector to the left or right to where you want the column located.

3. Release the mouse button when the heavy vertical line appears where you want the column located.

Category	Author	Title
Technical	Elliott	Stand Hdbk Power
Technical	Kleinert	Troublesht & Rep M

RENAME A COLUMN

1. Double-click the column selector of the column whose name you want to change.

–Or–

Right-click the column selector of the column whose name you want to change, and select **Rename Column**.

–Or–

Select a field in the column, and in the Datasheet (Table Tools) tab, click **Rename**.

2. Type a new name, and either press **ENTER** or click elsewhere in the table.

You can change the default settings for how new datasheets (including tables) appear. Click the **Office Button**, click **Access Options**, and click the **Datasheet** option. Change color, gridline, cell effects, and font options. Click **OK** when finished.

QUICKSTEPS

CHANGING HOW THE CURRENT DATASHEET LOOKS

Unlike spreadsheets and Word tables, formatting is applied to an entire datasheet—you cannot format individual fields, rows, or columns when working in Datasheet View. (The one exception is fields with the Memo data type and whose Text Format field property is set to Rich Text, as described in chapter 8.) The formatting options for the open table (or datasheet) are found in the Home tab Font group and the Datasheet Formatting dialog box, shown in Figure 4-16.

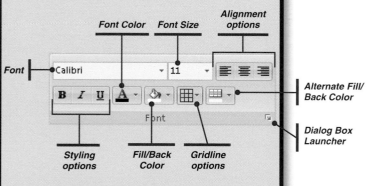

CHANGE TEXT ATTRIBUTES

The following options are found in the Font group:

- To change the typeface, click the **Font** down arrow, scroll through the list, and select a new typeface.

Continued . . .

Figure 4-16: The Datasheet Formatting dialog box, in combination with the Font group, contains options that apply formatting to the entire table.

HIDE AND UNHIDE COLUMNS

Hidden columns provide a means to temporarily remove columns from view without deleting them or their contents. (See the "Selecting Records, Fields, and Columns with the Mouse" QuickSteps for information selecting columns.)

1. Select the column(s) to be hidden.

2. In the Home tab Records groups, click **More** and click **Hide Columns**.

   –Or–

   Right-click the selection, and click **Hide Columns**.

3. To unhide columns, in the Home tab Records groups, click **More** and click **Unhide Columns**.

   –Or–

   Right-click a column selector, and click **Unhide Columns**.

CHANGING HOW THE CURRENT DATASHEET LOOKS *(Continued)*

- To change the text size, click the **Font Size** down arrow, scroll through the list, and select a new size.

- To bold, italicize, or underline selected field contents, click the respective button.

- To change text color, click the **Font Color** down arrow, and select a color from the palettes. (Chapter 8 provides more information on working with standard, custom, and theme-controlled colors.) The most recently used color appears on the Font Color button.

ALIGN TEXT IN A COLUMN

Click the **Left**, **Center**, or **Right** alignment buttons in the Font group.

CHANGE BACKGROUND COLORS

To provide contrast to your data, alternating rows in a table can have different colors applied. By default, the colors are drawn from the current formatting theme in effect (see Chapter 8 for more information on using themes). You can change this default appearance by changing either or both of the two colors used in the Datasheet Formatting dialog box.

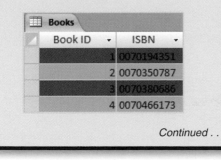

Continued . . .

In either case, click the check box next to hidden column(s) you want to show, and click **Close**.

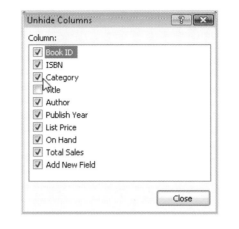

Lock and Unlock Columns

You can lock (or *freeze*) one or more columns to the leftmost side of the table so that they are visible no matter where in the table you might be.

1. To lock columns, select the column(s) you want to lock. Then, in the Home tab Records group, click **More** and click **Freeze**.

   –Or–

   Right-click a column selector, and click **Freeze Columns**.

2. To unlock frozen columns, in the Home tab Records group, click **More** and click **Unfreeze**.

   –Or–

   Right-click a column selector, and click **Unfreeze All Columns**.

   In either case, you will have to move the columns back to their original locations.

1. Click the Font group **Dialog Box Launcher** (the arrow in the lower-right corner of the group):

   - To change the background color, click the **Background Color** down arrow, and select a color from the palettes.

   - To change the color of alternating rows, click the **Alternate Background Color** down arrow, and select a color from the palettes. Click **No Color** to apply the fill/back color as a solid background.

   - To change the color of the gridlines, click the **Gridline Color** down arrow, and select a color from the palettes.

   - To return to the default theme colors, click **Automatic** at the top of each color menu.

2. Click **OK** when finished.

CHOOSE A GRID APPEARANCE

In the Font group, click the **Gridline** down arrow, and select the combination of vertical and horizontal gridlines you want from the menu.

ADD EFFECTS TO CELLS

1. Click the Font group **Dialog Box Launcher** (the arrow in the lower-right corner of the group).

2. Under Cell Effect, select a type of effect. The result appears in the Sample area.

3. Click **OK** when finished.

Adjust Row Height

You can adjust the height of all rows in the table by using the mouse, by typing a precise value, or by choosing a default height:

- To change row height with the mouse, point at the bottom border of a record selector. When the pointer changes to a cross, drag the border up or down to the height you want.

- To change row height precisely, right-click a row selector, and click **Row Height**. In the Row Height dialog box, type a row height. To use the default row height (14.25 is the default height for the Calibri font), click the **Standard Height** check box. Click **OK**.

How to...

- Sort Records in a Table
- Sort Records in a Form
- Choosing a Filter
- Filter by Selecting
- Filter for an Input
- Filter by Form
- Use Operators and Wildcards in Criteria
- Removing, Clearing, or Reapplying a Filter
- Use Advanced Filters
- Create a Simple Query with a Wizard
- Create or Modify a Query in Design View
- View the Query Results
- Save and Close a Query
- Using the Expression Builder
- Set Query Properties

Chapter 5
Retrieving Information

A great deal of Access is geared toward getting data into tables. In earlier chapters, you learned how to create tables, set field properties, and enter the data. Those are all worthwhile skills you need to develop, but the *value* of data lies in finding ways to extract from it just the information you want for a particular need. In this chapter you will learn how to organize data by sorting; how to filter data so that you see only the fields you want; and how to create queries, which can do everything filters do and much more.

Sort Data

Sorting allows you to reorganize your data by taking values in one or more fields and placing their corresponding records in an ascending or descending order. There are no permanent changes made to the data, data in each record is unchanged, and you can easily return your data to the view you started with.

✄	Cu̱t
📋	Copy
📋	Paste
A↓	Sort A to Z ⟍
Z↓	Sort Z to A
	Clear filter from Publish Year
	Text Filters ▸
	Equals "1991"
	Does Not Equal "1991"
	Contains "1991"
	Does Not Contain "1991"

Sort Records in a Table

Typically, records are sorted sequentially by the primary key as they are entered. You can alter this *sort order* by choosing to sort all records based on the values in a different field, or even in multiple fields.

SORT ON ONE COLUMN

1. In the database whose data you want to sort, open the table in Datasheet View (see Chapter 4).

2. Right-click anywhere in the column for the field that you want to sort your data on. Click **A-Z** to sort ascending—from smaller to larger numbers, oldest to newest dates and times, and alphabetically from A to Z.

–Or–

Click **Z-A** to sort descending—from larger to smaller numbers, newest to oldest dates and times, and alphabetically from Z to A.

(Alternatively, in the Home tab Sort & Filter group, click the **Ascending** or **Descending** buttons.)

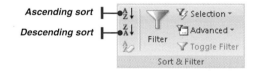

In all cases, records are reordered in the table to conform to the sort. A small up arrow (ascending sort) or down arrow (descending sort) appears next to the right side of the column header.

Last Name ⬆	First Name ▾
Andersen	Elizabeth

3. When you close the table, you will be asked if you want to change the table design. Clicking **Yes** will save the sort order. The next time you open the datasheet, the data will display with its new sort order.

SORT ON MULTIPLE FIELDS

You can sort on two or more fields by sorting them in a specific order. First, sort the most specific (or *innermost*) field. Sort the least specific (or *outermost*) field last, and sort any intermediate fields in the most-to-least hierarchy. For example, if you wanted an ascending sort for the prices in several categories of books, you would first perform an ascending sort of the List Price field, and then perform an ascending sort of the Category field. Records are then

NOTE

Sorting on multiple fields by the innermost and outermost concept is a *complex* sort, since you can select an ascending or descending sort for each field. If you want to sort multiple fields so that they are all ascending or all descending, move the columns so that they are adjacent, with the leftmost being the outermost field and the rightmost the innermost field. Select the columns (see Chapter 4 for information on moving and selecting columns), and select an ascending or descending sort.

organized by category, with the list prices in an ascending sort within each category. Figure 5-1 shows the results of this example.

1. In the database whose data you want to sort, open the table in Datasheet View (see Chapter 4).

2. Right-click the innermost field, and click an ascending or descending sort.

3. Repeat step 2 for any other fields you want to sort on, ending with the outermost field.

4. When you close the table, you will be asked if you want to change the table design. Clicking **Yes** will save the sort order. The next time you open the table, the data will display with its new sort order.

The least specific, or outermost, field is sorted last

Records are first sorted by the most specific, or innermost, field

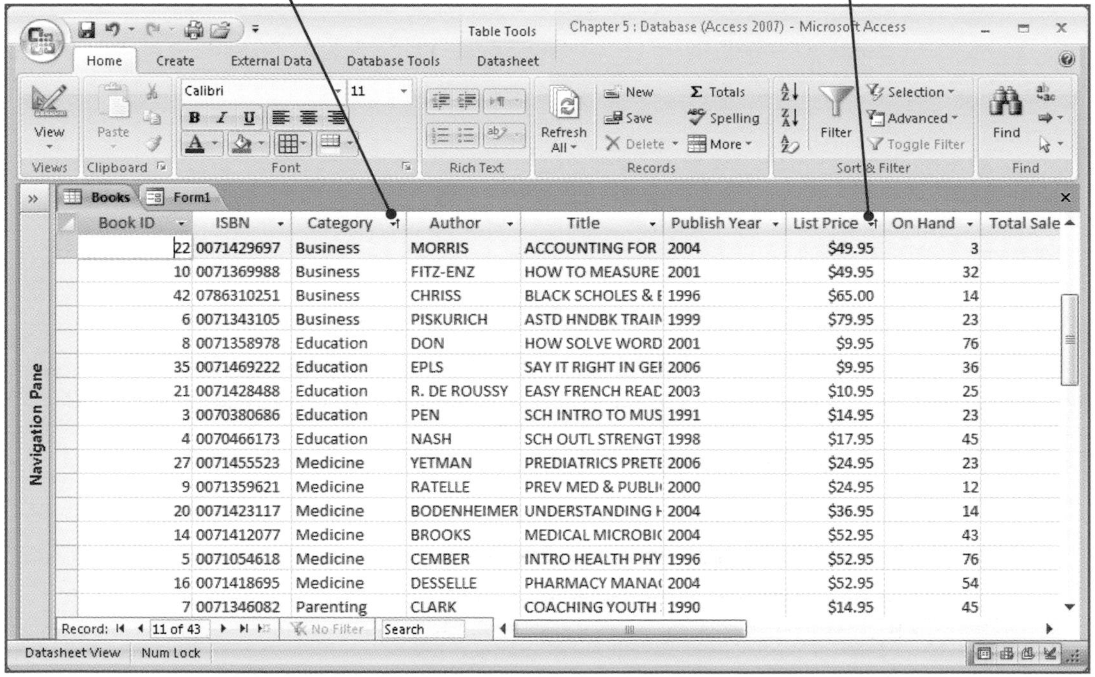

Figure 5-1: *You can sort a table on one or more fields to present the data in just the form you need.*

Sort Records in a Form

You can sort records using a form in Form View, and then move through them in the new sort order.

1. In the database whose data you want to sort, open the form in Form View (see Chapter 6 for information on working with forms).

2. Right-click the field in the form that you want to sort on. Click **A-Z** ↕ to sort ascending—from smaller to larger numbers, oldest to newest dates and times, and alphabetically from A to Z.

   –Or–

   Click **Z-A** ↕ to sort descending—from larger to smaller numbers, newest to oldest dates and times, and alphabetically from Z to A.

   Depending on your choice of sort order, you will see either the first or last record in the table or form, as shown in Figure 5-2.

Figure 5-2: **Performing a descending sort on the Last Name field reorders the records, with last names at the end of the alphabet now appearing first in the new sort order.**

NOTE

You can filter records in a datasheet/subdatasheet, form/subform, or query. The procedures, figures, and illustrations in this chapter use tables as the primary example object. However, the filtering techniques work similarly for each object.

TIP

All filters are "saved" with the table or form in which they were created until they are replaced with a new filter. When you close the table or form, you will be asked if you want save changes to the design of the object. Clicking **Yes** will retain the filter for the next time you open the object. Also, if you switch views when a filter is applied, for example, switching from Datasheet View to Form View, the filtering in place is retained. Advanced filters can also be saved as a query and be run irrespective of subsequent filters you've created. See "Save an Advanced Filter," later in the chapter.

Filter Data

Filtering by one of several methods lets you focus on specific records you want to see while hiding from view the rest of the data in the table. Setting up a filter can be as simple as selecting a value in a field (table column) and clicking a button, or you can apply complex criteria to multiple columns and save the filter design as a *query* (working with queries is discussed later in

CHOOSING A FILTER

The filter you choose will depend on the size of your data and the complexity of your filtering criteria. The main functionality for the filter types are as follows:

- **Filter By Selecting** lets you select a value in the table or form.

- **Filter By Form** lets you select values from a drop-down list or enter your own.

- **Filter For An Input** lets you type your criteria in a text box.

- **Advanced Filter** lets you design the filter in a grid, where you can sort the data, use operators and wildcards to set criteria, and save the filter as a query.

NOTE

You can filter data by selecting only a portion of a field. The options you are presented with vary, according to the type of data selected, as well as which portion of data is selected.

✂	Cut	$16.95
📋	Copy	$24.95
📋	Paste	$79.95
A↓	Sort Smallest to Largest	$14.95
		$19.95
Z↓	Sort Largest to Smallest	$16.95
	Clear filter from List Price	$16.95
	Number Filters ▸	$16.95
		$16.95
	Equals 16	$9.95
	Does Not Equal 16	$39.99
	Less Than or Equal To 16	$24.99
	Greater Than or Equal To 16	$60.00

the chapter). In a filter, you enter a value (and/or add *criteria*) in a field that you want to find in all other records that have the same value (or that meet the criteria you set) in the same field. For example, you might want to find all salespersons that have the value "Washington" in their Territory field. You would filter on "Washington" in the Territory field, and only those records that satisfied that criteria would be displayed. The record for a salesperson named "Joe Washington" whose territory is New York would not be displayed, since "Washington," in this case, is not in the filtered field.

Filter by Selecting

Filtering by selecting values is the easiest filter to perform, especially in small databases. The main reason for using this filter is that you can quickly locate the value on which the filter is based. Access offers several filtering options based on common criteria applicable to the data type of the column or field. You can identify data that contains a filter by looking for icons displayed in the column header that contains the filtered value ▾⊽ and on the navigation bar at the bottom of a table in Datasheet View or a form in Form View.

HIGHLIGHT A VALUE OR PORTION OF A VALUE

1. Open a table in Datasheet View or a form in Form View.

2. Select the value in the field that you want to filter on, as shown in Figure 5-3. The part of the value you select will determine the breadth and focus of the options made available.

3. Right-click the value and click one of the most common filtering criteria in the context menu.

   –Or–

   In the Home tab Sort & Filter group, click **Selection** and click one of the common filters.

   In any case, the filtered records are displayed, as shown in Figure 5-3.

4. To remove or delete the filter and return the data to its pre-filtered state, see the "Removing, Clearing, or Reapplying a Filter" QuickSteps later in the chapter.

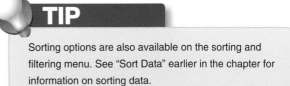

Figure 5-3: *Selecting a field and choosing a filter is a quick and easy way to view only the data you want.*

Select a field and a filter...

Equals "2004"
Does Not Equal "2004"
Contains "2004"
Does Not Contain "2004"

Book ID	ISBN	Category	Author	Title	Publish Year
12	0071377964	Technical	EDWARDS	BEAUTIFUL BUILT-II	2002
13	0071408959	Business	ALLAIRE	OPTIONS STRATEGI	2003
14	0071412077	Medicine	BROOKS	MEDICAL MICROBIC	2004
15	0071413014	Technical	WELLS	AIRPORT PLANNINI	2003
16	0071418695	Medicine	DESSELLE	PHARMACY MANAC	2004
17	0071418717	Business	PAGE	HOPE IS NOT A STR	2003
18	0071421947	Business	KADOR	50 HIGH IMPACT SP	2004

Record: 16 of 4

Datasheet View   Num Loc

...to display only the records that contain the value in the same field

Book ID	ISBN	Category	Author	Title	Publish Year	Lis
14	0071412077	Medicine	BROOKS	MEDICAL MICROBIC	2004	
16	0071418695	Medicine	DESSELLE	PHARMACY MANAC	2004	
18	0071421947	Business	KADOR	50 HIGH IMPACT SP	2004	
19	007142251X	Technical	KINNISON	AVIATION MAINTEI	2004	
20	0071423117	Medicine	BODENHEIMER	UNDERSTANDING I	2004	
22	0071429697	Business	MORRIS	ACCOUNTING FOR	2004	
24	0071441719	Technical	WOODSON	BE A SUCCESSFUL R	2004	
38	0072231246	Technical	MEYERS	A+ GUIDE TO OPER/	2004	
39	0072232021	Technical	PHILLIPS	IT PROJECT MANAC	2004	
*	(New)					

Record: 1 of 9   ▶ ▶I ▶⊞   Filtered   Search

Datasheet View   Num Lock   Filtered

TIP

Sorting options are also available on the sorting and filtering menu. See "Sort Data" earlier in the chapter for information on sorting data.

FILTER BY SELECTING FIELD VALUES

1. Open a table in Datasheet View or a form in Form View.

2. In the Home tab Sort & Filter group, click **Filter**.

   –Or–

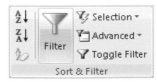

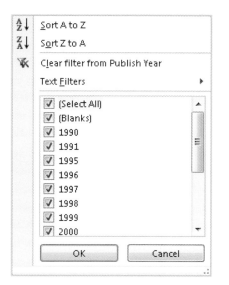

In Datasheet View, click the column header down arrow.

In either case, a sorting and filtering menu appears.

3. Click **Select All** in the values list to remove the check marks next to all values in the column.

4. Click the values whose records you want to display. Click **OK** to display the filtered records.

FILTER BY EMPTY CELLS

1. Open a table in Datasheet View or a form in Form View.

2. In the Home tab Sort & Filter group, click **Filter**.

   –Or–

   In Datasheet View, click the column header down arrow.

   In either case, a sorting and filtering menu appears.

3. Click **Select All** to remove the check marks next to all values in the column.

4. Click **(Blanks)** at the top of the values list. Click **OK**, and those records with blank values in the column will be displayed.

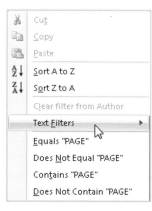

Filter for an Input

You can type a value, operators, and wildcards in a text box to quickly filter your data.

1. Open a table in Datasheet View or a form in Form View.

2. Right-click the value in the field that you want to filter on.

   –Or–

   In the Sort & Filter group, click **Filter**.

3. Click **Data type Filters** to see a more expanded list of filters based on the data type of the field, as shown in Figure 5-4.

4. Click the filter you want, and a custom filter dialog box appears, with one or two text boxes to accept the value you want to filter on, or you can type additional criteria (see "Use Operators and Wildcards in Criteria" later in the chapter).

5. To remove or delete the filter and return data back to its prefiltered state, see the "Removing, Clearing, or Reapplying a Filter" QuickSteps later in the chapter.

NOTE

Filtering By Exclusion—that is, displaying all records that *don't* contain the filtered-on value in the same field—is performed in the same way as "Highlight a Value or Portion of a Value" earlier in the chapter, except for the command to start the filter. In this case, click the **Does Not Equal** *Value* to start the filter.

> Equals...
> Does Not Equal...
> Begins With...

TIP

To clear values that are displayed in the table or form, right-click a cell or field, and click **Clear Grid**.

Filter by Form

You can create a filter by choosing a value to filter on from a drop-down list of all values in the field, or you can type the value and/or add operators and wildcards. (See "Use Operators and Wildcards in Criteria" later in the chapter.)

1. Open a table in Datasheet View or a form in Form View.

2. In the Home tab Sort & Filter group, click **Advanced** and click **Filter By Form**. You will see a one-line blank record in Datasheet View, or you will see a blank set of fields in Form View.

Books: Filter by Form				
Book ID	ISBN	Category	Author	Title
▾				

3. Click the field you want to filter on. A down arrow will appear at the right end of the field, as shown for Form View in Figure 5-5. Click the down arrow and select the value you want to filter on from the drop-down list.

   –Or–

   Type the value you want to filter on in the field.

   –Or–

   Type operators and wildcards in addition to typed or selected values.

4. Click **Toggle Filter** in the Sort & Filter group to apply the filter.

5. To remove or delete the filter and return data back to its prefiltered state, see the "Removing, Clearing, or Reapplying a Filter" QuickSteps.

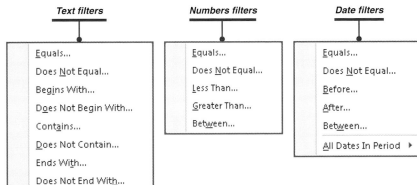

Figure 5-4: *Filtering options that accept criteria in a dialog box vary according to the field's data type.*

Use Operators and Wildcards in Criteria

You can "juice up" how records are filtered by using *operators* and *wildcards*. These are symbols and other characters that tell the filter or query to return certain results. For example, if you use "12.95" in a Price field, the filter or query would return only those records that contained a $12.95 price. If you entered the greater-than-or-equal-to operator—">=12.95"—Access would return those records greater than or equal to $12.95.

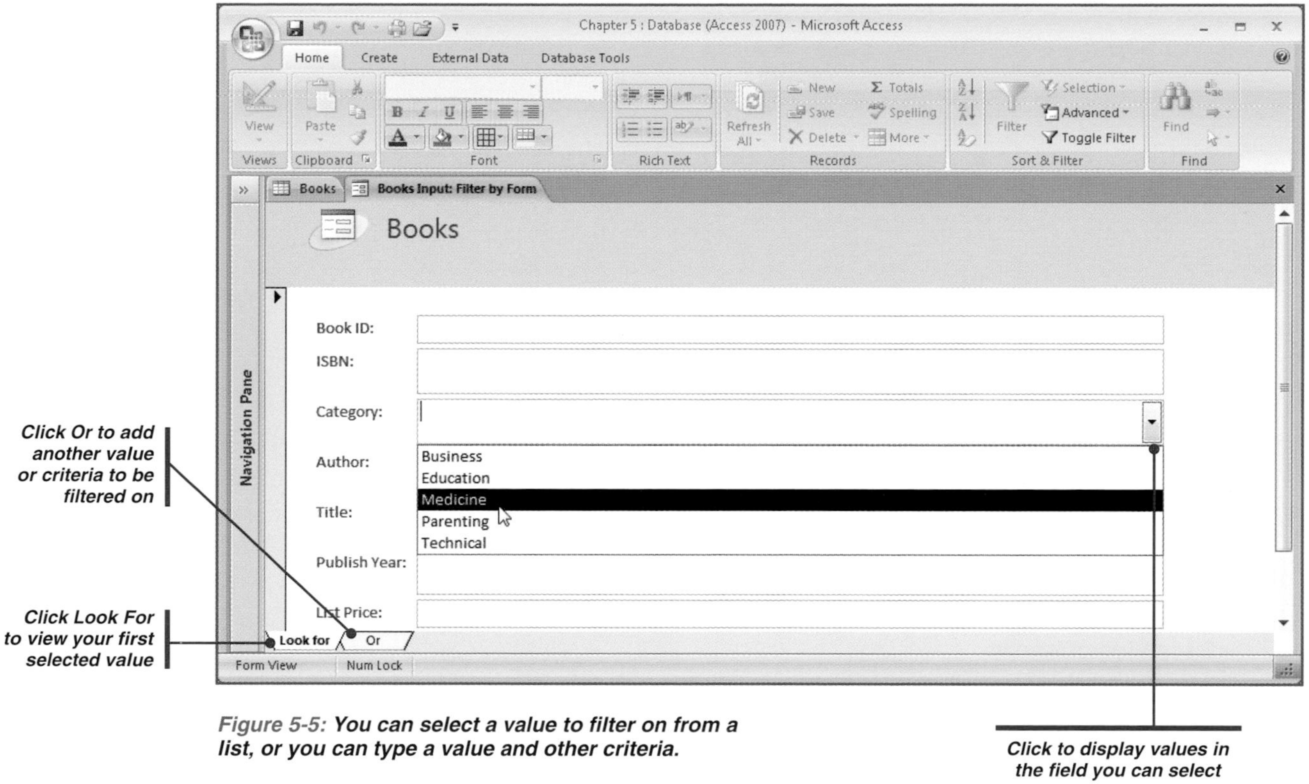

Books Input: Filter by Form

Books

Book ID:	
ISBN:	
Category:	
Author:	Business Education
Title:	Medicine Parenting Technical
Publish Year:	
List Price:	

Click Or to add another value or criteria to be filtered on

Click Look For to view your first selected value

Look for / Or

Figure 5-5: *You can select a value to filter on from a list, or you can type a value and other criteria.*

Click to display values in the field you can select

NOTE

You can select directly from menus filters that use most of the common comparison operators. See "Highlight a Value or Portion of a Value" earlier in the chapter.

TIP

For a complete listing of operators, use the Expression Builder, described later in this chapter.

USE COMPARISON OPERATORS

Table 5-1 provides a list and descriptions of common operators you can use to compare values.

USE ARITHMETIC OPERATORS

Table 5-2 provides a list and descriptions of common operators you can use to calculate a value.

USE LOGICAL OPERATORS

Table 5-3 provides a list and descriptions of common operators you can use to apply logical comparisons.

COMPARISON OPERATOR	DESCRIPTION
>	Greater than
>=	Greater than or equal to
<	Less than
<=	Less than or equal to
=	Equal to
<>	Not equal to
Between	The inclusive values between two values (for example, "between 9 and 12" would return 9, 10, 11, and 12)

Table 5-1: **Comparison Operators**

ARITHMETIC OPERATOR	DESCRIPTION
+	Addition
*	Multiplication
/	Division
-	Subtraction

Table 5-2: **Arithmetic Operators**

LOGICAL OPERATOR	DESCRIPTION
AND	Both values must be satisfied
OR	Either value must be satisfied
NOT	The value is not satisfied

Table 5-3: **Logical Operators**

USE WILDCARDS

Wildcards are characters that act as placeholders in expressions used in filters or queries when you are trying to find a particular word or string of characters and only know limited information about the value. Typically used in text fields, you can use them in other data types. Table 5-4 lists the most commonly used wildcards.

TIP

You can also use wildcards in the Find and Find And Replace dialog boxes (click **Find** or **Replace** in the Home tab Find group). See Chapter 4 for information on finding and replacing text in a table.

UICKSTEPS

REMOVING, CLEARING, OR REAPPLYING A FILTER

When you *clear* a filter, you permanently strike it from the object it's associated with. When you merely *toggle* a filter, it can be reapplied. To re-create a cleared filter, you have to start from scratch.

Continued . . .

WILDCARD	DESCRIPTION
*	Used as a placeholder for all characters that occupy the space. For example, filtering on a value of *son would return values that started with any characters as long as they ended in "son," such as Robertson and comparison.
?	Used as a placeholder for a single character. For example, filtering on a value of r??der would return values that contained any characters in the second and third positions, such as reader and Ridder.
[ ]	Returns values that match any characters you type between the brackets. For example, the[mr]e would return there and theme, but not Thebe.
!	Returns values that don't match the characters you type between brackets. For example, the[!mr]e would return Thebe, but not there or theme.
-	Returns values that match a range of characters between brackets. For example, the[m-z]e would return there and theme, but not Thebe.
#	Used as a placeholder, similar to ?, but used to replace a single numeric character.

Table 5-4: **Common Wildcards**

REMOVE A FILTER

1. Open the table or form that contains the filter you want to remove.

2. In the Home tab Sort & Filter group, click the **Toggle Filter** button.

   –Or–

   Click the **Filtered** icon on the navigation bar.

   In either case, the data is returned to its pre-filtered state.

REAPPLY THE MOST RECENT FILTER

1. Open the table or form that contains the filter you want to reapply.

2. In the Home tab Sort & Filter group, click the **Toggle Filter** button.

   –Or–

   Click the **Unfiltered** icon on the navigation bar.

   In either case, the data is filtered according to the criteria used in the most recent filter.

CLEAR A FILTER

1. Open the datasheet or form that contains the filter you want to delete.

2. In the Home tab Sort & Filter group, click **Advanced** and click **Clear All Filters** (this option, as the label implies, clears the current filter and any saved filters).

   –Or–

   Select a cell in the column that contains the filter, right-click the cell, and click **Clear Filter From Field Name**.

Use Advanced Filters

Advanced filters allow you to easily use multiple criteria in multiple fields (columns) to find and sort records.

You can also use *expressions* to set up criteria. Expressions used in filters are typically short combinations of values, operators, wildcards, and other terms that return a value. Access has an Expression Builder tool that you can use to build the expression using lists and buttons. Right-click a criteria field, and select Build to open the Expression Builder window. See the "Using the Expression Builder" QuickSteps for more information.

CREATE AN ADVANCED FILTER

1. Open a table in Datasheet View or a form in Form View.

2. In the Home tab Sort & Filter group, click **Advanced** and click **Advanced Filter/Sort**. The advanced filter design pane opens with a default name, including the table name and a sequential filter number.

3. Click the **Field** down arrow in the leftmost column of the grid in the lower half of the pane. Select the first field that you want to search. (See "Work in the Grid" later in this chapter for other ways to choose the field you want.)

4. If you want to sort your results, click the **Sort** field, and open its drop-down menu. Click the sort order you want.

5. In the Criteria field, type the first criteria you want to apply in the current field. (See "Use Operators and Wildcards in Criteria" earlier in the chapter.)

6. Type a second criteria, as necessary, in the "or" field. Records that satisfy either condition will be returned. Repeat for any other criteria you want to add.

7. Repeat steps 3–6 to apply criteria in multiple fields, as shown in Figure 5-6.

8. In the Home tab Sort & Filter group, click **Toggle Filter** to display the results.

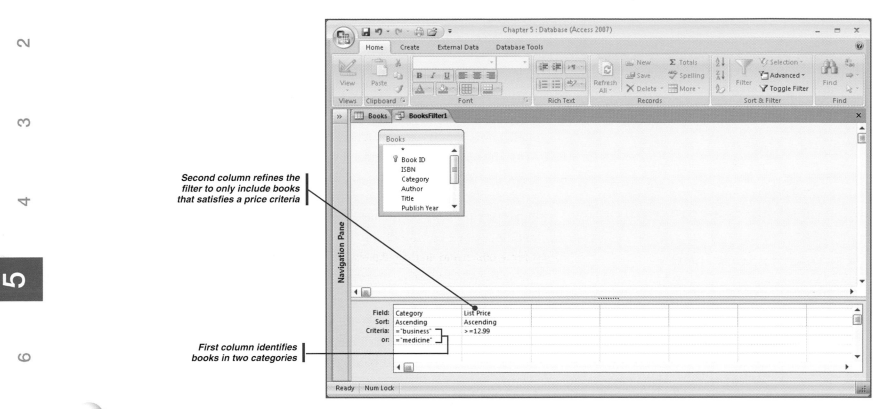

Second column refines the filter to only include books that satisfies a price criteria

First column identifies books in two categories

Figure 5-6: The advance filter pane lets you set up complex filters and sort the results.

TIP

For a more complete description on how to use the advanced filter pane, see "Create or Modify a Query in Design View" later in the chapter.

TIP

To clear any existing criteria in the grid, in the Sort & Filter group, click **Advanced** and click **Clear Grid**; or right-click an area of the pane outside the grid, and click **Clear Grid.**

SAVE AN ADVANCED FILTER

You can save a filter you set up in the advanced filter pane as a query and run it at a future time.

1. Set up the filter in the advanced filter pane.

2. Prior to applying the filter, in the Sort & Filter group, click **Advanced** and click **Save As Query**.

   –Or–

   Right-click an area of the pane outside the grid, and click **Save As Query**.

3. In the Save As Query dialog box, type a name for the query. Click **OK**. (To run the query, see "View the Query Results" later in the chapter.)

Work with Queries

Queries offer the most powerful and flexible way to work with the data in your database. They allow you to retrieve, change, add to, and analyze data from one or more tables or other queries. Queries respond to the criteria you set and display the resultant data in a table or datasheet. The *Select* queries family— such as Simple, Find Duplicates, and Find Unmatched—do so without changing any underlining data. *Action* queries (such as Make-Table, Update, Append, and Delete) cause the underlying data to change. You can also *join* data from multiple tables and analyze data by using Crosstab queries (see Chapter 10 for information on Crosstab queries).

Create a Simple Query with a Wizard

The easiest way to create a Select query is to let Access guide you using the Simple Query Wizard. The operant word in the wizard name is "Simple." The wizard doesn't try to help you establish criteria, other than letting you choose what fields (columns) you want to include. After finishing the query, you will most likely need to modify the design (see "Create or Modify a Query in Design View" later in the chapter).

1. Open the database in which you want to create the query.

2. In the Create tab Other group, click **Query Wizard**.

3. In the New Query dialog box, click **Simple Query Wizard**, and click **OK**.

4. In the first page of the Simple Query Wizard, shown in Figure 5-7, click the **Tables/Queries** down arrow, and select the table or query from where you first want to select the fields that will appear in your query results.

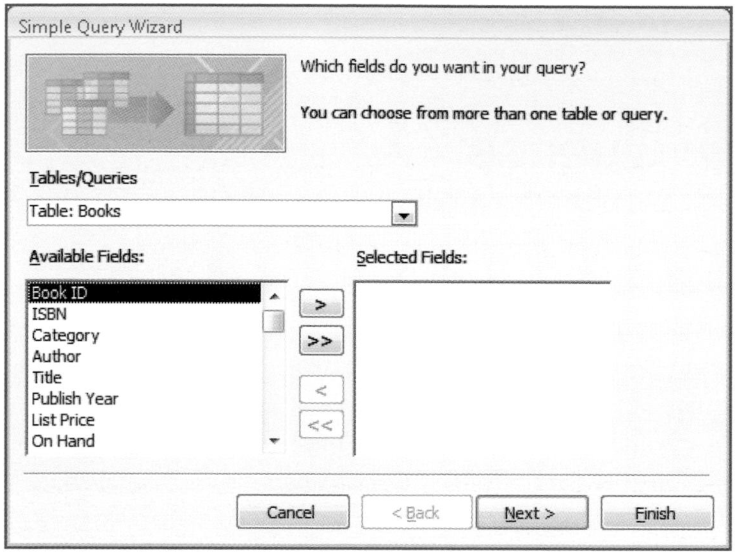

Simple Query Wizard

Which fields do you want in your query?

You can choose from more than one table or query.

Tables/Queries

Table: Books

Available Fields:

Book ID
ISBN
Category
Author
Title
Publish Year
List Price
On Hand

Selected Fields:

[>] [>>] [<] [<<]

[Cancel] [< Back] [Next >] [Finish]

*Figure 5-7: **The Simple Query Wizard lets you select the fields of data you want from tables or queries in the database.***

5. Move the fields you want from the Available Fields to the Selected Fields list by either double-clicking the fields you want or by using the select/ remove buttons between the two lists to add or remove fields (single arrows move the selected field; double arrows move all fields).

6. Repeat steps 4 and 5 if you want to include fields from other tables or queries. Click **Next** when finished adding fields.

7. In the last page of the wizard, type a title or name for the query, and choose whether to open (run) the query as is or to modify its design. Click **Finish** when done. Depending on the choice you selected, the new query will appear as a table or datasheet with the resultant fields you selected earlier in the wizard.

–Or–

The new query will open in Design View, ready for adding criteria and making other changes.

In either case, the new query will be listed under the Queries group in the Navigation Pane.

Queries
- Add Books
- Year 2000 Titles

Create or Modify a Query in Design View

Queries use a Design View pane, shown in Figure 5-8, where you can modify an existing query (for example, a query created using the Simple Query Wizard) or start one from scratch.

1. Open the database where you want to create or modify a query.

2. In the Create tab Other group, click **Query Design** to open a blank query in Design View.

Query Wizard   Query Design   Macro

Other

–Or–

NOTE

Depending on the field(s) you select in the Simple Query Wizard, you might see an additional page that lets you choose whether to display detailed or summary results.

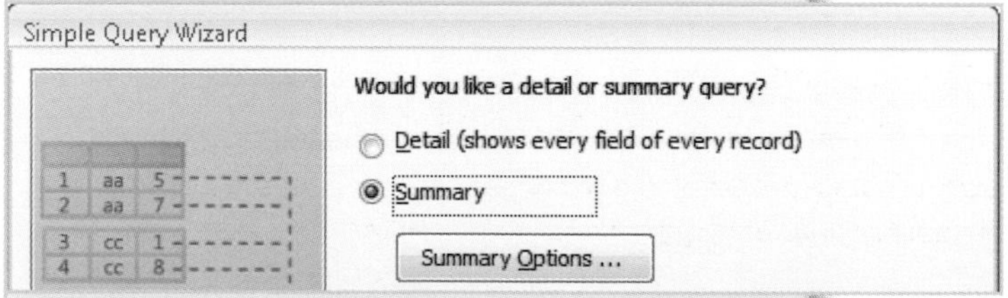

Simple Query Wizard

Would you like a detail or summary query?

○ Detail (shows every field of every record)

● Summary

[Summary Options ...]

1	aa	5
2	aa	7
3	cc	1
4	cc	8

Design area

Contextual tab of query-related tools

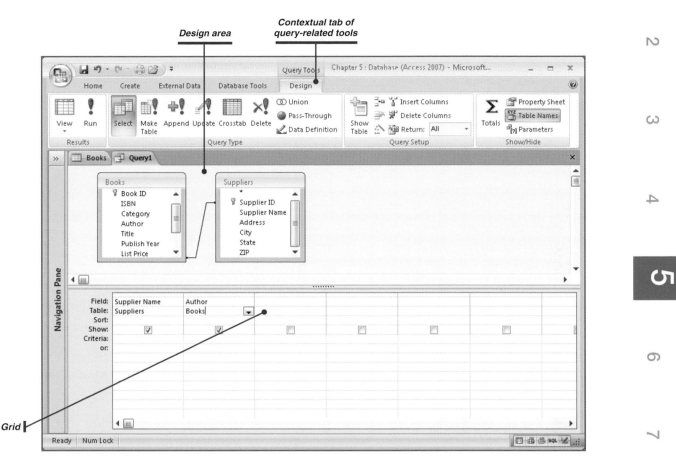

Figure 5-8: *The Query Design View pane provides everything you need to set up or change a query.*

CAUTION

If you add multiple tables to a query, they may not function as designed unless they have a *relationship*. Right-click a blank portion of the design area, and click **Relationships** to view any related tables (see Chapter 2 for information on joining tables into relationships).

1. In the Navigation Pane, click the pane's title bar, and under Navigate To Category, click **Object Type**. Under Filter By Group, click **All Access Objects**.

2. In the Queries group, right-click the name of the query you want to change, and click **Design View**. The query opens in Design View, and the ribbon displays the Design tab (Query Tools).

Figure 5-9: *Add tables and queries to the design area.*

WORK IN THE DESIGN AREA

The top portion, or *design area*, of the query Design View pane displays the fields, tables, and queries that you want the query to use in performing the actions you ask of it. (Existing queries will show their associated tables and queries; new queries will show a blank palette.)

1. If not displayed, click **Show Table** in the Design tab (Query Tools) Query Setup group to display the Show Table dialog box, shown in Figure 5-9. Choose which tables and/or queries you want to include (press **CTRL** while clicking objects to select multiple objects).

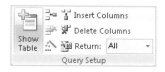

2. Click **Add**. The objects are added to the design area. Click **Close** when finished.

3. In the Query Type group, click the query you want. Depending on your selection, you will see a tailored grid at the bottom of the pane and/or be presented with a dialog box requesting more information from you.

4. To remove an object from the design area, right-click the object and select **Remove Table**.

WORK IN THE GRID

The lower portion of the query Design View pane, or *grid*, contains columns that you set up, on a field-by-field basis, using the fields from the tables and queries in the design area. Each column has several parameters you can apply to fully build your query.

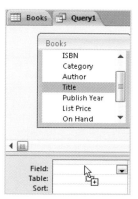

1. If working with a blank grid, add the first (or only) field to the leftmost column by locating it in the table or query in the design area and dragging it into the field labeled Field. You can also click the field in the grid, click the down arrow that appears, and select the field you want.

2. If you want to sort your results, click the **Sort** field, click its down arrow, and select the sort order you want.

3. Select the **Show** check box if you want the values from this field to display after the query is run.

TIP

A popular use for queries is to calculate a total. Click **Totals** in the Design tab (Query Tools) Show/Hide group to add a Total row to the grid. Click the **Total** field in the column where you want to apply it, click the down arrow that appears, and choose the type of total you want. If you choose **Expression**, type the expression in the Criteria field; or right-click the field, and select **Build** to use the Expression Builder.

4. Type expressions, values, or other criteria in the Criteria field; or click **Builder** in the Query Setup group to have the Expression Builder help you construct an expression (see the "Using the Expression Builder" QuickSteps later in the chapter).

Query Setup
Insert Rows Insert Columns
Delete Rows Delete Columns
Show Table Builder Return: All

5. Repeat steps 1–4 for other fields you want to include in the query.

6. Modify the structure of the grid by changing the number of rows and columns using the applicable Insert and Delete tools in the Query Setup group. (See Chapter 4 for information on selecting, inserting, and deleting rows and columns in a table.)

View the Query Results

In order to view the results of a query, you can *run* it from Design View, *switch* to Datasheet View, or *open* a saved query in the Navigation Pane.

1. With the query in Design View, click **Run** in the Results group.

–Or–

Switch to Datasheet View by clicking the **View** button in the Results group or clicking **Datasheet View** in the Views area at the right end of the status bar.

–Or–

In the Navigation Pane, click the pane's title bar, and under Navigate To Category, click **Object Type**. Under Filter By Group, click **All Access Objects**. In the Queries group, right-click the query you want to open, and click **Open**.

2. Depending on the query type you are using, you will either see the results displayed in a table or datasheet or you will need to supply additional criteria in a dialog box.

Save and Close a Query

Queries, unlike advanced filters, can be saved as objects to be used over and over again (of course, you can save the advanced filter as a query and use it "over and over" again).

TIP

To stop a query while it is running, press CTRL+BREAK.

TIP

To return to Design View after running the query, click **View** in the Results group (Design tab).

TIP

To better arrange the design area and the grid in the query Design View pane, resize the pane by collapsing the Navigation Pane and/or resizing the Access window. You can also change the proportion each area occupies in the pane by dragging the bar between the areas up or down.

TIP

You can simultaneously move all fields in a table or query from the design area to the columns in the grid, rather than dragging them or choosing them individually. From the top of each field list in the table or query object, drag the asterisk (*) to the first field in the grid (see the Suppliers table in Figure 5-8).

SAVE A QUERY

You can save the query in Design View or in Datasheet View with the query results.

1. Right-click the tab corresponding to the query's name, and click **Save**.

   –Or–

   Press **CTRL+S**.

2. Type a query name in the Save As dialog box, and click **OK**. The query will be displayed in the Queries group in the Navigation Pane.

CLOSE A QUERY

1. Right-click the tab corresponding to the query's name.

   –Or–

   In Design View, right-click a blank spot in the design area.

2. Click **Close**.

3. If changes to the query have not been saved, click **Yes** when prompted. In addition, if the query is new, type a query name in the Save As dialog box, and click **OK**.

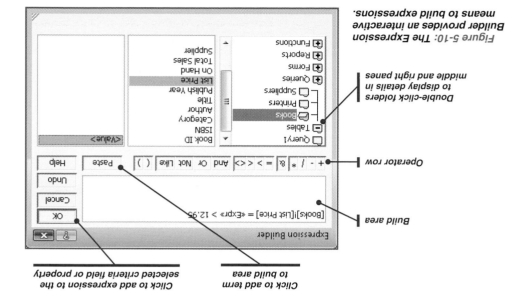

Figure 5-10: The Expression Builder provides an interactive means to build expressions.

Expression Builder

Build area

Operator row

[Books]![List Price] = «Expr» > 12.95

Double-click folders to display details in middle and right panes

Click to add term to build area

Click to add expression to the selected criteria field or property

Query1
Tables
Books
Printers
Suppliers
Queries
Forms
Reports
Functions

Book ID
ISBN
Category
Author
Title
Publish Year
List Price
On Hand
Total Sales
Supplier

<Value>

OK Cancel Undo Help Paste

+ - / * & = < > <= >= <> And Or Not Like ( )

QUICKSTEPS

USING THE EXPRESSION BUILDER

The Expression Builder, shown in Figure 5-10, provides listings and buttons for the expression terms that you select to build your own expression.

CREATE OR EDIT AN EXPRESSION

• In query Design View or in an advanced filter, right-click a criteria field, and click **Build**.

   –Or–

• In query Design View, place the insertion point in a criteria field, and click the Query **Builder** in the Query Setup group on the Design tab (Query Tools).

Continued . . .

TIP

The Expression Builder, typically opened by clicking the three-dot Builder button [⋯] in certain property fields, is used in several other areas of Access. Its functionality is the same when used in filters and queries.

Microsoft Office Access

Do you want to save changes to the design of query 'Query1'?

Yes No Cancel

USING THE EXPRESSION BUILDER

(Continued)

ADD AN EXPRESSION TERM

1. Double-click the folders containing database objects, functions, constants, operators, and common expressions you want in the left, and possibly middle, pane to see their details in the other pane(s) to the right.

2. Double-click the term you want in the middle or right pane, or click **Paste**. The term is added to the build area at the top of the dialog box.

3. Repeat steps 1 and 2 to add other terms to the expression.

ADD OPERATORS

- Click your insertion point in the build area where you want the operator added. Click the applicable button from the center row.

   –Or–

- Double-click **Operators** in the left pane, select a category in the middle pane, and double-click the operator in the right pane.

ADD VALUES

1. Click your insertion point in the build area where you want the value added. In most cases, however, the Expression Builder will correctly set up the build area expression for you after inserting an operator.

2. Type the value.

ADD THE EXPRESSION TO THE CRITERIA FIELD

Click **OK** in the Expression Builder dialog box.

Set Query Properties

You can fine-tune several characteristics of a query by changing the attributes of its properties, as shown in Figure 5-11.

Figure 5-11: The Query Properties Property Sheet lists several query properties whose settings you can choose or modify.

Property Sheet	×
Selection type: Query Properties	

General

Description	
Default View	Datasheet
Output All Fields	No
Top Values	All
Unique Values	No
Unique Records	No
Source Database	(current)
Source Connect Str	
Record Locks	No Locks
Recordset Type	Dynaset
ODBC Timeout	60
Filter	
Order By	
Max Records	
Orientation	Left-to-Right
Subdatasheet Name	
Link Child Fields	
Link Master Fields	
Subdatasheet Height	0"
Subdatasheet Expanded	No
Filter On Load	No
Order By On Load	Yes

OPEN THE QUERY PROPERTY SHEET

The Property Sheet can be used to display both field properties and query properties. Once you have the **Property Sheet** displayed, make sure you are viewing the query properties list.

1. Click a blank area of the Design View pane (do not place the insertion point in a field).

2. Open the query in Design View, and click **Property Sheet** in the Show/Hide group.

   –Or–

Top Values	All
Unique Values	5
Unique Records	25
Source Database	100
Source Connect Str	5%
Record Locks	25%
Recordset Type	All
ODBC Timeout	60
Filter	

Right-click a blank area the query Design View pane (avoid objects in the design area and the grid), and click **Properties**.

–Or–

Press **ALT+ENTER**.

In each case, the Property Sheet will display the list of query properties (see Figure 5-10).

SET OR MODIFY A PROPERTY

- Click the box to the right of the property you want to set or change. Depending on the property, type the setting you want to add or change.

  –Or–

- Click the down arrow that appears, and select the setting from the drop-down list.

CHOOSE ONLY TOP OR BOTTOM VALUES

When running a query that returns a large number of results, you can choose to only have returned a certain number or percentage of the top or bottom numeric values or newest or oldest dates (to display the bottom values, sort the applicable field in descending order).

1. In query Design View, open the Property Sheet (see "Open the Query Property Sheet"), and display the query properties.

2. Click the box next to the Top Values property, and click the down arrow. Click the number of values to display or a percentage of the total values.

   –Or–

   In the Query Setup group, click the **Return** down arrow, and click the number of values to display or a percentage of the total values.

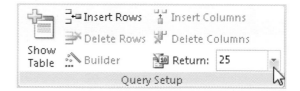

3. Run the query.

How to...

- Use the Form Tool
- Work with the Split Form Tool
- Setting the Location of the Splitter Bar
- Create a Form with Multiple Records
- Creating a Multiple-Table Form
- Employ the Form Wizard
- Understanding Form Views
- Use the Blank Form Tool
- Create a Form in Design View
- Adding Fields with the Field List
- Add Elements to a Form
- Selecting a Form Section
- Add Bound Controls
- Add Unbound Controls
- Copy or Delete a Control
- Select Controls
- Rearrange Controls
- Understanding Control Layouts
- Modify Controls
- Navigating in a Data Entry Form

Chapter 6

Creating Forms and Using Controls

6

You use forms to enter data or to display the information you have already entered. This chapter explains the several ways you can create a new form. Access 2007 provides several form tools, a Form Wizard, and you can create a form from scratch in Design View. You will learn how to modify form designs to meet your needs and how to choose the appropriate controls and set their properties.

Create Forms

Access forms have many uses. Mainly used for data entry and viewing, they are also utilized as user-interactive elements that offer additional choices or request additional information.

You have more than one way to create a new form. You can use one of several form tools, use the Form Wizard, or start from scratch in the form Design View. Whatever method you choose to create a form, you can tailor its appearance and behavior to exactly match the end use for the form.

Use the Form Tool

The Form tool lets you create a form with one mouse click. Because forms are often created to make data entry more efficient, the Form tool simply places each field from the table or query you select into an easy-to-read form. If there is another table that has a one-to-many relationship with your selected table (or query), that table is displayed as a datasheet under your new form. This is shown in Design View in Figure 6-1.

To create a form with the Form tool:

1. Open a table or query in Datasheet View.
2. In the Create tab Forms group, click **Form**. A new form is displayed in Layout View. You see the Form Layout Tools tabs displayed above the ribbon, as shown in Figure 6-2.

Work with the Split Form Tool

Access 2007 includes a new tool that displays both a Form View as well as the Datasheet View of the table with which you are working. The two views are coordinated so that you can make changes in either the Form View or the Datasheet View.

CREATE A SPLIT FORM

1. In the Navigation Pane, drag the table or query with which you want to work into the Access 2007 work area.
2. In the Create tab Forms group, click **Split Form**.

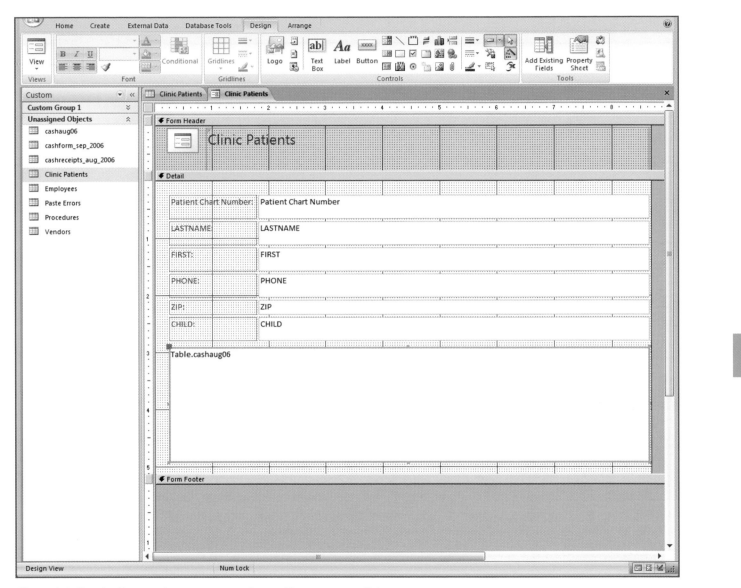

Figure 6-1: *Use the Form tool to create a new form with one mouse click.*

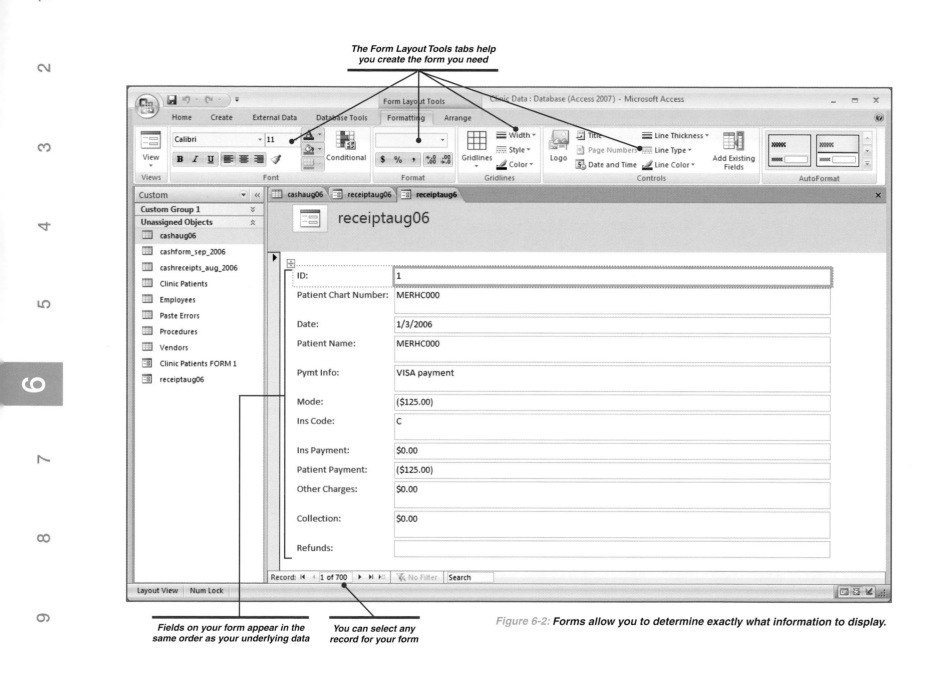

The Form Layout Tools tabs help you create the form you need

Figure 6-2: **Forms allow you to determine exactly what information to display.**

Fields on your form appear in the same order as your underlying data

You can select any record for your form

SETTING THE LOCATION OF THE SPLITTER BAR

You may want to fix the location of the splitter bar so that those who use your form in Form View cannot change it. To permanently set the location of the splitter bar in a split form:

1. Right-click the form's tab, and click **Design View**.

2. Press **F4** to open the Property Sheet. "Form" should be displayed at the top of the Property Sheet. If not, click the down arrow, and click **Form**.

3. Click the **Format** tab, click the **Split Form Splitter Bar** property, and click **Yes** on the drop-down menu. If you click **No**, the splitter bar is hidden from users.

4. Scroll to the **Save Splitter Bar Position** property, and click **Yes** from the drop-down list. If you want to set an exact position, scroll up to the **Split Form Size** property, and type the exact setting you want for the height of the form pane.

Split Form Size	2.1458"
Split Form Orientation	Datasheet on Bottom
Split Form Splitter Bar	Yes
Split Form Datasheet	Allow Edits
Split Form Printing	Datasheet Only
Save Splitter Bar Position	Yes

5. Right-click the form's tab, and click **Layout View**. Drag the splitter bar to where you want it located if you have not set an exact position in step 4.

6. Right-click the form's tab, and click **Form View** to see how your split form looks.

3. Your new form appears in Layout View, and the underlying data appears at the bottom of the Access work area in Datasheet View, as shown in Figure 6-3.

4. To move the form separator line (called a *splitter bar*) up or down, place your mouse on the line until you see the double-headed arrow. Hold down the mouse button, and drag up or down to move the splitter bar and display more of either view.

WORK WITH SPLIT FORM PROPERTIES

You can set several properties of your new split form from the Property Sheet. See the "Setting the Location of the Splitter Bar" QuickSteps for additional properties.

1. From within your split form, press **F4** to open the Property Sheet.

2. In Layout View or Design View, set these properties:

- Click **Split Form Orientation** to set the location of the datasheet. It can be on the left, the right, above, or below the form.

- Click **Split Form Datasheet**, and click **Allow Edits** to enable editing directly on the datasheet. Click **Read Only** to prevent editing on the datasheet.

- Click **Split Form Size** to specify the width and/or height of the form.

- Click **Split Form Printing** to specify what is printed when the user prints the form.

Create a Form with Multiple Records

The Form tool creates a form that displays one record at a time. If you need a form that displays more than one record, you can use the Multiple Items tool. With a multiple-item form, you can show all of your records, but add a logo or other graphics, change text box sizes, or add controls—things you cannot do in a table or datasheet.

1. From the Navigation Pane, open the table or query with which you want to work.

2. In the Create tab Forms group, click **Multiple Items**.

[Multiple Items icon]

![QuickSteps clock icon] **QUICKSTEPS**

CREATING A MULTIPLE-TABLE FORM

You can choose fields from more than one table if the tables are related (see Chapter 2).

1. In the Create tab Forms group, click **More Forms** and click **Form Wizard**.

2. Click the **Tables/Queries** down arrow, and select the main table from the Tables/Queries list.

3. Double-click each field you want. The fields are moved to the Selected Fields list box.

4. Repeat step 3 and select the related table from the Tables/Queries list.

5. Select the fields from that table.

6. Click **Finish** or click **Next** to continue the wizard (see "Employ the Form Wizard").

![Note pushpin icon] **NOTE**

If you haven't specified which table or query to use in the new form, the Form Wizard shows the first object in the alphabetic list of tables and queries in the current database. You can change that in the first dialog box.

3. Your new form is displayed with all the records from the table or query you selected.

Multiple Items Clinic Patient					×
Clinic Patients					
Patie: LASTNAME	FIRST	PHONE		ZIP	CHILD
7 Wiggins	Sally	360-555-4577		98175	Sam
8 McCarthy	Chuck	206-555-1177		98001	Maggie
9 Nosster	Kelly	360-555-1744		98125	Kim

Record: ◄ ◄ 1 of 10 ► ►I ►▄ 🗏 No Filter | Search

4. Make any changes you want for this form. See "Modify the Form Design" later in this chapter for more information.

5. Right-click the form tab, and click **Save** to display the Save As dialog box. Type a name for this form, and click **OK**.

6. Right-click the form's tab again, and click **Close** to close your new form.

Employ the Form Wizard

If you have used earlier versions of Access, you are familiar with the Form Wizard. You can still use the Form Wizard in Access 2007. The wizard helps you specify how your information is sorted and displayed, and you can use fields from several related tables or queries. For more information on establishing relationships, see Chapter 2.

1. To start the Form Wizard, in the Create tab Forms group, click **More Forms** and click **Form Wizard**.

2. In the first Form Wizard page, click the **Tables/Queries** down arrow, and select the table or query you want as the basis for the form.

3. In the Form Wizard page shown in Figure 6-4, move the fields you want from the Available Fields list to the Selected Fields list by either double-clicking the fields you want or by using the select/remove buttons between the two lists (single arrows move the selected field; double arrows move all fields).

4. Repeat steps 2 and 3 if you want to include fields from other tables or queries. Click **Next** when finished adding fields.

📋 More Forms ˅	Form Design
📝	Form Wizard
▦	Datasheet
▭	Modal Dialog
📑	PivotTable

Left margin numbers: 1 2 3 4 5 **6** 7 8 9 10

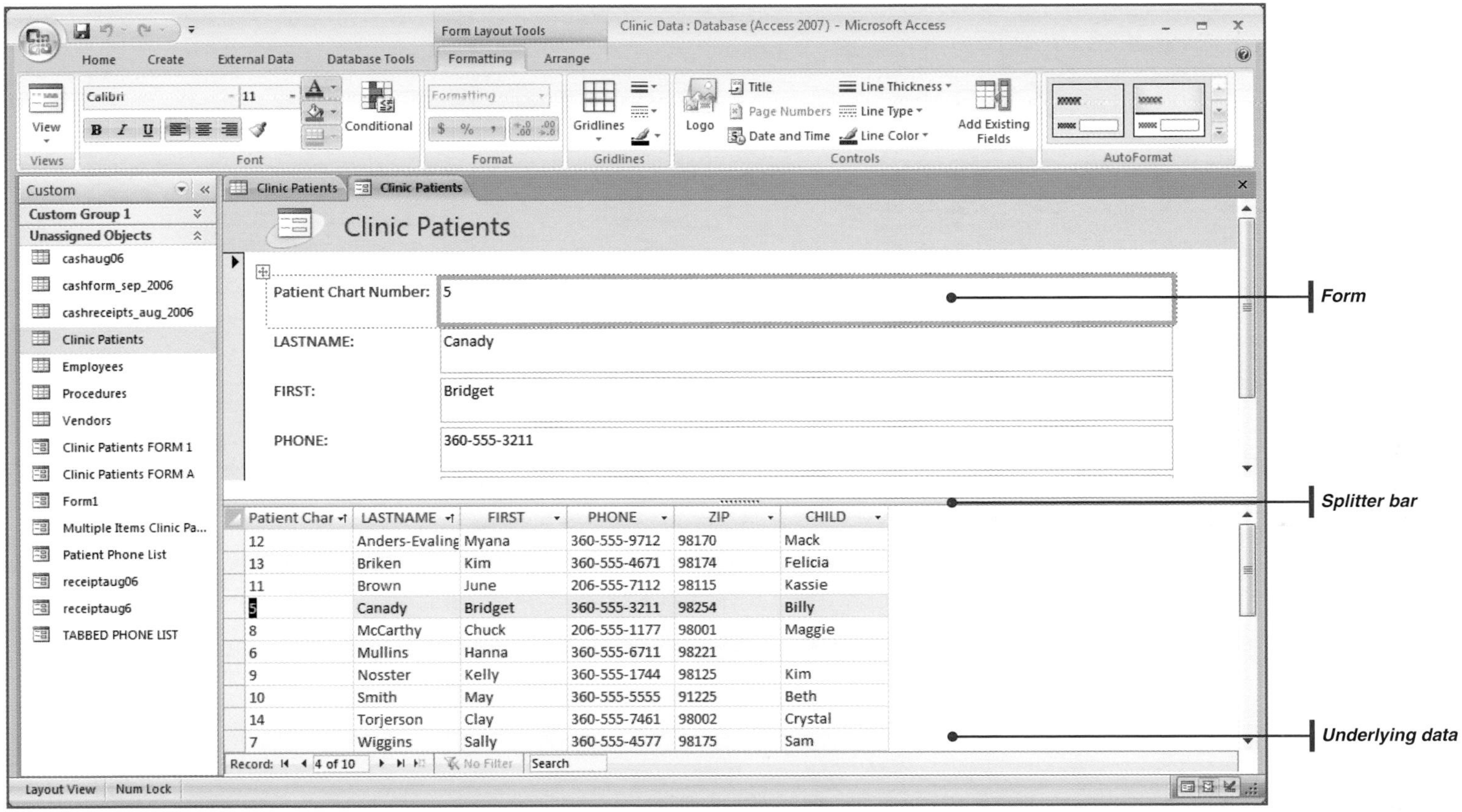

Figure 6-3: *The Split Form tool allows you to see both your form and its underlying data.*

5. The next two Form Wizard pages offer you choices of layout and style (see Figure 6-5). Choose the layout and style you want, and click **Next** after each choice.

6. In the final page of the Form Wizard, type a title for the form. Then:

   • Click **Open The Form To View Or Enter Information** to start entering data at once.

   –Or–

   • Click **Modify The Form's Design** to change to Design View, where you can edit the design. See "Create a Form in Design View" later in the chapter.

7. Click **Finish**. The completed form resembles that shown in Figure 6-6.

TIP

If the form is blank, there may not be any data in the table or query you chose as the basis for the form. Open the table to check for data. If you based the form on a query, the query may not return any records because of conflicting criteria. Run the query to see if any records are returned. (See Chapter 5 for more information on working with queries.)

QUICKFACTS

UNDERSTANDING FORM VIEWS

Three views are available when you use a form. These are Form View, Layout View, and Design View. Each has its uses.

USE FORM VIEW

Form View allows you to enter data more efficiently. With Form View, you can:

- Sort and filter your data

- Quickly find specific records

- Change the formatting of specific text boxes

- Check spelling of the data within the form (and its underlying table)

USE LAYOUT VIEW

Layout View is the view you first see when using the Form tool. With it you can:

- See the data as you are working with the form so that you can make changes that fit your requirements

- Add and edit controls to the form

- Add fields using the Field list (see "Adding Fields With The Field List" QuickSteps elsewhere in this chapter)

USE DESIGN VIEW

Design View allows you to see more parts of your form; however, unlike Layout View, you don't see any of your data. With Design View you can:

- Add labels, lines, rectangles, and other such *controls* to your form.

- Edit text boxes directly within each text box, without using a Property Sheet. (See Chapter 5 for information about Property Sheets.)

Continued . . .

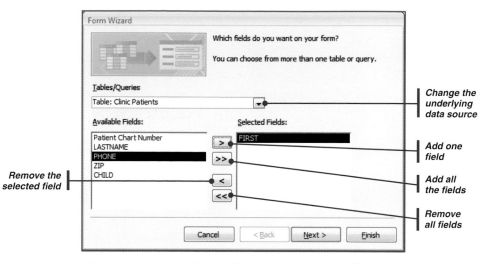

Change the underlying data source

Add one field

Add all the fields

Remove the selected field

Remove all fields

Figure 6-4: **The Form Wizard allows you to select the fields you want to include in a form.**

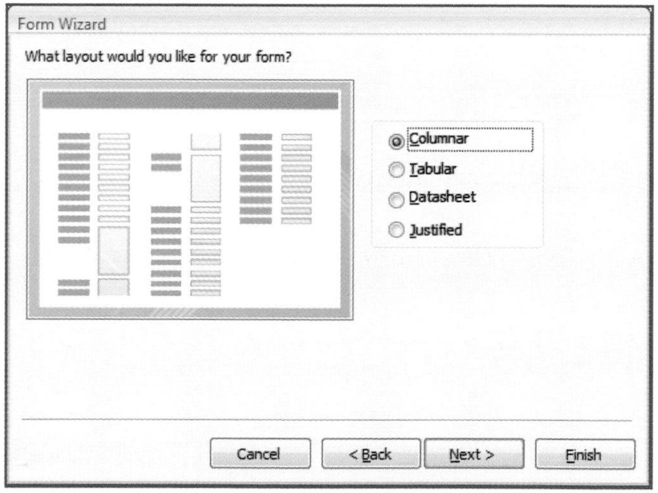

Figure 6-5: **You have a choice of four different layouts for your form.**

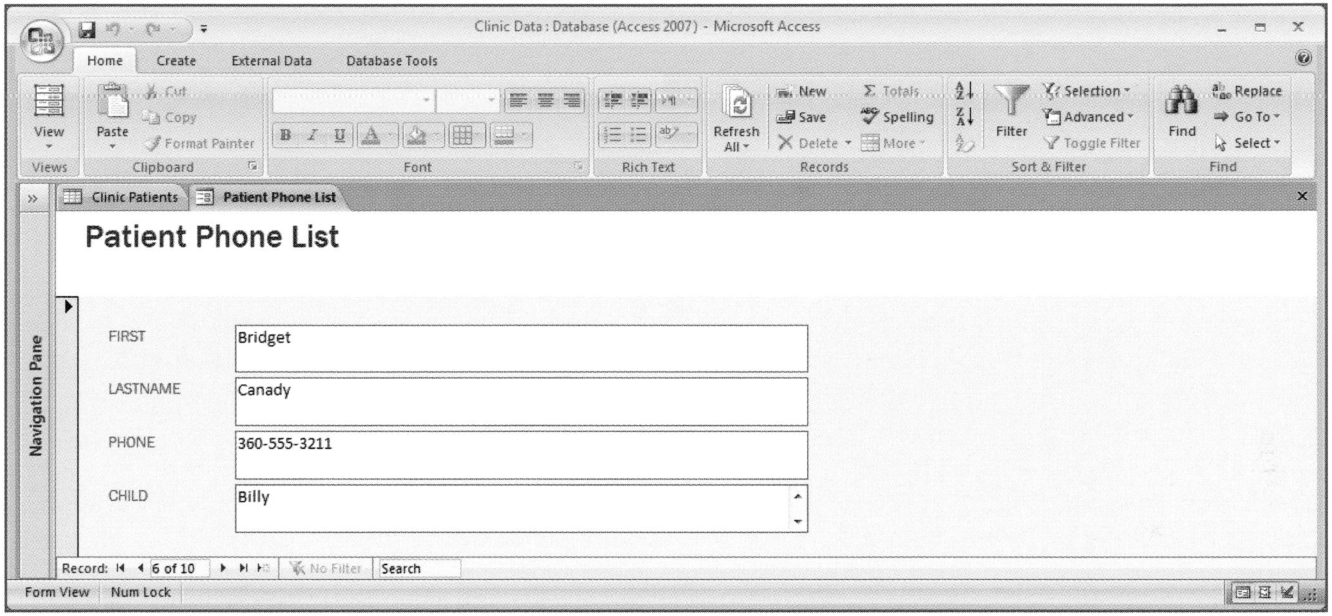

Figure 6-6: View the finished form in Form View.

QUICKFACTS

UNDERSTANDING FORM VIEWS

(Continued)

- Add new fields and controls to your form right on the design grid.
- Resize sections of your form, such as the form header or footer.

SWITCH VIEWS

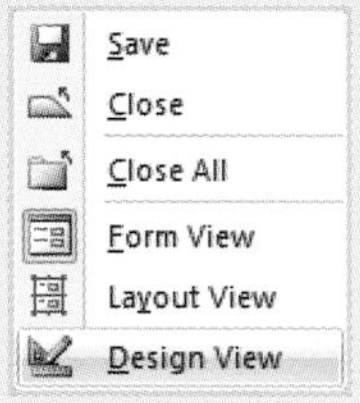

- To switch between views in your form, right-click your form tab, and click the view with which you want to work. The icon for the current view will be highlighted in the View button on the Format tab (Form Layout Tools).

Use the Blank Form Tool

If you have only a few fields with which you want to work, you can quickly create a form using the Blank Form tool.

1. In the Create tab Forms group, click **Blank Form.**

2. A blank form window opens in Layout View, as shown in Figure 6-7. The Field List pane opens on the right side of the Access work area, displaying each table in your database.

3. Click the plus sign to the left of the table with which you want to work. The Field list displays each of the fields within that table (see Figure 6-7).

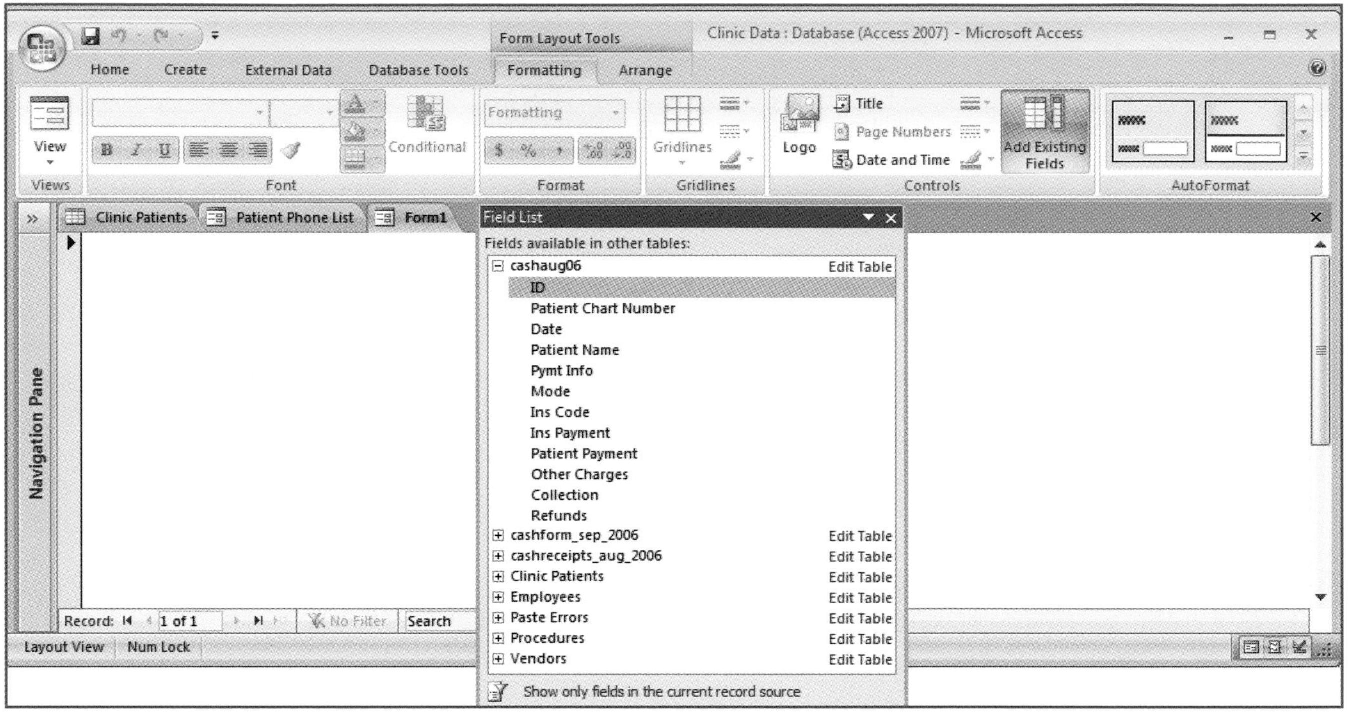

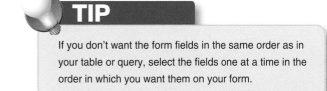

Figure 6-7: *The Blank Form tool opens a blank form and the Field list, from which you can choose your own fields.*

Create a Form in Design View

You can begin designing a new form without the help of the form tools or the wizard. You also have the option of choosing a table or query as the basis for the new form or creating a form not linked to existing data at all.

1. In the Create tab Forms group, click **Form Design**. A blank form grid opens with the Field List pane on the right side of the Access work area.

2. Click the plus sign to the left of the table you want to use as the basis for your new form. The Field list displays each of the fields within that table. See "Adding Fields with the Field List" QuickSteps elsewhere in this chapter.

TIP

If you don't want the form fields in the same order as in your table or query, select the fields one at a time in the order in which you want them on your form.

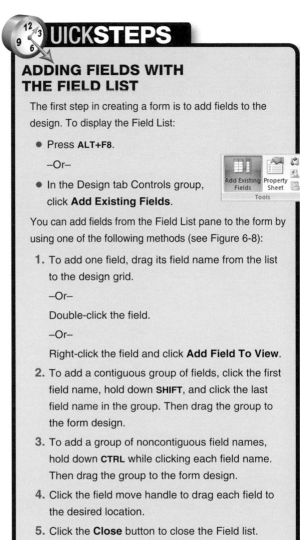

QUICKSTEPS

ADDING FIELDS WITH THE FIELD LIST

The first step in creating a form is to add fields to the design. To display the Field List:

● Press **ALT+F8**.

–Or–

● In the Design tab Controls group, click **Add Existing Fields**.

You can add fields from the Field List pane to the form by using one of the following methods (see Figure 6-8):

1. To add one field, drag its field name from the list to the design grid.

   –Or–

   Double-click the field.

   –Or–

   Right-click the field and click **Add Field To View**.

2. To add a contiguous group of fields, click the first field name, hold down **SHIFT**, and click the last field name in the group. Then drag the group to the form design.

3. To add a group of noncontiguous field names, hold down **CTRL** while clicking each field name. Then drag the group to the form design.

4. Click the field move handle to drag each field to the desired location.

5. Click the **Close** button to close the Field list.

6. In all cases, your new field appears on the blank form, as seen in Figure 6-8. After you have entered all the fields you want to use, right-click the form's tab, and click **Save**.

7. Type a name in the Save As dialog box, and click **OK**.

8. Right-click the tab again, and click **Close**.

ADD FIELDS USING CONTROLS

In the previous section, we chose the field and Access provided the control. Now we'll talk about adding the control (the empty container) for a field. Later, we will assign a field (bound control) to it with a wizard or with a Property Sheet. You can also use the controls to add command buttons, list and combo boxes, and other controls. For more information on controls, see "Use Controls" later in this chapter.

1. Open the form, right-click the form tab, and click **Design View** to display the form grid design.

2. In the Design tab Controls group, click **Use Control Wizards** to have Access provide assistance, when available.

3. In the Design tab Controls group, click the control you want to place on your form. A small icon appears by your mouse pointer.

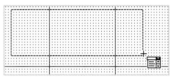

4. Click the position on the grid approximately where you want the control on the form. If there is a wizard associated with this control, follow its steps.

5. After you have added all the controls you want, right-click the form's tab, and click **Save**.

MODIFY THE FORM DESIGN

When you have completed the form design—either with the help of the Form Wizard or on your own—you can still make changes to it. Forms have many properties that determine their appearance and behavior. There are properties for the form itself, properties for controls, properties for the title, and so forth. Verify that "Form" is in the Selection box at the top of the Property Sheet. For ways to change properties, see the "Selecting a Form Section" QuickSteps.

1. Open the form in Design View.

2. In the Design tab Tools group, click **Property Sheet**.

3. Click the **Format** tab. Figure 6-9 shows a partial list of the format properties you can set for your form. Other tabs in the Property Sheet offer data, event, and other properties.

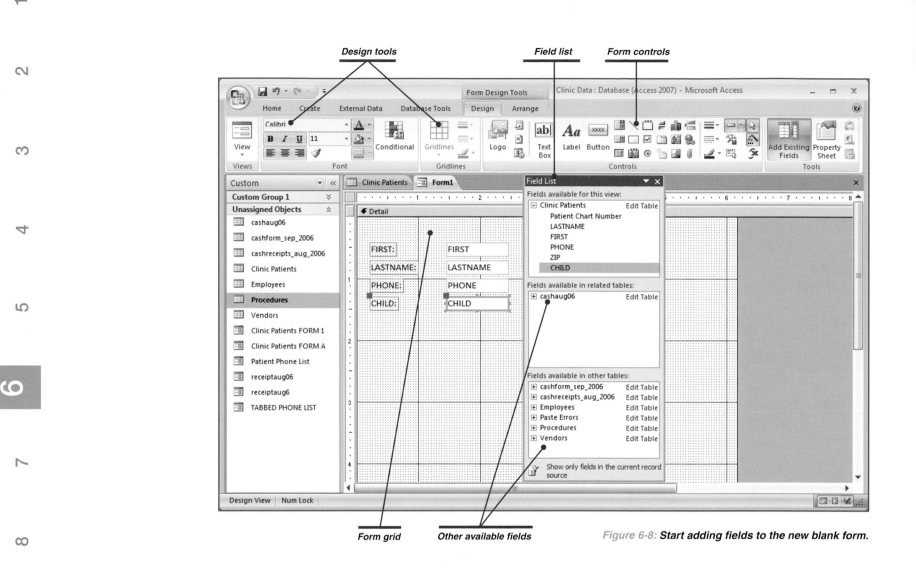

Design tools   **Field list**   **Form controls**

Form grid   **Other available fields**

Figure 6-8: **Start adding fields to the new blank form.**

4. Select the property from the list, and enter a value; or click the property's down arrow, and choose from the list of options.

5. When you have finished, right-click the form tab, and click **Layout View** to see how your changes affect your form.

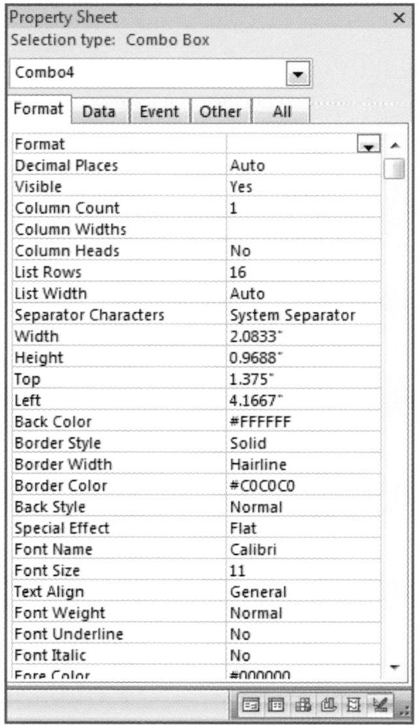

Figure 6-9: *Set the form properties with the Property Sheet.*

Add Elements to a Form

You can add elements such as a title, the date and time, and page numbers to your form.

ADD A TITLE

Titles are located in a form header. If you did not use the Form Wizard to create a title, you can manually add a title and create a form header.

1. Open the form in Design View.

2. In the Design tab Controls group, click **Title**. A title is created in the form header, as seen in Figure 6-10. By default, the caption is "Form 1." 🔲

3. Click inside the caption, and type a title name. Press **ENTER** to save your new title.

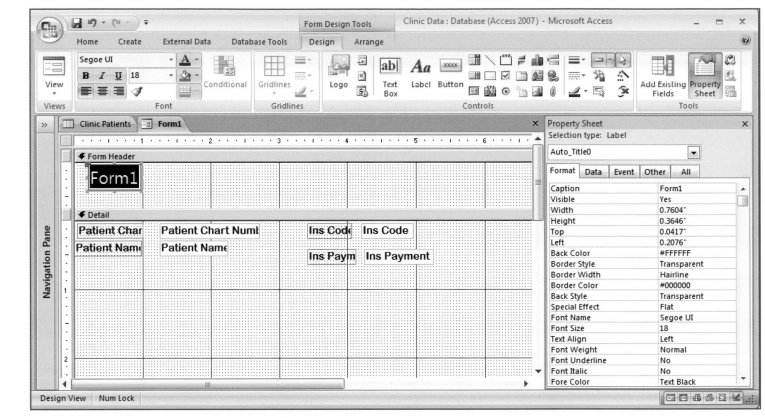

Figure 6-10: *The title you create will appear in the form header.*

CHANGE THE APPEARANCE OF A TITLE

1. In Design View, right-click the label box for your title, and click **Properties** to display the Property Sheet, if it is not shown.

2. Click the **Format** tab. From the Properties list:

   - Click the **Font Name** down arrow to display a list of fonts from which to choose.

   - Click the **Font Size** down arrow to choose from a list of sizes, or type the size you want to use.

   - Click the **Fore Color** down arrow to choose another color for your title.

3. Press **ENTER** or **TAB** to accept any changes you have made. You might need to increase the size of the control to accommodate an increased font size.

If you choose to display page numbers, a special section called "Page Footer" or "Page Header" is created on your form. You see these sections in Design View and Print Preview.

Date and Time

☑ Include Date
◉ Thursday, November 02, 2006
◯ 02-Nov-06
◯ 11/2/2006

☑ Include Time
◉ 7:11:09 PM
◯ 7:11 PM
◯ 19:11

Sample:
Thursday, November 02, 2006
7:11:09 PM

[OK]   [Cancel]

Figure 6-11: **You can choose to display both the date and time on your form.**

Page Numbers

Format
◉ Page N
◯ Page N of M

[OK]
[Cancel]

Position
◉ Top of Page [Header]
◯ Bottom of Page [Footer]

Alignment:
Center ▼

☑ Show Number on First Page

By default, Access puts the date and time control in the form header. You can drag this control to another location on your form if you choose.

INCLUDE THE DATE AND/OR TIME ON A FORM

From time to time, you may need to include a date and time on your forms. The date and time that appear are the system date (the date on your computer) at the time the form is opened.

1. Open the form in Design View.

2. In the Design tab Controls group, click **Date And Time** to open the Date and Time dialog box. 🔟

3. Click **Include Date** to display the date. Choose from the three available formats, as seen in Figure 6-11. An example of how the format will look is shown in the Sample area.

4. Click **Include Time** if you want to display the time as well. Choose from the three available time formats.

5. Click **OK** to close the dialog box. The date (and time, if you included it) controls appear in the form header.

6. Right-click the form tab, and click **Save** to save the changes to your form.

ADD PAGE NUMBERS

You can insert page numbers on your form in either the header or footer.

1. Open the form in Design View.

2. In the Design tab Controls group, click **Insert Page Numbers** to display the Page Numbers dialog box. 🔟

3. In the Format section, click **Page N** to display the page number. Click **Page N Of M** to display each page number as well as the total number of pages—for example, "Page 7 of 12."

4. In the Position section, click **Top Of Page [Header]** to display your page number in the form header.

   –Or–

   Click **Bottom Of Page [Footer]** to have the page number appear in the form footer.

5. Click the **Alignment** down arrow to choose how your page number aligns on the form, that is, in the center, right, or left.

6. Click the **Show Number On First Page** check box if you don't want to have the page number appear on the first page of your form.

7. Click **OK** when finished.

QUICKSTEPS

SELECTING A FORM SECTION

Before you can work on a particular section of a form (or report), you need to select it.

SELECT THE FORM

- To select the form itself, click the form selector (the small square at the intersection of the horizontal and vertical rulers). A small black square appears when the form is selected.

–Or–

- On the Property Sheet, click the **Selection Type** down arrow, and click **Form**.

SELECT FORM SECTIONS

The form header, footer, and detail sections also have selectors at the intersection of the section bar and the vertical ruler:

- Click the selector for the section you want selected. The section bar is reverse-highlighted (white text appears on a black background).

–Or–

- On the Property Sheet, click the **Selection Type** down arrow, and click the section (or control) from the list.

TIP

You can change the size of the design area sections by dragging the top of the section bars up or down.

Use Controls

Form designs include three types of controls:

- **Bound** controls contain data stored directly in an Access table. For example, text boxes, combo boxes, and list boxes are bound controls.

- **Unbound** controls are design elements unrelated to table data. For example, labels, command buttons, images, lines, and rectangles are unbound controls. These are discussed in the next section, "Add Unbound Controls."

- **Calculated** controls are a type of bound control that contain data that is an *expression* of several elements, similar to a formula in Microsoft Excel. See "Add Bound Controls" later in this chapter.

Some of the control types used in Access 2007 are shown in Table 6-1.

Add Bound Controls

You can set up bound controls from a wizard or manually using the Field list. The easiest way to add table or query data to the design is to use the Field list, as described in the "Adding Fields with the Field List" QuickSteps earlier in this chapter. To add other types of controls, see "Add Fields Using Controls" earlier in the chapter:

ADD A COMBO BOX CONTROL WITH THE WIZARD

Combo and list boxes are both bound to the underlying table data. The only difference between them is the amount of space they take up in the form:

- A list box displays a number of values in the field. How many values depend on the height of the control you draw in the form design. If not all values fit in the box, a scroll bar is added.

- A combo box displays a single value with a down arrow that expands the list. Again, if there are more values than fit in the drop-down list, a scroll bar is added.

Control wizards are available for many of the control types. For example, you can add a combo box control that shows a list from which the user can choose, based on values in the underlying table or query or on values you create.

CONTROL NAME	DESCRIPTION
Text box	A control that displays the values stored in fields in the underlying table or query, including calculated fields
Label	A block of text, such as a title, a description, or instructions for the user
Command button	A button that starts an action—such as opening a report, running a macro, or initializing a VBA procedure
Combo box	A control that displays a drop-down list of values, with a text box for data entry
List box	A control that displays a list of choices for user interaction (this can represent a field value or search criteria)
Subform/subreport	A control that displays data from more than one table
Line	A control that allows you to emphasize information on a form
Rectangle	A control that can be used for graphic effects
Bound object frame	A control for objects that are stored in a field in the underlying table's data
Option group	A set of mutually exclusive options within a frame (can contain toggle buttons, option buttons, or check boxes)
Check box	A control that specifies a Yes/No value from the underlying record source
Option button	A control that displays a Yes/No value
Toggle button	A button that shows an on or off position
Tab control	A control that can be used to create a form with several pages so that the user can move from section to section by clicking the tab
Insert page	This tool allows you to insert a new page into your form
Insert chart	A control that can be used to display Access data in chart form
Unbound object frame	A control used to display an OLE object
Image	An unbound picture, such as a company logo, that has no ties to the underlying data in the form
Insert/remove page break	A control used to start a new screen on your form or a new page on a printed form
Insert hyperlink	A control used to insert a link, whether to another location or file on the user's computer, a Web site, or an e-mail address
Attachment	A control that allows the form to access the files stored in the underlying database as attachments

Table 6-1: **Controls Commonly Used in Form Design**

1. Open a form in Design View. In the Design tab Controls group, click **Combo Box [Form Control]** . Your mouse pointer turns into a crosshair, with a combo box icon.

2. Drag a rectangle on your form design where you want this list located. When you release the mouse button, you will see both a label and an unbound control box, and the Combo Box Wizard appears, as seen in Figure 6-12.

Combo19:   Unbound

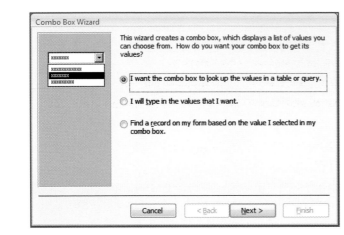

Figure 6-12: *Use the Combo Box Wizard to easily set up a combo box control.*

NOTE

You can use several formatting tools to change the appearance of a form. See Chapter 8 for more information.

3. Click **I Want The Combo Box To Look Up The Values In A Table Or Query** if you want your list based on information in the underlying data source.

–Or–

Click **I Will Type In The Values That I Want** if you want to add values from an outside data source.

In either case, click **Next** (the rest of these steps assume you are using data from a table or query; the steps to add values are similar and easily followed).

4. Select the table or query where the values are stored. Click **Next**.

5. Select the fields you want to see in the list, and click **Next**.

6. Set the sort order for your items, if you choose. Click **Next** to continue.

7. Drag the right edge of the column border to adjust the column widths to fit the field values, as shown in Figure 6-13, and choose whether to show or hide the primary key field. Click **Next**.

8. If desired, enter a label for the combo box control in the text box at the top of the page to replace the default label, and click **Finish**. Then switch to Form View to see the new combo box control.

ADD A CALCULATED CONTROL

Calculated controls combine values from several text, number, currency, or date fields that are included in the underlying table or query. A calculated control is a

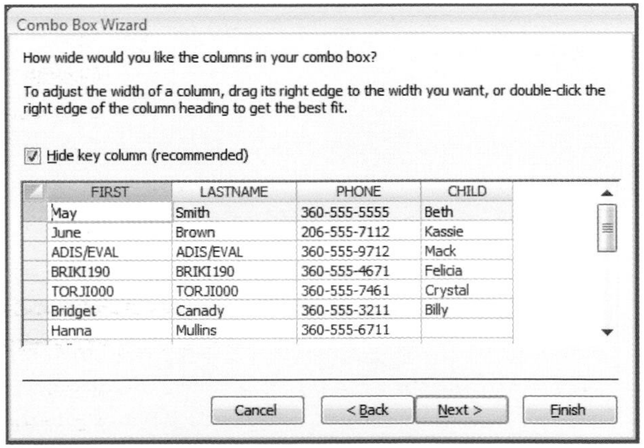

Figure 6-13: *You can adjust your column widths when using the Combo Box Wizard.*

text box control whose control source property is set to an expression. Here are some examples:

- **=[price]*[onhand]** displays the total value of the inventory.
- **=[Expiration Date]-Date()** displays the number of days until the expiration date.
- **=[First Name] & " " &[Last Name]** displays both the first name and last name with a space between.

Depending on the data type of the calculated control, you may need to change some of its formatting properties. For example, if the result is a currency field, you may want to see a dollar sign. If you want to see the result in a different font or bold, change those properties after creating the calculated control.

1. Open your form in Design View. In the Design tab Controls group, click the **Text Box** tool. ab|

2. Click the form design area where you want the new control. The control and its label are displayed.

3. In the Property Sheet, click the **Data** tab. (If the Property Sheet is not displayed, double-click the control.)

4. Click **Control Source** and type the expression you want.

Format	Data	Event	Other	All
Control Source		=[FIRST] & " " & [LASTNAME]		

–Or–

Click the **Builder** button [...] to use the Expression Builder to help you set up the expression (see Chapter 5 for more information on using the Expression Builder).

5. Click the **Format** tab to set the formatting properties that suit your needs, such as formatting currency or fonts. For example, to format for currency, in the Format tab, click the **Format** down arrow, and choose **Currency**. The data will appear in U.S. currency format.

6. Click the label of your new text box. On the Property Sheet, click the **Format** tab, and type the name for your label in the Caption property box.

7. Right-click the form's tab, and click **Save**. Right-click the form's tab again, and click **Form View** to see the results.

NOTE

Controls are used in both forms and reports. Reports are discussed in Chapter 7.

Yes/No controls—such as toggle buttons ⇄, check boxes ☑, and option buttons ⊙—can appear on a form as single controls or as part of an option group control ⊡. (An option group control combines a set of Yes/No controls in a group within a frame. When the user selects one of the options, that value is stored in the field associated with the option group control.) When you select or clear one of these buttons, the Yes or No value is displayed in the underlying table or query. The way it is displayed depends on the format property set in the table design.

1. In a form open in Design View, in the Design tab Controls group, click the control you want to use.

2. Position your mouse pointer in the form design where you want the control to appear, and click. Check boxes and option buttons include a generic label, while the toggle buttons show no label or image.

3. If you have chosen a control with a generic label, click the control label (not the Yes/No control itself).

4. On the Property Sheet, click the **Format** tab, and type the desired text in the Caption property text box.

5. Switch to Form View to see the results.

Yes/No controls can be grouped within an option group control that offers a list of mutually exclusive alternatives. The control itself is the frame around the Yes/No controls. The Option Group Wizard is on hand to guide you through adding an option group, as seen in Figure 6-14.

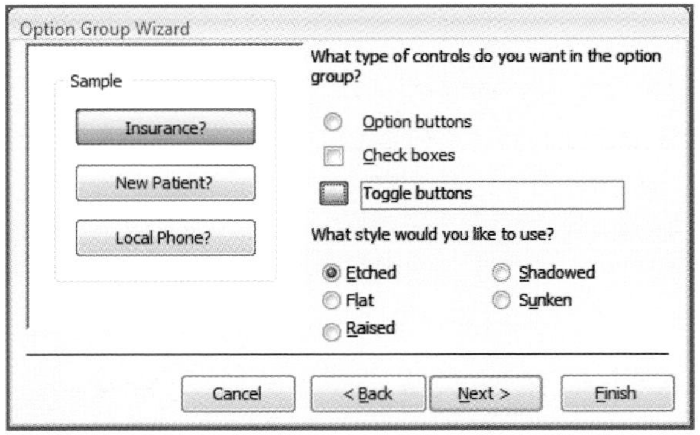

Figure 6-14: **The Option Group Wizard helps set Yes/No controls.**

Add Unbound Controls

Unbound controls can be used to improve the appearance of the form and add some user interfacing tools, such as command buttons. You can also add the current date, time (see "Include the Date and/or Time on a Form" earlier in the chapter), and images to the form.

ADD A COMMAND BUTTON

Command buttons are true user interactive tools. For example, you can add a command button that opens or closes a form, moves to the next or to a new record, or deletes the current record. Through the Command Button Wizard, you can create over 30 different types of command buttons. To add a command button that moves to the next record in Form View:

1. Open the form in Design View.

2. In the Design tab Controls group, click **Use Control Wizards** to ensure the wizards are active. Click the **Button** tool .

3. Click in the form design area where you want to place the button, and draw a rectangle. The Command Button Wizard opens. Figure 6-15 shows the first Command Button Wizard page, with the categories of commands in the left pane and groups of related individual commands in the right pane. The Sample pane displays the button's default image.

4. In the left pane, click the **Record Navigation** category.

5. Select **Go To Next Record** in the Actions pane. Click **Next**.

6. In the next page, the wizard lets you choose between text and a picture to show on the button. Accept the default text name, or enter a different name in the text box.

   –Or–

   Choose **Picture** and accept the default picture.

   –Or–

   Click **Show All Pictures**, and choose another image from a list that includes all the Access icons.

   In all cases, click **Next**.

7. Type a name for your button, if you choose, and click **Finish**.

INSERT IMAGE CONTROLS

You can add images that will remain constant on your form. To add an image from a file on your computer:

1. In an open form in Design View, in the Design tab Controls group, click the **Image** tool, and draw a frame in the form design area.

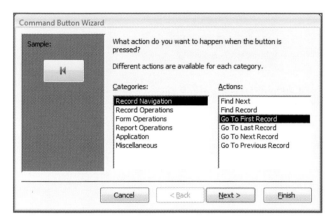

Figure 6-15: **Create interactive tools with command buttons.**

Figure 6-16: *You can add images to your form with the image control.*

2. In the Insert Picture dialog box, locate the picture you want on your form, as seen in Figure 6-16. Once you have located the file you want to use on your form, double-click the file.

3. Your image is displayed on the form. Use the sizing handles to adjust the frame, if necessary.

4. Right-click the form's tab, and click **Save** to save your form.

Copy or Delete a Control

After you have built a control and set its special properties, you can create copies of it to add to the form design and remove controls you no longer need.

COPY A CONTROL

1. Click the control itself, not the label. An orange selection border surrounds the control.

> Patient Chart Number: | Patient Chart Number

2. Right-click the control and click **Copy**.

   –Or–

   In the Home tab Clipboard group, click **Copy**.

3. Position your mouse pointer where you want the copy to be on the form, right-click again, and click **Paste**.

   –Or–

   In the Home tab Clipboard group, click **Paste**.

4. Drag the copy to where you want it on your form.

DELETE A CONTROL

To remove a control from the form design:

1. Click the control.

2. Click **DELETE** on your keyboard.

   –Or–

   Right-click the control and click **Delete**.

If you change your mind, click **Undo** on the Quick Access toolbar.

Select Controls

Even if you used wizards to create controls for your form (or report), you will probably want to make some changes. Before you can make any control changes, however, you will need to select the control.

When you select a control, you will see a border around it. In addition, there are sets of small darker squares in several locations on the border. These are the *handles*. The larger square in the upper-left area of the control is the *move handle*; the smaller ones are *sizing handles*. Once one or more controls have been selected, you can move, resize, align, adjust spacing, and change their properties, either individually (if only one is selected) or as a group.

SELECT A SINGLE CONTROL

1. Open your form in either Design View or Layout View.

2. Click the control you want to select.

   –Or–

   Click the **Selection Type** down arrow on the Property Sheet, and click the control you want to select.

SELECT MULTIPLE CONTROLS

Property Sheet
Selection type: Text Box

FIRST

CHILD_Label
Detail
FIRST
FIRST_Label
Form

If you want to make the same changes to several controls, select them all before making the changes. You may use one of the following methods:

● In either Layout View or Design View, hold down **SHIFT** while you click each control that you want to change.

- Press **CTRL+A** to select all controls on a form.

- Click any control in a group of selected controls, and you will notice a small four-headed arrow inside a box at the upper-left area of the controls. Click it to select all the controls.

Patient Chart Number:	Patient Chart Number
LASTNAME	LASTNAME

- In Design View only, you may select controls using these methods:

- To select a column or row of controls, click the horizontal ruler above the controls or the vertical ruler left of the controls when your mouse pointer turns into a bold arrow.

- To select a block of controls, drag to draw a rectangle in the form design area around the controls. This selects all controls within or partially within the rectangle. (Make sure Select is toggled on in the Controls group.)

Rearrange Controls

When you insert a control onto your form, you may want to move the controls, arrange them differently, or realign them. Some controls have two move handles (text boxes, option buttons, and check boxes, for example), so you can move the edit region and label together or separately.

Text24:	Unbound

MOVE AND RESIZE CONTROLS

- To move a control, select the control and point the mouse pointer either on the upper-left move handle or anywhere on the border until it turns into a four-headed arrow. Drag the control to another location.

- To move a control with both an edit region and a label, drag any border to move them together.

- To move just the label by itself or the edit region by itself, drag either move handle to move just that part of the control, independent of the other.

- If you have selected a group of controls, moving one control moves all the controls together.

- To resize a control, drag one of the sizing handles. Dragging a corner sizing handle can change both the height and width at once. If you have selected a group of controls, they are all resized at once.

UNDERSTANDING CONTROL LAYOUTS

Control layouts can be compared to a table that is aligned both vertically and horizontally so that your form will have a professional appearance. These layouts help you to present your information. There are two types of control layouts, each of which arranges your data differently.

USE A TABULAR CONTROL LAYOUT

In tabular layouts, your controls are organized like an Excel spreadsheet. Headers or labels are across the top. For example, if you created a text box control for a telephone number, in a tabular layout, the label for your text box would be in the form header, and the control would be beneath it in the detail section of your form.

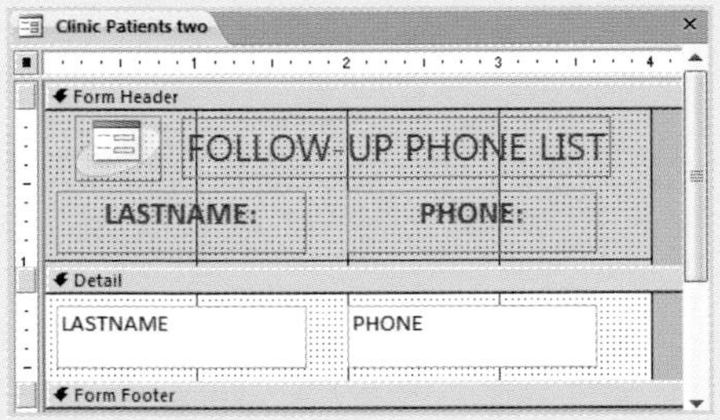

USE A STACKED CONTROL LAYOUT

When you use a stacked control layout, each of the labels appears on the left of the form, with the control containing the information to its right.

ARRANGE CONTROLS

In Design View, in the Arrange tab (Form Design Tools) Size group, you can adjust the position of one or more controls as follows:

- **To Fit** resizes a control to fit its contents.
- **To Grid** resizes a control so that all four corners reach the nearest grid points.
- **To Tallest**, **To Shortest**, **To Widest**, and **To Narrowest** adjust the size of all other members of the group to fit one.
- Click the **Anchoring** down arrow to move a control or a group of controls in one or more directions, as shown in Figure 6-17.

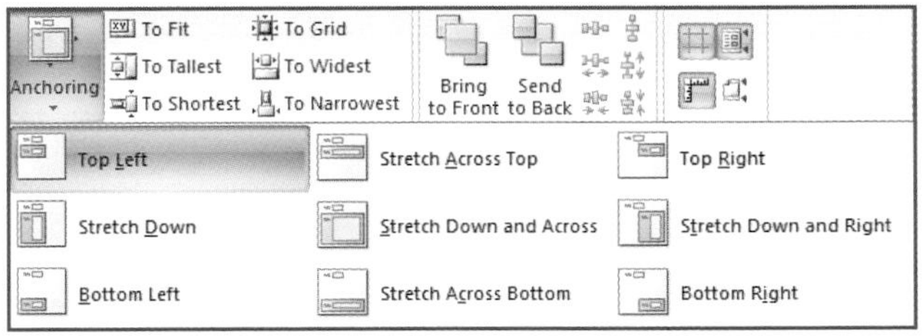

Figure 6-17: **You can arrange a group of controls on your form in several directions.**

ALIGN AND SPACE CONTROLS

The aligning and spacing options apply to groups of controls. Forms look more professional when the elements are lined up evenly and are equally spaced.

1. With a form open in Design View, select a group of controls using any of the methods described in "Select Controls" earlier in this chapter.

2. In the Arrange tab Control Alignment group:
   - Click **Left** to place all controls in a column with the left sides lined up.
   - Click **Right** to place all controls in a column with the right sides lined up.
   - Click **Top** to place all controls in a row with the tops lined up.
   - Click **Bottom** to place all controls in a row with the bottoms lined up.
   - Click **To Grid** to place the upper-left corner of all controls on a grid mark.

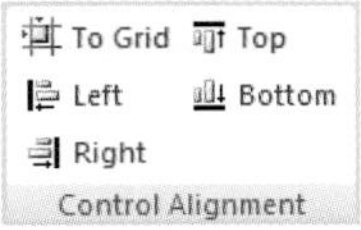

Modify Controls

Once controls are placed in the form design, you can still make changes to their appearance and behavior. To modify a control, select it (as described in "Select Controls," earlier in this chapter), and then change its properties, switch to a different control type, or copy its format to other controls.

OPEN THE PROPERTY SHEET

Controls in forms and reports all have properties that set their appearance and behavior. The Property Sheet contains lists of all the properties that apply to the selected control, arranged by category.

To open the Property Sheet for a control, in either Layout or Design View:

- Press **F4**.

  –Or–

- In the Arrange tab Tools group, click **Property Sheet**.
- In Design View only, you can double-click the control to open the Property Sheet.

The lists of properties in the sheet depend on the type of control you have selected. Click the tab that contains the type of property you want to set, or click the **All** tab to see them all. A scroll bar indicates there are more properties than are visible at the moment.

CHANGE A CONTROL

To change a property, click the property and type the setting in the property box.

–Or–

Click the down arrow, and select the setting from the list.

–Or–

Click the **Builder** button to get help from a gallery, Expression Builder, list, or dialog box with a choice of builders. What shows up depends on the type of control you have selected.

If you have selected more than one control, the properties displayed in the Property Sheet are limited to those common to all the selected control types.

Choose Builder

Macro Builder
Expression Builder
Code Builder

OK   Cancel

> **TIP**
>
> You can change the Windows visual theme and/or modify an existing theme to your liking. See *Windows Vista QuickSteps*, published by McGraw-Hill/Osborne, for more information on modifying Windows visual elements.

APPLY WINDOWS THEMES FOR CONTROLS

By default, Access 2007 applies the current Microsoft Windows visual theme to the controls you use in your forms. While this might make for a more consistent look to the user, you may not want to use the current theme for all of your new databases (see Chapter 8 for more information on formatting forms and reports). To turn Windows themes on or off:

1. Open a database and click the **Office Button**.
2. Click **Access Options** and click **Current Database**.
3. In the Application Options section, click **Use Windows-Themed Controls On Forms** to use these themes, or clear this check box so that the theme will not be applied to your form's controls, as shown in Figure 6-18.
4. Click **OK** to close the dialog box.

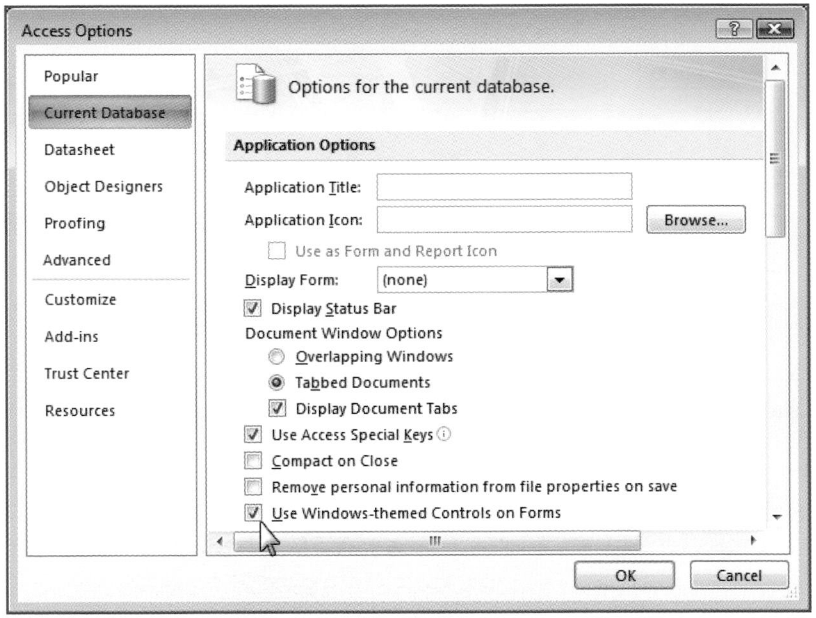

Figure 6-18: ***You can choose to use Windows themes on your form controls.***

QUICKSTEPS

NAVIGATING IN A DATA ENTRY FORM

When you use a form for data entry, you usually press **TAB** to move from one field to another. The order in which you move through the fields is determined by the sequence in which you add the fields to the design. If you have rearranged them, you may no longer have a smooth trail through the data. To fix this:

1. Open the form in Design View.

2. Select the **Detail** section by clicking its selection box in the vertical ruler.

3. In the Arrange tab Control Layout group, click **Tab Order**. ⊞ Tab Order

4. In the Tab Order dialog box, under Section, click **Detail**.

5. Click **Auto Order** to build a path left to right, then top to bottom.

   –Or–

   Under Custom Order, click the field selection box (the gray square at the left of the field name), and drag it to a new position in the list, as seen in Figure 6-19. Repeat with other fields as necessary.

6. Click **OK** when the fields are in the order you want.

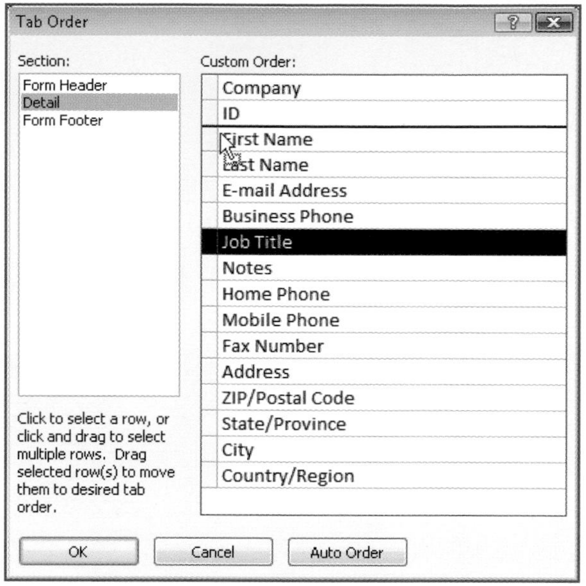

Figure 6-19: **You can arrange the order in which you move through the fields in a form.**

How to...

- *Viewing Reports*
- *Use the Report Tool to Create a Report*
- *Use the Report Wizard to Create a Report*
- *Understanding Grouping in Reports*
- *Use the Blank Report Tool*
- *Create a Report in Design View*
- *Format a Report*
- *Working with Data in Reports*
- *Use the Group, Sort, And Total Pane*
- *Calculate a Value*
- *Accomplishing Common Tasks in Reports*
- *Set Group Headers and Footers in a Report*
- *Create a Summary Report*
- *Create Labels*

Chapter 7
Working with Reports

Access provides numerous ways to display your information in printed format (see Chapter 8 for information on printing). For the best physical display, however, using *reports* is the way to go, as shown in Figure 7-1. Within reports, you can determine the size and appearance of each item, allowing you complete control over the spotlight of each page. This chapter will take you through the basics of creating reports, starting with using the built-in tools and wizards, and ending with a "do-it-yourself" approach using Design View.

Create Reports

Reports provide a method for presenting information residing within tables and queries. This information may be presented in its current format or manipulated to display comparisons, subtotals, and totals. Although the latter can be accomplished by using queries, reports achieve this task with much less effort. The construction of reports is similar to building forms. Because of this,

UICKSTEPS

VIEWING REPORTS

When working with reports, it is helpful to understand how to navigate through the different views and the purpose for each view. Open a database and the Navigation Pane to see all of the available reports. Reports are designated by the Report icon.

VIEW REPORTS IN REPORT VIEW

When you double-click your report on the Navigation Pane, it opens in Report View. In Report View, you can:

- Copy text to the Clipboard
- Create filters
- Remove filters

VIEW REPORTS IN DESIGN VIEW

Design View is the place to go when creating or modifying your reports. At first sight, Design View appears to bombard the eye with boxes, called controls, and dotted grid patterns, as shown in Figure 7-2. It is in this view that you are able to create or control the displayed report by changing anything from the underlying data source to the color of the text.

- From the Navigation Pane, right-click a report and click **Design View**.

  –Or–

- In an open report, right-click the report tab, and click **Design View**.

  –Or–

- Click **Design View** in the Views area on the status bar.

Continued . . .

CASH RECEIPTS JANUARY 2006

Date	IDENTIFICATION	TOTAL RECEIVED	INSURANCE	PATIENT	OTHER
1/3/2006	MAXCHO00	($125.00)	$0.00	($125.00)	$0.00
1/3/2006	ALEXLI000	($80.00)	$0.00	$0.00	($80.00)
1/4/2006	BRALK90	($120.00)	$0.00	$0.00	($120.00)
1/4/2006	EXELAB3B0	($100.00)	$0.00	$0.00	($100.00)
1/7/2006	TRELP122	($50.00)	$0.00	($50.00)	$0.00
1/7/2006	KNOLKT00	($200.00)	$0.00	($200.00)	$0.00
1/7/2006	JOHNLB00	($100.00)	$0.00	($100.00)	$0.00
1/7/2006	RASTBK00	($180.00)	$0.00	($180.00)	$0.00
1/7/2006	CARSJB100	($20.00)	$0.00	($20.00)	$0.00
1/7/2006	THMLBB100	($100.00)	$0.00	$0.00	($100.00)
1/7/2006	THOLJB00	($3,500.00)	$0.00	($3,500.00)	$0.00
1/7/2006	BEEKBS00	($200.00)	$0.00	($200.00)	$0.00
1/7/2006	KENNTD00	($74.00)	$0.00	($74.00)	$0.00
1/7/2006	WATKCM00	($300.00)	$0.00	($300.00)	$0.00
1/7/2006	BRAD000	($200.00)	$0.00	($200.00)	$0.00
1/7/2006	SULTIB000	($78.00)	$0.00	($78.00)	$0.00
1/7/2006	OSBJR000	($1,498.00)	($1,498.00)	$0.00	$0.00
1/11/2006	BROWMK000	($500.00)	$0.00	($500.00)	$0.00
1/11/2006	OWEMIJ00	($156.00)	$0.00	($156.00)	$0.00
1/11/2006	BRONEB00	($95.00)	$0.00	$0.00	($95.00)
1/13/2006	CASTMM00	($100.00)	$0.00	($100.00)	$0.00
1/13/2006	BEBO100	($100.00)	$0.00	$0.00	($100.00)
1/13/2006	AKLE000	($100.00)	$0.00	$0.00	($100.00)
1/13/2006	MCJAC00	($1,172.00)	($1,172.00)	$0.00	$0.00
1/13/2006	RALHC100	($3,424.00)	($3,424.00)	$0.00	$0.00
1/13/2006	JALTSS000	($15.00)	$0.00	($15.00)	$0.00
1/13/2006	CARSPK00	($200.00)	$0.00	($200.00)	$0.00
1/13/2006	BRANTO000	($1,175.00)	$0.00	($1,174.70)	$0.00
1/13/2006	SMIBC100	($253.00)	$0.00	($253.00)	$0.00
1/13/2006	DEFK100	($80.00)	$0.00	$0.00	($80.00)
1/13/2006	WILLRA100	($80.00)	$0.00	($80.00)	$0.00
1/13/2006	GREGOP100	($100.00)	$0.00	($100.00)	$0.00
1/13/2006	CIVERL000	($110.00)	$0.00	$0.00	$0.00

Page 1 of 21

Figure 7-1: *Reports present and calculate data in an easy-to-understand format.*

many of the detailed techniques used when working with the similar tools or objects are the same as those provided in Chapter 6.

Use the Report Tool to Create a Report

The quickest way to create a report is to use the Report tool. It creates a report that displays all fields and records in the underlying table or query. Using this tool necessitates that the report be based on a single table or query.

1. In the Navigation Pane, click the table or query on which you want your report based.
2. In the Create tab Reports group, click **Report**. The report is displayed in Layout View.
3. Press **CTRL+S** to save the report. The Save As dialog box appears.
4. Enter the name for your new report, and click **OK**. The saved report appears in the Navigation Pane in the Reports group and in other groups with its underlying data.

Use the Report Wizard to Create a Report

If you would like to include more than one table or query in one report, the Report Wizard is your quickest way to achieve this.

1. In the Create tab Reports group, click **Report Wizard**. [Report Wizard]
2. The Report Wizard opens, asking which fields you want on your report.

SELECT FIELDS FOR YOUR REPORT

In the first page of the Report Wizard, shown in Figure 7-3, you will select the fields you want in your report.

1. Click the **Tables/Query** down arrow, scroll through the list, and select a table or query.
2. Click the single right arrow to choose individual fields from the Available Fields list, or click the double right arrow to choose all fields. The fields will be displayed in the Selected Fields box.
3. If you are unsatisfied with the chosen results, click the double left arrow to remove all the fields, or click the single left arrow to remove individual fields from the Selected Fields box.
4. Repeat steps 1–3 if you want to include fields from other tables or queries. Click **Next** when finished adding fields.

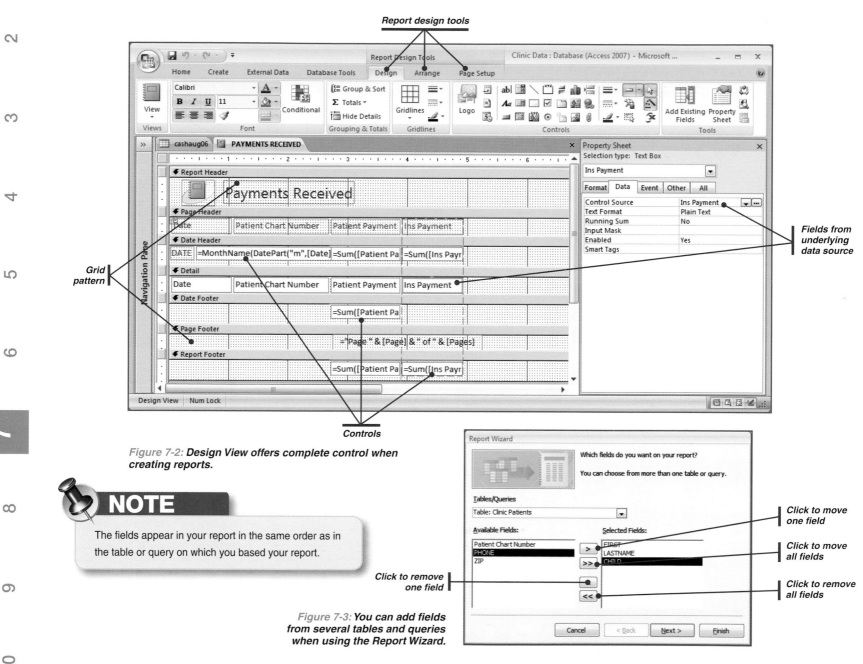

Report design tools

Fields from underlying data source

Grid pattern

Controls

Figure 7-2: **Design View offers complete control when creating reports.**

NOTE

The fields appear in your report in the same order as in the table or query on which you based your report.

Click to remove one field

Figure 7-3: **You can add fields from several tables and queries when using the Report Wizard.**

Click to move one field

Click to move all fields

Click to remove all fields

ADD GROUPING LEVELS AND INTERVALS

The second step allows you to add *grouping levels*. See the "Understanding Grouping in Reports" QuickFacts for more information.

1. Select the item by which you want to group your data, if any. Click the single right arrow to set up the first level of grouping.

2. To create grouping intervals, click **Grouping Options**. You can customize how the detail for your report is grouped. Each type of field has different choices, appropriate for that field type. For example, if a group level is a currency field, you are offered the option of grouping by 10s, 50s, and so forth.

3. Make any selections for each of your group levels. Click **OK** to close the Grouping Intervals dialog box.

4. Click Next to move to the third page of the wizard.

SET THE SORT ORDER AND SUMMARY INFORMATION

1. Select a field in the sort order box. (Note that the choices do not include any of the fields by which you elected to group.)

2. If you would like to change the sort method from ascending to descending, click **Ascending** and it will toggle to Descending.

3. If you would like to add additional sort fields, repeat steps 1 and 2. You can choose up to four sort fields.

4. To create summary values in the group footers, click **Summary Options**. This opens a dialog box that makes it easy to calculate and display summary values for any grouped numeric fields that the wizard finds in the Detail section, as seen in Figure 7-4. Do one or more of the following:

   ● Click the calculation you would like for each detail field. You can select multiple options.

   ● If you only want to see the totals for each group, click **Summary Only** in the Show area. If individual detail amounts are preferred, click **Detail And Summary**.

Figure 7-4: ***You can choose to display both detail and summary values in your report.***

QUICKFACTS

UNDERSTANDING GROUPING IN REPORTS

When you create a report, you often want to present your information in the most organized manner possible, such as sorting alphabetically or chronologically. Access 2007 allows another level of organization called *groups*. A group is a set of records that can include a header, footer, and other such introductory information, as well as summary data. Grouping allows you to present your data in a way that separates records into classifications that you determine. For example, you could create a report that displays sales representatives by territory and include a total of sales for each month. By grouping your information, you can:

- Create separate sections for each of your classifications, including a separate header and footer.

- Show a total for each section.

- Group on up to 10 fields. Access 2007 will nest each group according to its level.

- By clicking the **Calculate Percent Of Total For Sums** check box (when you have selected the Sum option), the wizard will display an additional field that shows the percent of the grand total this sum represents.

- Click **OK** to close the Summary Options dialog box.

5. Click **Next** to continue.

ESTABLISH THE REPORT'S LAYOUT AND ORIENTATION

The next page of the Report Wizard offers choices of layout and style. Select the layout descriptions to view the examples.

1. Select the layout that best fits your design needs. If you are not sure which one you want, click each option to see how your report would be presented.

2. Choose the page orientation, and determine whether to adjust the field widths so that all fields fit on a page. Click **Next**.

CHOOSE THE STYLE

The next page of the wizard allows you to choose the style for your font, title, label detail, and so on from a list of predetermined settings.

1. Scroll through the list of options. Each option displays a small preview.

2. Click the option you want. Click **None** if you want to configure your own settings in Design View.

3. Click **Next**, and you will have the option to use the default title, or you can create your own (see the next section).

–Or–

4. Click **Finish**, and Access 2007 will create a title for your report.

CREATE THE REPORT TITLE AND PREVIEW YOUR REPORT

1. Specify the report title by accepting the default title or typing a new one in the text box.

2. Choose to preview the report or to open it in Design View to make additional modifications.

3. Click **Finish**. Access 2007 creates your new report. You will see the structural framework of your report before the data is displayed.

Use the Blank Report Tool

To quickly create a report from scratch, especially if you want only a few fields on your report, use the Blank Report tool. □ Blank Report

1. In the Create tab Reports group, click **Blank Report**. A blank report in Layout View is displayed with the Field List pane visible on the right. You may receive a message to show all tables. If so, click to display the Field list.

2. Click the plus sign (+) to the left of the table or query that has the fields you want to use on your report.

Field List	×
Fields available in other tables:	
⊞ cashaug06	Edit Table
⊞ cashform_sep_2006	Edit Table
⊞ cashreceipts_aug_2006	Edit Table
⊞ Clinic Patients	Edit Table
⊞ Employees	Edit Table
⊞ Procedures	Edit Table
⊞ Vendors	Edit Table

3. Double-click each field you want to use in your report. They will appear in the order that you select.

4. You can also use your **CTRL** and **SHIFT** keys to choose several fields, and then drag them as a group onto your report.

5. Add a title, logo or other image, or page numbers, as described in "Format a Report" later in this chapter.

6. Press **CTRL+S** to save your new report. In the Save As dialog box that appears, type a name and click **OK**.

Create a Report in Design View

When creating a report in Design View, it is helpful to see the framework of the report. Figure 7-5 shows an example of the view you will see when first entering Design View. There are seven sections to the report, each with its own purpose, as listed in Table 7-1.

The Design tab Controls group contains the report controls provided in Access 2007. These controls can be selected and placed in the grid accordingly. The controls may be *bound* (linked directly to underlying data) or *unbound* (not connected to a

---

TIP

To add multiple fields quickly from the Field list to the Detail pane, hold the **CTRL** key and click non-adjacent fields to select them. To select adjacent fields, click the first field in the group, hold the **SHIFT** key and click the last field in the group. Drag any of the selections to the Detail pane to include all selected fields.

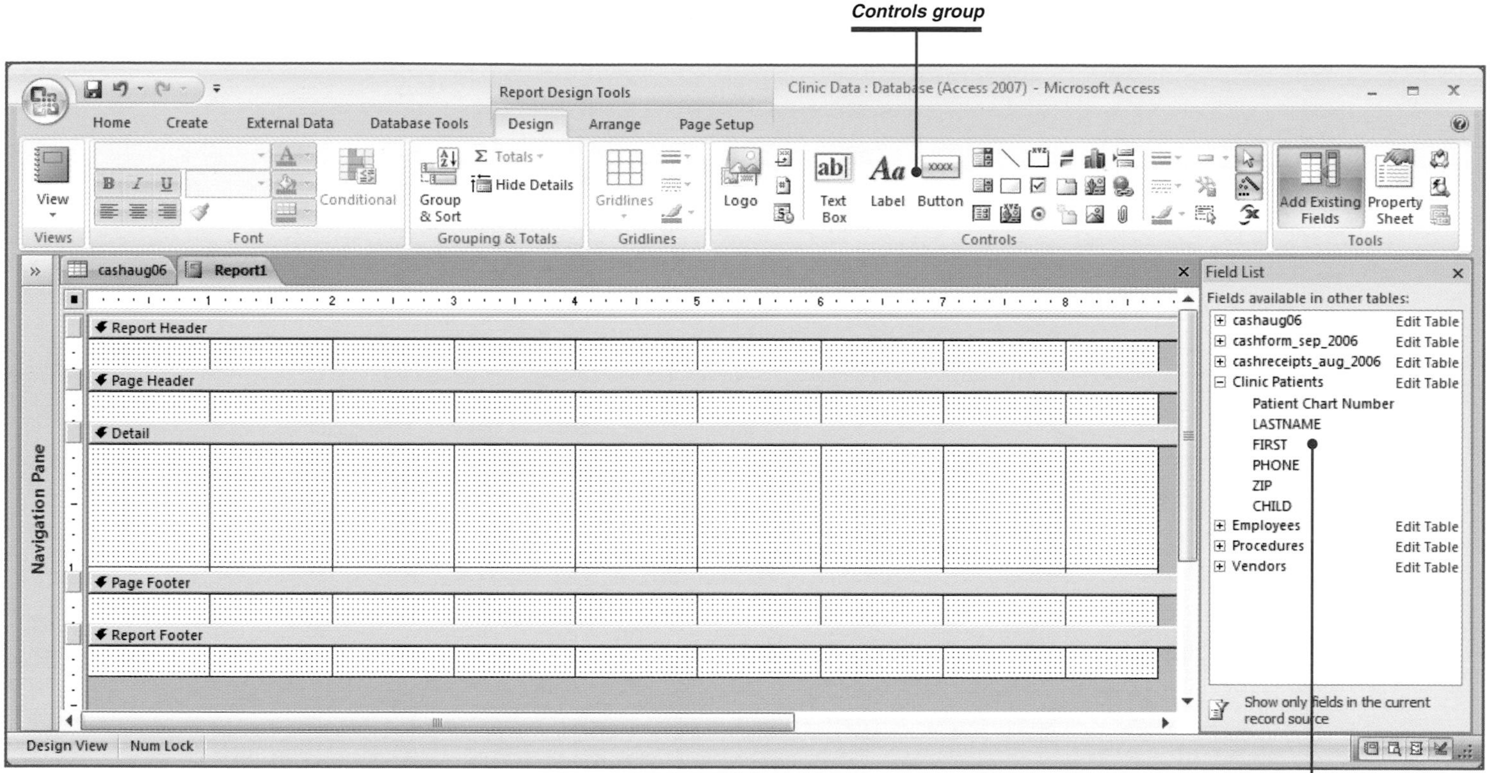

Controls group

Figure 7-5: *Click the controls you want to use, and select a space on the grid to begin designing your report.*

Choose fields and drag them to the grid

SECTION	DESCRIPTION
Report Header	Contains information printed once at the beginning of the report. This includes such information as the report title, company logo, author, and so on.
Page Header	Contains information that is printed at the top of every page, such as the page number and dates.
Group Header	Contains information that is printed at the beginning of each new group of records, such as the group name.
Detail	Contains records from a table or results from a query.
Group Footer	Contains information that is printed at the end of each group of records, such as summary details for each group.
Page Footer	Contains information printed at the bottom of each page.
Report Footer	Contains information printed once at the bottom of the last page, such as report totals.

Table 7-1: *Report Sections*

record source). See Chapter 6 for more information about commonly used controls and their purpose. The Field list provides the names of fields from an underlying table or query. When creating a basic report, you can simply drag fields to the grid. Controls can then be added to enhance your basic report.

1. In the Create tab Reports group, click **Report Design**. A blank report design grid appears.

2. Press **ALT+F8** to open the Field list if is not already displayed.

3. Drag a field name from the Field list to the desired location within the report's design grid. Repeat this process until you are satisfied with the report contents.

4. Right-click the report tab, and click **Save** to save your new report. If this is the first time that you have saved this report, the Save As dialog box will appear. Type a name for this report, and click **OK**.

Modify Reports

Many of the modifications made to a report (or form) revolve around controls and the customization of them. To view specific information on controls and making changes within the controls, see Chapter 6. Other modifications, such as grouping data, are only found in reports.

Format a Report

You can customize how the text looks in your report with custom formatting.

1. In Layout View, work with the Format tab Font group.

    –Or–

    In Design View, work with the Design tab Font group.

2. Select the field where you want to apply the formatting. See Table 7-2 for a review of your formatting tool choices.

CHANGE THE FIELD WIDTH

1. In either Design or Layout View, click the field you want to size. An orange border appears around either the detail information or the field name, whichever you have clicked.

2. Position your mouse pointer on either side of the border until you see a double-headed arrow.

3. Drag until the field size is the way you want it.

TIP

Most modifications on your reports can be done in Layout View; however, if an option is dimmed, this means it is unavailable. Switch to Design View.

FORMATTING TOOL	ICON	DESCRIPTION
Font	Calibri	Used to change the font that appears on your report. The default is Calibri
Font Size	11	Used to change the size of your font. The default is 11 points
B	**B**	Used to display your font in **bold**
I	*I*	Used to display your font in *italics*
U	U	Used to display your font with an underline
Align Left	≡	Aligns data to the left in a control or label
Center	≡	Aligns data in the center of a control or label
Align Right	≡	Aligns data to the right in a control or label
Font Color	A ▾	Sets the color for your font
Fill Color	◇ ▾	Fills in the background of a control or label
Format Painter	◇	Copies the format of a selected control to another control
Conditional	Conditional	Applies conditional formatting to the data in your finished report. (See Chapter 8 for information on conditional formatting)
Alternate Fill/Back Color	▦ ▾	Used with conditional formatting to change fill or background colors when the data meets a certain condition

Table 7-2: Font Group Commands

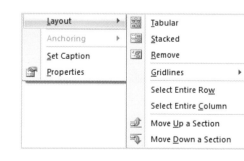

SELECT AN ENTIRE ROW OR COLUMN

1. In Layout View, right-click the row or column you want to select.

2. Click **Layout**.

3. Click **Select Entire Row**.

–Or–

Click **Select Entire Column**.

DELETE A FIELD

1. In Layout View, right-click the field you want to delete.

2. Click **Delete**.

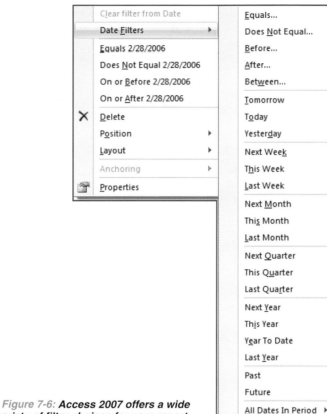

QUICKSTEPS

WORKING WITH DATA IN REPORTS

One way that reports differ from forms is in their ability to display information in groups. In Access 2007, you can quickly sort, group, or filter fields in your report.

SORT A SINGLE FIELD

1. In the Navigation Pane, right-click the report you want to work with, and click **Layout View**.

2. Right-click the field by which you want to sort

3. Click **Sort A To Z** to create an ascending sort. (The sort label reflects the data type of the field. For more information, see Table 7-3.)

   –Or–

   Click **Sort Z To A** to create a descending sort. The report reflects your change.

GROUP BY A SINGLE FIELD

1. In an open report in Layout View, right-click the field you want to group by.

2. Click Group On *field name*. ⌊≡ Group On PYMT

FILTER A FIELD

1. In Layout View, right-click the record by which you want to filter.

2. Click the filter property you want. You have several choices, as shown in Figure 7-6. (For more information on applying filters, see Chapter 5.)

Figure 7-6: *Access 2007 offers a wide variety of filter choices for your report.*

Use the Group, Sort, And Total Pane

You can also add or modify groups, sorts, and totals on your report from the Group, Sort, And Total pane, as shown in Figure 7-7. Before and after examples of a report are shown in Design and Report Views in Figures 7-8 and 7-9.

Depending on the type of data in your underlying table, each grouping and sorting level has several options from which you can choose. To display all of the options, click **More** on the level you want to change. To hide these options, click **Less**.

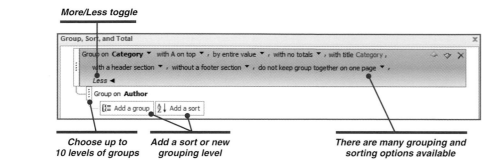

More/Less toggle

Choose up to
10 levels of groups

Add a sort or new
grouping level

There are many grouping and
sorting options available

Figure 7-7: **The Group, Sort, And Total pane lets you
group and sort by up to 10 levels.**

OPEN THE GROUP, SORT, AND TOTAL PANE

1. Open a report in either Layout View or Design View.

2. In Layout View, in the Formatting tab Grouping & Totals group,
click **Group & Sort**.

–Or–

In Design View, in the Design tab Grouping & Totals group,
click **Group & Sort**.

In either case, the Group, Sort, And Total pane will appear on
the bottom of the report area.

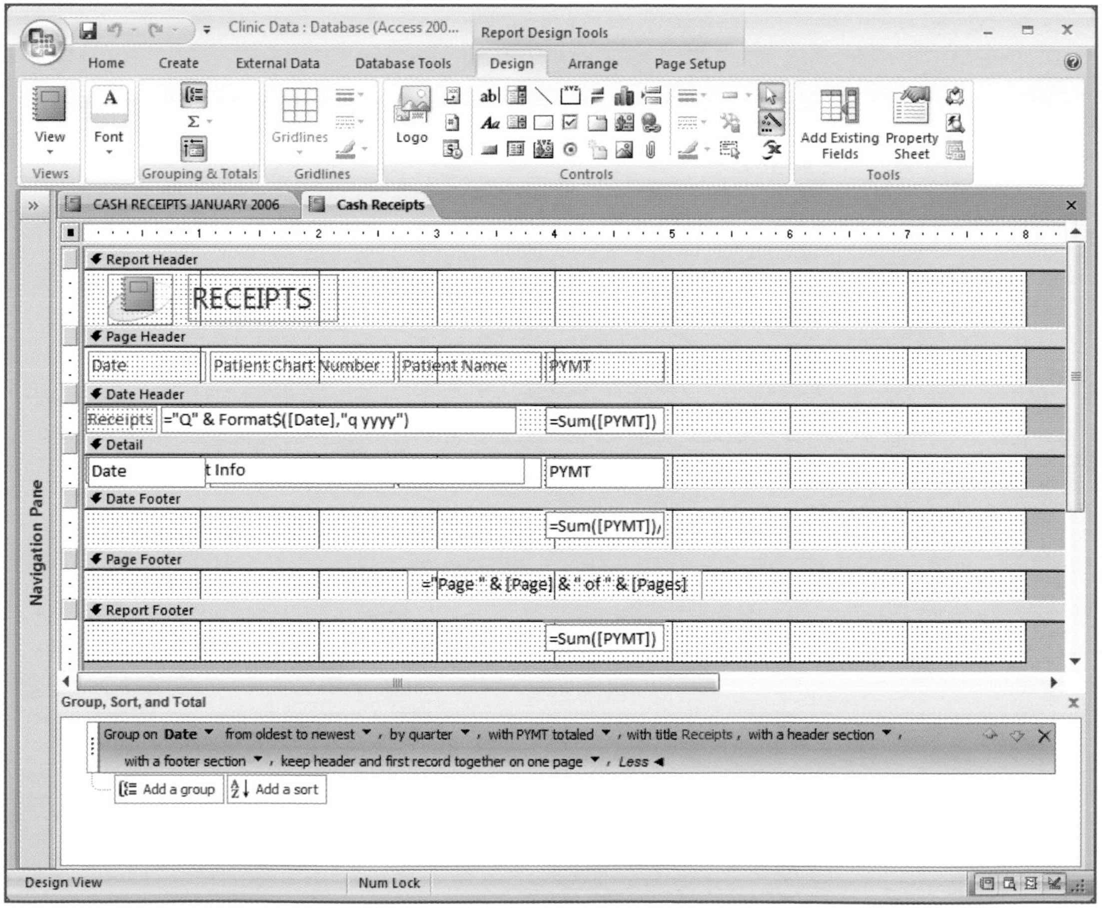

Figure 7-8: **Design View shows
your report's controls,
grouping levels, and sorts.**

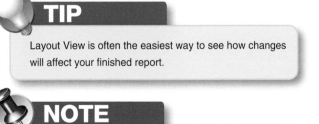

Figure 7-9: *Report View shows the results of controls, sorts, and grouping levels.*

7

TIP

Layout View is often the easiest way to see how changes will affect your finished report.

NOTE

While you can add up to 10 levels of groups in a report, if you have more than one or two, you may have to scroll down to see the Add A Group button.

ADD A NEW GROUP LEVEL

1. In the Group, Sort, And Total pane, click **Add A Group**.

2. A list of the available fields in your report is displayed, and a new line is added to the Group, Sort, And Total pane.

3. Click the field by which you want to group. The grouping level is added to your report, and, in Layout View, you can see the change to your report.

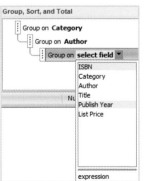

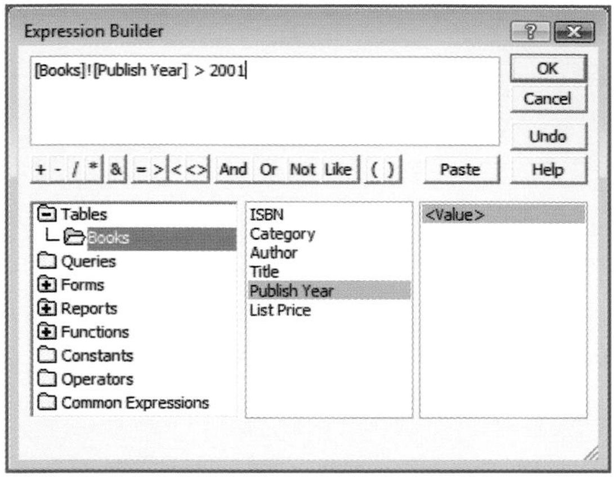

Figure 7-10: *You can create an expression for your group.*

DATA TYPE	SORT OPTIONS
Text	With A on top With Z on top
Date	From oldest to newest From newest to oldest
Number	From smallest to largest From largest to smallest
Expression	Ascending Descending

Table 7-3: *Sort Options in Group Levels*

USE AN EXPRESSION TO GROUP BY

In addition to choosing grouping levels, you can create a group using an *expression*. An expression is a calculation. It is the comparable to a formula in Microsoft Excel.

1. Click the down arrow next to the field name in the grouping level on which you want to build an expression.

2. From the drop-down list, click **Expression** at the bottom.

3. Complete your expression using the Expression Builder, as shown in Figure 7-10 (see Chapter 5 for information on using the Expression Builder).

ADD A NEW SORT LEVEL

1. In the Group, Sort, And Total pane, click **Add A Sort**.

2. Select the field in your report that you would like to establish as the main group. The sort order field will automatically default to **With A On Top** in Text data type fields. To change this, click the **With A On Top** down arrow to display a drop-down list, from which you can choose **With Z On Top** to create a descending order. Options for other data types are shown in Table 7-3.

CHANGE A GROUP TITLE

1. In the Group, Sort, And Total pane, click the group level for which you want to change the title, and then click **More** to display the options.

2. Next to With Title, click **Click To Add**. (The default title of a grouping is the field name.) The Zoom dialog box appears. Type the title you want.

3. Click **Font** to display the Font dialog box. Make any changes and click **OK** to return to the Zoom dialog box.

4. Click **OK** when you are done.

DETERMINE HOW DATA IS GROUPED

1. Click the group level you want to change, and click **More**.

2. Click the **By Entire Value** down arrow to make the changes. The default is **By Entire Value**; however you can choose just the first one or two characters or create a custom group of characters.

3. If you are in Layout View, your changes will appear immediately on your report.

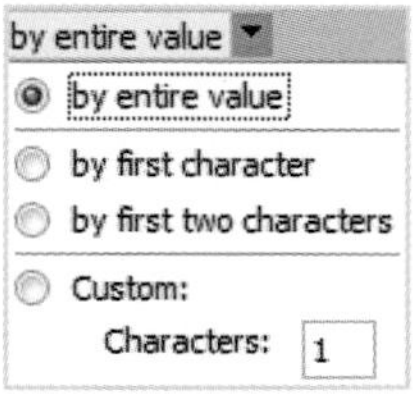

Calculate a Value

Reports, like queries, have the ability to perform calculations of field values within their designs. The benefit of using a report is its further ability to display the information in a customized and formatted printable fashion.

ADD CALCULATIONS TO A REPORT

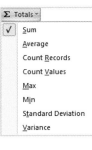

1. Open a report in Layout View, as this view is the quickest way to add calculations.
2. Click the field to which you want the calculation applied.
3. In the Format tab Grouping & Totals group, click **Totals**. Σ Totals ▾
4. Select one of the calculations from the menu.
5. A total appears in the group footer. Its control source is an expression reflecting your chosen calculation. You can see this expression in Design View.

📌

NOTE

If you have established grouping levels, adding a total to a field will add the same calculation on each group level.

CALCULATE A GROUP TOTAL

1. Open your report in Layout View.
2. From the Format tab Grouping & Totals group, click **Group & Sort** to open the Group, Sort, And Total pane.
3. Click the grouping or sort level where you want to create totals. Click **More** and click **With *Field Name* Totaled** to open the Totals dialog box:

   - Click **Total On** to display the drop-down list of fields from which you can choose. Click the field you want to use for totals.
   - Click **Type** to display the list of calculations you can perform. Click the type of calculation you want Access 2007 to perform.
   - Click **Show Grand Total** to add a grand total in the report footer at the end of the report.
   - Click **Show Group Totals As % Of Grand Total** to add a calculated percentage of the grand total for each group.
   - Click **Show In Group Header** or **Show In Group Footer** if you want this total displayed in each group.

4. Click outside the Totals dialog box to close it. Your report reflects your changes at once.

ACCOMPLISHING COMMON TASKS IN REPORTS

Open a report in Design View.

INSERT PAGE BREAKS

1. In the Design tab Controls group, click the **Page Break** icon.

2. Click where you want the page break on the report. You will see a yellow line with dots at the far left side of the report. Category When you open the report again, you will only see a series of small dots to indicate the page break in Design View. Category

CREATE A REPORT TITLE

In the Design tab Controls group, click the Title icon. The default title name is highlighted in the report header. Type a new title. Press **ENTER** to save your new title.

FORMAT A REPORT TITLE

1. Right-click the report title.

2. Click **Fill/Back Color** to set the background or fill color of your title.

   Fill/Back Color
   Font/Fore Color

3. Click **Font/Fore Color** to set the color of the title font.

ADD PAGE NUMBERS

1. In the Design tab Controls group, click the **Insert Page Number icon**.

2. The Page Numbers dialog box appears. Select how you want page numbers to display.

3. Click **OK**.

Continued . . .

Set Group Headers and Footers in a Report

You can create headers and footers within groups.

1. In Design or Layout View, open the Group, Sort, And Total pane, and select the group level with which you want to work.

2. Click **More**.

ADD OR REMOVE A GROUP-LEVEL HEADER OR FOOTER

with a header section
with a header section
without a header section

1. Click **With A Header Section** to open a drop-down list.

2. Click **Without A Header Section** to remove the default header. If the header section contains controls other than the grouping field, a dialog box appears, warning you that these controls will be removed. Click **Yes** if that is all right. Click **No** to retain the controls.

Microsoft Office Access

Do you want to delete the group section for the database object 'List Price' and its contents?
The group header or footer you want to delete contains controls which will be deleted along with the section.

Yes   No

3. Follows steps 1–3 for **With A Footer Section**.

CHANGE OR DELETE GROUPING OR SORT LEVELS

1. In the Group, Sort, And Total pane, click the group level you want to change.

2. Click the up or down arrow at the right side of the group level to move it either up or down.

3. To delete a group level, click **Delete** at the end of the row.

Create a Summary Report

Sometimes, you may want your report to show only totals. A summary report displays only the totals that appear in header or footer rows. To create a summary report:

1. Open a report in Layout View.

2. In the Format tab Grouping & Totals group, click **Hide Details**. Hide Details Only the summary information will appear.

3. Click **Hide Details** again to display the detailed information.

ACCOMPLISHING COMMON TASKS IN REPORTS *(Continued)*

ADD THE DATE AND TIME

1. In the Design tab Controls group, click the **Date & Time** icon.

2. Choose the format from the Date And Time dialog box.

3. Click **OK**.

TIP

See the packaging that came with your purchased labels. There should be a product number shown on its cover. Reference this in the first page of the Label Wizard.

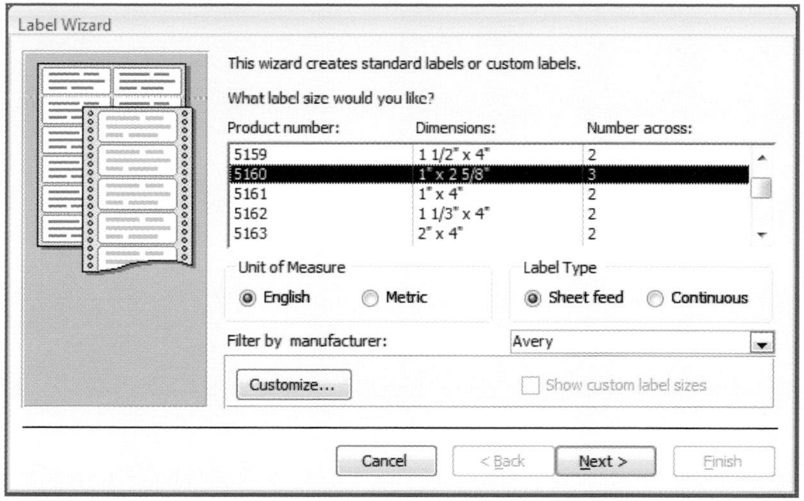

Figure 7-11: **With the Label Wizard, creating new mailing labels is accomplished in just a few mouse clicks.**

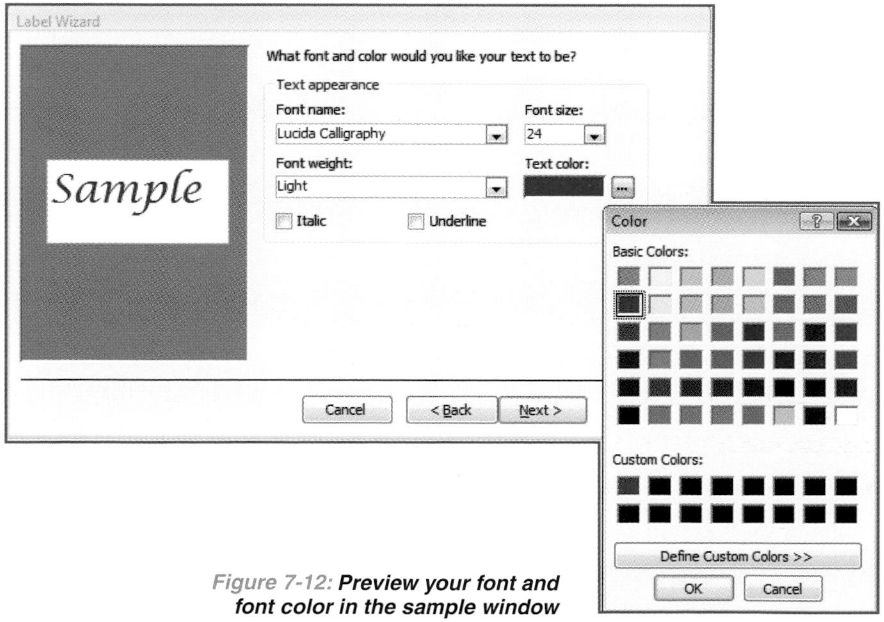

Figure 7-12: **Preview your font and font color in the sample window**

Create Labels

Within Access 2007 is a quick way to create labels.

1. Open the table or query where your information is stored.

2. In the Create tab Reports group, click **Labels**. The Label Wizard will start.

3. Select the size and type of label you would like to print, as seen in Figure 7-11. If you can't find the right size in the preset label sizes, click **Customize** and set your own parameters by creating a new label definition. Click **Close** to return to the Label Wizard.

4. Click **Next** when finished choosing or creating a label.

5. Choose the font and color you would like applied to your text, as shown in Figure 7-12. To see the available color choices, click the **Builder** button to the right of the Text Color text box. Click a basic color, or click the **Define Custom Colors** button to select a custom hue. Click **OK** to return to the Label Wizard.

6. Click **Next**.

7. Select a field you want on the label, and click the right arrow to move it to the Prototype Label list box. If you are creating a mailing label or a label containing more than one line of text, press **ENTER** to move to the next line of the Prototype Label box. Continue selecting and moving fields until the label is designed to your liking. Click **Next**.

What would you like on your mailing label?

Construct your label on the right by choosing fields from the left. You may also type text that you would like to see on every label right onto the prototype.

Available fields:

| Patient Chart Number |
| LASTNAME |
| FIRST |
| PHONE |
| ZIP |
| CHILD |

Prototype label:

{FIRST} {LASTNAME}

8. Select the fields you would like to sort by, and click the right arrow to move it to the Sort By box. Use the direction arrows to move or remove fields from the Sort By box. Click **Next** to move to the final page.

Available fields:

| Patient Chart Number |
| LASTNAME |
| FIRST |
| PHONE |
| CHILD |

Sort by:

ZIP

9. Type a report name in the text box, or accept the default name. Select whether to view the labels in Print Preview as they will be printed or to continue modifying the label design in Design View. Click **Finish**.

NOTE

Refer to Chapters 6 and 8 for additional information about other formatting features for your reports and forms.

How to...

- *Modify Images*
- *Use Conditional Formatting*
- *Add a Chart*
- *Use Graphics*
- *Modify the Form or Report Design*
- *Understanding Formatting Rules*
- *Using Windows Themes*
- *Work with Rich Text Formatting*
- *Set Up the Print Job*
- *Review Data Before Printing*
- *Output the Print Job*

Chapter 8
Preparing Your Data for Presentation

You can make several visual enhancements to your forms and reports before you release them to be used (in the case of forms) or printed (in the case, typically, of reports). The first part of this chapter describes many of these features in addition to how you can format forms and reports in Design View. The latter part of the chapter describes further options you have for printing your data.

Improve the Data's Appearance

The judicious use of color, graphics, and lines can transform a drab collection of data into an appealing presentation for people who enter or analyze your data. The features and techniques described in this section apply to both Form and Report Design Views, unless otherwise noted.

FILE TYPE	EXTENSION
Bitmap/Device Independent Bitmap	.bmp/.dib
Graphics Interchange Format	.gif
Icon	.ico
Joint Photographic Experts Group	.jpg
Portable Network Graphic	.png
Windows Metafile/Enhanced Metafile	.wmf/.emf

Table 8-1: **Graphic File Types Used in Forms or Reports**

Modify Images

Chapter 6 describes how to insert images into Design View, directly or by use of an image control. This section describes changes you can make to the image after it has been placed in a form or report in Design View.

CHOOSE AN IMAGE FORMAT

Image controls support many graphic formats. Some of the common graphic types supported are listed in Table 8-1.

CHANGE IMAGE PROPERTIES

There are a number of properties specifically associated with images that you can use to change the characteristics of images you add to a form or report. As shown in Figure 8-1, you can change the setting of each property on the Property Sheet. To change a property's setting, do one of the following:

- Type a value. For example, to precisely change the location of an image in the form or report section that it is in, type units of measurement in the Top and Left property text boxes. The intersection of these two numbers defines the location of the upper-left corner of the image.

Width	1.75"
Height	0.875"
Top	0.0833"
Left	2.2083"

- Click the property's down arrow, and select a setting from the drop-down list. For example, to decrease the size of your database, you could change each image file picture type from being *embedded* (each file becomes part of the .accdb file) to being *linked* (a pointer is placed in the database to the actual location of the image file outside the database). See Chapter 10 for more information on linking.

Picture Type	Embedded
Width	Embedded
Height	Linked

- Click the **Builder** button to open a dialog box for supplementary information. For example, clicking the Picture property Builder button opens the Insert Picture dialog box, where you can change the location of the present image or browse to a new image.

Picture	BOOKS.jpg ...
Size Mode	Zoom
Picture Alignment	Center
Picture Type	Embedded

Property Sheet

Selection type: Image

Auto_Logo0

Format	Data	Event	Other	All

Visible	Yes
Picture	BOOKS.jpg
Size Mode	Zoom
Picture Alignment	Center
Picture Type	Embedded
Width	1.4958"
Height	1.2458"
Top	0.1667"
Left	5.2083"
Back Color	#E4EEF3
Border Style	Solid
Border Width	Hairline
Border Color	#E4EEF3
Back Style	Transparent
Special Effect	Flat
Hyperlink Address	
Hyperlink SubAddress	
Gridline Style Top	Transparent
Gridline Style Bottom	Transparent
Gridline Style Left	Transparent
Gridline Style Right	Transparent
Gridline Color	#73A8D4
Gridline Width Top	1 pt
Gridline Width Bottom	1 pt
Gridline Width Left	1 pt
Gridline Width Right	1 pt
Top Padding	0.0208"
Bottom Padding	0.0208"
Left Padding	0.0208"
Right Padding	0.0208"
Display When	Always

Figure 8-1: **Many properties are available when working with images.**

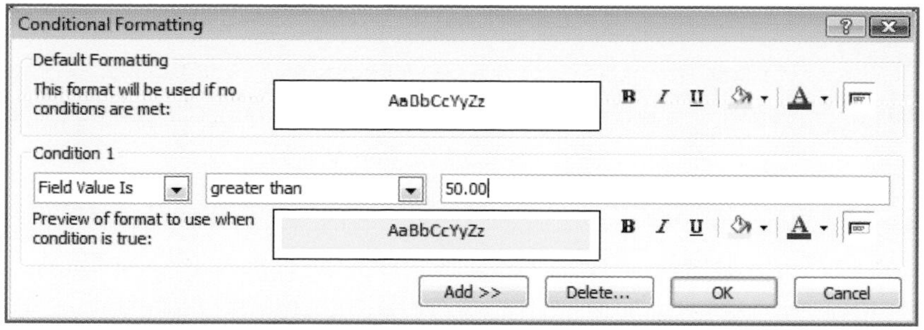

Use Conditional Formatting

You can use *conditional formatting* to change how your controls look in a form or report by applying formatting to data that satisfies a set of criteria you select. For example, you can have each value over $50.00 be on a yellow background, as seen in Figure 8-2.

Figure 8-2: *Conditional formatting draws attention to data on your form or report.*

SET CONDITIONAL FORMATTING

You can set conditional formatting in both reports and forms. The following instructions refer to a report. To set a conditional format:

1. In the Navigation Pane, right-click the report you want to change, and click **Design View** or **Layout View**.

2. Click the control on which you want conditional formatting applied. In the Font group, click **Conditional**. The Conditional Formatting dialog box appears, as seen in Figure 8-3.

3. Under Condition 1, click the down arrow, and select the whether the control contains a value or expression.

NOTE

The pictures (or *images*) and graphics that are described in this chapter are *unbound* objects, meaning they are stored in the design of the form or report and do not change when you move from record to record or from page to page. *Bound* pictures, such as photos that identify each item in your antique collection, are bound to the underlying data.

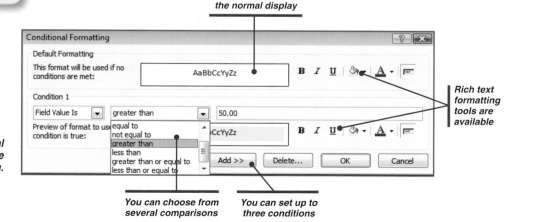

Figure 8-3: *You have several comparisons from which to choose when selecting conditional formatting.*

The default format is the normal display

Rich text formatting tools are available

You can choose from several comparisons

You can set up to three conditions

4. If the control contains a value, click the comparison down arrow (the default is **Between)** to choose from a list of comparison operators. Type a constant value in the text box (the third box) and, depending on what you chose as your comparison operator, type another constant value in the fourth box.

   –Or–

   If the control contains an expression, type the expression in the single text box.

5. Click the formatting you want to appear for values (or expressions) that are true for the condition you set:

   - Click **B** to make the font bold.
   - Click **I** to set the font in italics.
   - Click **U** to underline the text.
   - Click the **Fill/Back Color** tool down arrow to display a choice of background colors (clicking the tool itself applies the color displayed on the tool).
   - Click the **Font/Fore Color** tool down arrow to choose the font color.

6. Click **Add** to set additional conditions. You may set up to three. To remove a condition, click **Delete**.

7. Click **OK** to complete the conditional formatting.

8. Right-click the form tab, and click **Report View** to see how your report looks with the conditional formatting applied, as seen in Figure 8-4.

DISPLAY HIDDEN BACKGROUND COLORS

If you have set a background color and cannot see it, you may have to change the field property.

1. In the Design tab Tools group, click **Property Sheet**.

2. Click the **Format** tab.

Back Style	Normal
Special Effect	Transparent
Scroll Bars	Normal

3. Click the **Back Style** down arrow, and change the setting to **Normal**.

4. Right-click the form tab, and click **Report View**. You should see the background color.

Add a Chart

You can add *charts* by copying them from other programs, such as Microsoft Excel; by creating your own using the Excel menus and tools within Access; or by using the Access Chart Wizard.

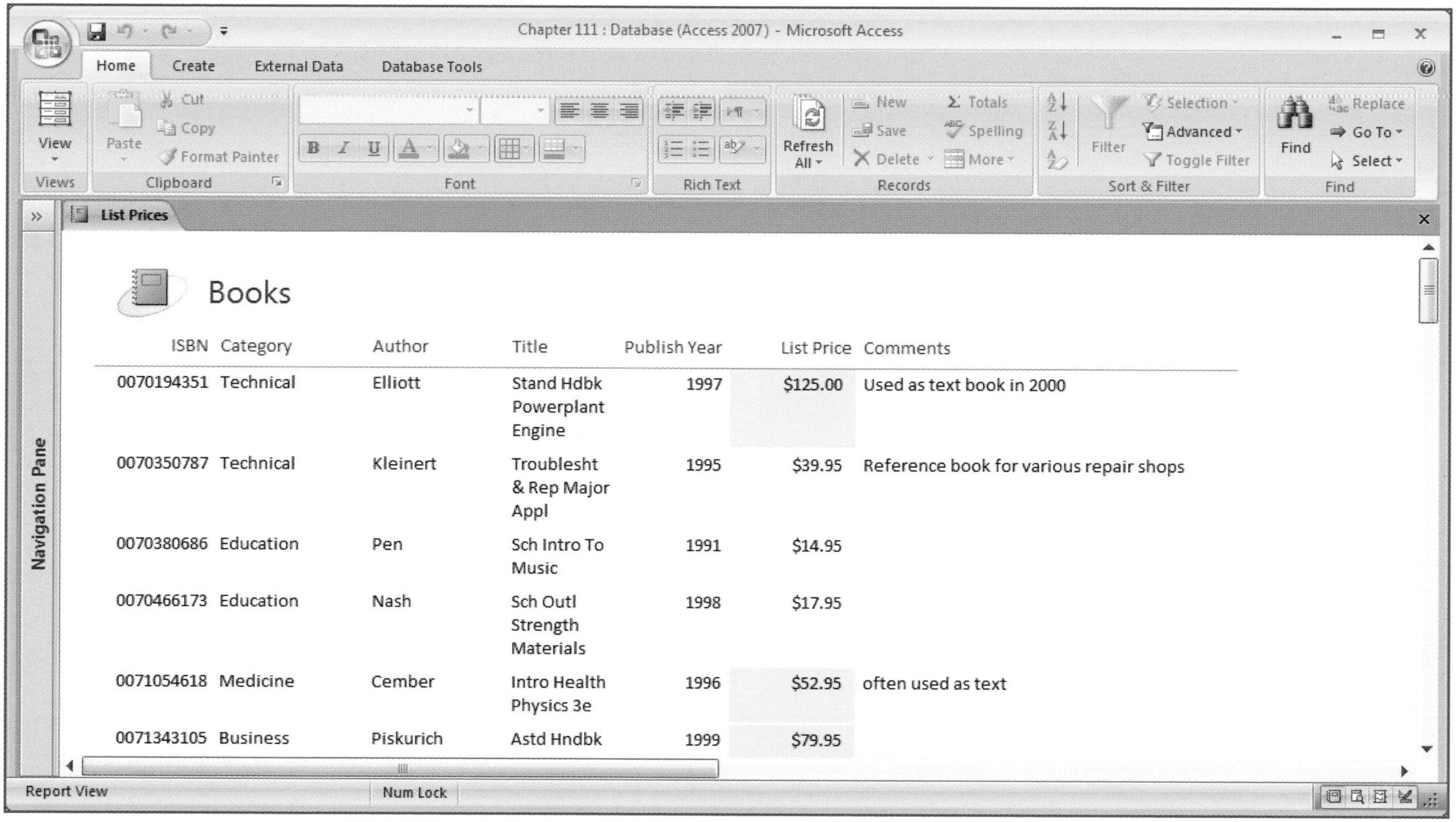

![Access window showing Books report in Report View. Columns: ISBN, Category, Author, Title, Publish Year, List Price, Comments.]

ISBN	Category	Author	Title	Publish Year	List Price	Comments
0070194351	Technical	Elliott	Stand Hdbk Powerplant Engine	1997	$125.00	Used as text book in 2000
0070350787	Technical	Kleinert	Troublesht & Rep Major Appl	1995	$39.95	Reference book for various repair shops
0070380686	Education	Pen	Sch Intro To Music	1991	$14.95	
0070466173	Education	Nash	Sch Outl Strength Materials	1998	$17.95	
0071054618	Medicine	Cember	Intro Health Physics 3e	1996	$52.95	often used as text
0071343105	Business	Piskurich	Astd Hndbk	1999	$79.95	

Report View   Num Lock

Figure 8-4: *After setting conditional formatting, select data on your report is emphasized.*

INSERT AN EXCEL CHART

1. Open Microsoft Excel and locate the chart you want to insert.
2. Right-click the chart and click **Copy**.
3. Open the report or form in Design View, and right-click where you want to place the chart. (See "Select Design View Components," later in the chapter.)
4. Click **Paste**. The chart is placed in an Unbound Object Frame box, which you can resize and move as necessary.

CAUTION

Excel charts cannot be linked or imported. They must be copied manually into your form or report.

CREATE A CHART USING EXCEL FEATURES

1. Open the report or form in Design View.

2. In the Design tab Controls group, click the **Unbound Object Frame** icon. The Unbound Object Frame mouse pointer will appear.

3. Drag a rectangle on your form or report where you want to place the chart. The Microsoft Office Access dialog box appears.

4. Click **Create New**. In the Object Type list box, click **Microsoft Office Excel Chart**, and then click **OK**. A sample chart opens and the Access ribbon is replaced with the

Use Excel tools to design your chart

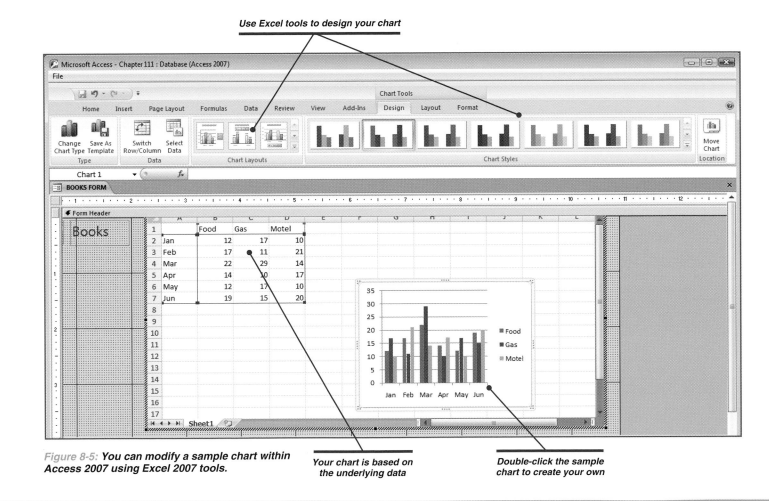

Figure 8-5: *You can modify a sample chart within Access 2007 using Excel 2007 tools.*

Your chart is based on the underlying data

Double-click the sample chart to create your own

NOTE

To learn more about using Excel and charting, see *Microsoft Office Excel 2007 QuickSteps,* also published by McGraw-Hill.

ribbon from Microsoft Office Excel 2007, containing charting tools and features, as shown in Figure 8-5.

5. Click **Change Chart Type** in the Chart Tools Design tab Type group, or use the other tools to build the chart.

6. Click outside the chart to return to full Access functionality. To edit the chart with Excel features, double-click it.

CREATE A CHART USING A WIZARD

1. Open the report or form in Design View.

2. In the Design tab Controls group, click the **Insert Chart** icon.

3. Drag a rectangle in the location where you want the chart.

4. The Chart Wizard appears. Choose the table or query whose data you want to use. Click **Next**.

5. Select the fields from the table or query that contain the data you want to see charted. Click **Next**.

6. Choose a chart type. Click a chart type to see its description displayed in the wizard, as shown in Figure 8-6.

Which fields contain the data you want for the chart?

Available Fields:
- ISBN
- Category
- Author
- Title

Fields for Chart:
- List Price
- Publish Year

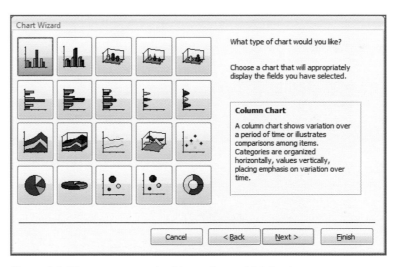

Figure 8-6: ***There are many chart types from which to choose.***

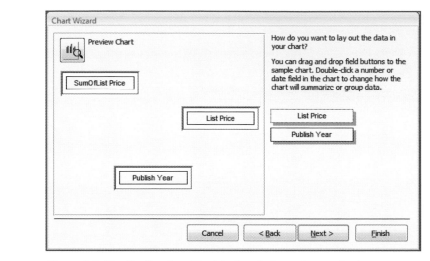

Figure 8-7: *Use the Preview Chart feature to lay out your chart.*

7. To lay out your chart, drag the field buttons into the field boxes on the sample chart, as seen in Figure 8-7. Click **Preview Chart** to see how you're doing. If you don't like the layout of the chart, change the location of the fields, and click **Preview Chart** again. When you are satisfied with your chart, click **Next**.

8. To have the chart reflect changes record-by-record, link the fields in the form or report to the fields on the chart. Click **Next**.

If you want the chart to change from record to record, select the fields that link the document and the chart.

Report Fields   Chart Fields:

ISBN   ISBN

9. Type a title for the chart, and choose whether to display a legend for the data series. Click **Finish**. Figure 8-8 shows the results of a chart created using the Chart Wizard.

Use Graphics

Though Access doesn't provide the full breadth of drawing tools available in other Office programs, you can still be quite creative by using lines and rectangles to separate, encompass, or emphasize areas in your forms and reports. An example of how lines and rectangles can enhance a form is shown in Figure 8-9.

ADD LINES AND RECTANGLES

1. Open the report or form in Design View.

2. In the Design tab Controls group, click the **Line** or **Rectangle** tool, and drag in the Design View section to the approximate size and location to more precisely modify the graphic:

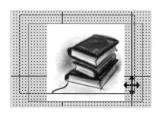

- Drag one of the eight sizing handles on the border of the graphic to resize it.
- Point to the border of the graphic, and when the mouse pointer changes into a cross, drag the graphic to reposition it.

  –Or–

- Use the applicable property in the Property Sheet to set width, height, and location (see the next section, "Modify Graphics Properties").

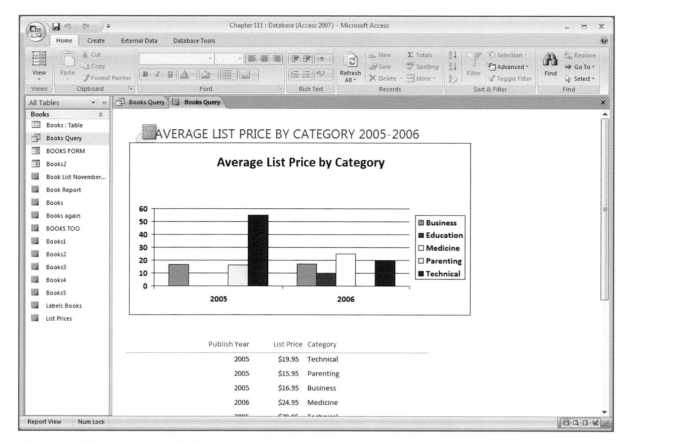

Figure 8-8: **A chart can be a useful on a form or report.**

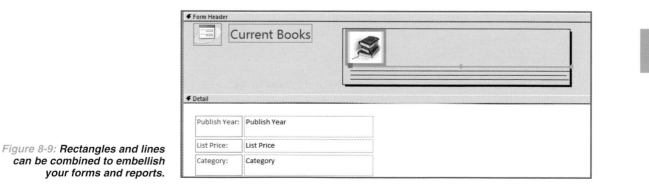

Figure 8-9: **Rectangles and lines can be combined to embellish your forms and reports.**

Build Event...
Build...
Change To ▶
Tab Order...
✂ Cut
📋 Copy
📋 Paste
📋 Paste Formatting
Align ▶
Size ▶
Position ▶
Layout ▶
✕ Delete
Anchoring ▶
Fill/Back Color ▶
A Font/Fore Color ▶
Special Effect ▶
Properties

MODIFY GRAPHICS PROPERTIES

1. In Design View, click the graphic to select it.

2. In the Design tab Tools group, click **Property Sheet**.

   –Or–

   Right-click the graphic and select **Properties**.

3. Change the settings for the property you want (see "Change Image Properties" earlier in the chapter for ways to change property settings).

Modify the Form or Report Design

Forms and reports have several properties that determine their appearance and behavior.

SELECT DESIGN VIEW COMPONENTS

Before you can work on a particular section of a form or report, you need to select it. In the Navigation Pane, drag the form or report to the Access work area to open it. Right-click the object and click **Design View**:

● To select the object itself (form or report), click the object selector (the box at the intersection of the rulers), ▣ or click anywhere in the background outside the form/report design area.

● Check bullet size. It is smaller than the other bulletsTo select a form or report section, click the form/report section selector—the small square in the vertical ruler next to the section divider. (If the ruler is not displayed, in the Arrange tab Show/Hide group, click the **Ruler** icon 🗒 to turn it on; or right-click anywhere in the report or form, and click **Ruler**.)

● To select controls, click a single control, and hold down SHIFT while clicking multiple controls; or drag a selection rectangle around the controls you want.

● To select all components on the report or form, press CTRL+A.

CHANGE FORM AND REPORT PROPERTIES

1. Open the form or report in Design View.

2. Click the form/report selector at the intersection of the horizontal and vertical rulers.

TIP

See Chapter 6 for more information on working with controls, such as how to move, resize, and arrange them.

UNDERSTANDING FORMATTING RULES

There are several rules you need to remember regarding formatting:

- The format that is applied to a field in your table is applied to all form and report controls that you link or bind to that field. It also will apply to any query you create with the Query Designer.

- The display format you set affects the appearance of your data, not how someone enters it. For example, if you set a field to display a number in a currency format, the user need not enter the dollar sign.

- When you set an input mask for a field as well as a display format, Access applies the display format only after that record is saved.

- To enable rich text formatting in a Memo field, the Text Format property must be set to Rich Text (see "Enable Rich Text Formatting").

3. In the Design tab Tools group, click **Property Sheet**, if it is not selected, to display the Property Sheet.

4. In the Property Sheet, click the **Format** tab. Figure 8-10 shows a list of the format properties you can set for a report. Other tabs in the Property Sheet offer data, event, and other properties.

5. Click the text box next to a property, and click the down arrow or the **Builder** button to see a list, gallery, or dialog box of choices.

–Or–

Type a value.

6. When finished, close the Property Sheet, and in the Design tab Views group, click **View** and change to either Report View or Layout View to see your changes.

Property Sheet	▼ ×
Selection type: Report	
Report	▼

Format	Data	Event	Other	All

Caption	Book Report
Default View	Report View
Allow Report View	Yes
Allow Layout View	Yes
Picture	(none)
Picture Tiling	No
Picture Alignment	Center
Picture Type	Embedded
Picture Size Mode	Clip
Width	8.4479"
Auto Center	No
Auto Resize	Yes
Fit to Page	Yes
Border Style	Sizable
Scroll Bars	Both
Control Box	Yes
Close Button	Yes
Min Max Buttons	Both Enabled
Moveable	No
Show Page Margins	Yes
Grid X	24
Grid Y	24
Layout for Print	Yes
Grp Keep Together	Per Column
Picture Pages	All Pages
Page Header	All Pages
Page Footer	All Pages
Orientation	Left-to-Right
Palette Source	(Default)

Figure 8-10: **You have many chances to customize a form or report through its Property Sheet.**

8

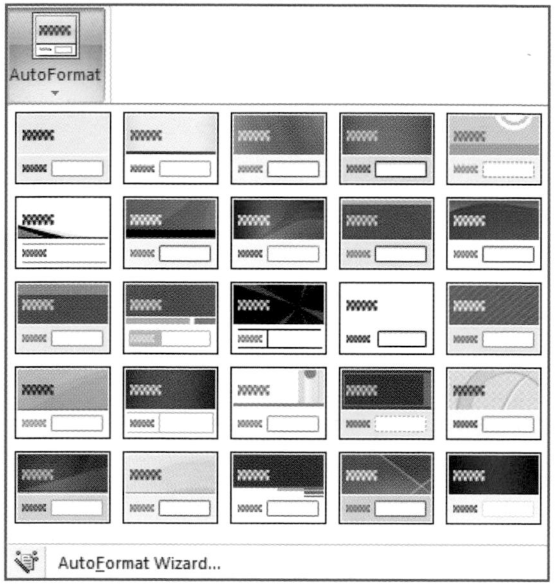

Figure 8-11: *Change the style of either a form or a report with AutoFormat.*

FORMAT AUTOMATICALLY

When you created a form or report with its respective wizard, you had a choice of layout and style. You can modify these designs manually, as described earlier in this chapter, or you can select from one of the Access 2007 predefined formats.

1. Open the form or report in either Layout or Design View.

2. In Design View, in the Arrange tab AutoFormat group, click **AutoFormat**.

–Or–

In Layout View, in the Format tab AutoFormat group, click **AutoFormat**.

In both cases, you will see the 25 predefined formats for your form or report, as shown in Figure 8-11.

3. Click the style you want to immediately apply it to your report or form.

APPLY A PREDEFINED FORMAT

You can apply any of the 25 predefined formats for your form or report, and you can create a new AutoFormat based on your current form or report. The explanation included here refers to forms, but the same procedure work in reports as well.

To apply a new AutoFormat:

1. Open your form in Design View.

2. In the Arrange tab AutoFormat group, click **AutoFormat** to display the predefined formats.

3. Double-click the format you want to use.

CREATE A NEW AUTOFORMAT

You can apply font, color, and border attributes to a new AutoFormat based on a form (or report) you have created.

1. Open the form on which you want to base your new format.

2. In Design View, in the Arrange tab AutoFormat group,

–Or–

In Layout View, in the Format tab AutoFormat group,

click the **AutoFormat** down arrow, and click **AutoFormat Wizard**.

USING WINDOWS THEMES

The overall appearance of Access 2007 (and all programs run in a Windows operating system) is determined by *themes*. A theme is a predefined style of icons, fonts, mouse pointers, sounds, colors, screen savers, and background colors. You can use any of the themes included with Windows, and you can customize a theme after it is applied.

SET THE THEME IN WINDOWS XP

To set or change the theme when working with Windows XP:

1. Right-click a blank area of the desktop, and click **Properties**. The Display Properties dialog box appears.

2. Click the **Themes** tab, and click the **Theme** down arrow to choose from the predetermined themes. Click the theme you want to use.

3. Click **OK** to close the Display Properties dialog box.

SET THE THEME IN WINDOWS VISTA

1. Right-click a blank area of the desktop, and click **Personalize**. The Personalization window opens.

2. Click **Theme** to display the Theme Settings dialog box.

3. Click the **Theme** down arrow to choose from predefined settings.

4. Make your choice from the displayed settings, and click **OK**.

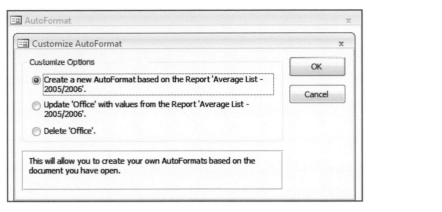

Figure 8-12: ***Use the Customize AutoFormat dialog box to create new formats.***

3. The AutoFormat dialog box will appear with one of the formats highlighted. Click **Customize**. The Customize AutoFormat dialog box will appear, as seen in Figure 8-12:

- To create a new AutoFormat based on the attributes you have set on your form, click **Create A New AutoFormat Based On The Form** *"Your Form Name."*

- To update the highlighted format, click **Update** *'Format Name'* **With Values From The Form** *"Your Form Name."*

- To delete the highlighted format, click **Delete 'Format Name.'**

Work with Rich Text Formatting

Access 2007 has several types of formatting you can use to display your data. You can set how your data appears on-screen and when printed. As discussed in Chapter 3, you can set input masks to force database users to enter information in a preset manner, such as (***) ***-**** in a telephone number. Both of these format options affect only the appearance of the data, not how it is stored in Access 2007. New to Access 2007, you can apply rich text formatting to text blocks in much the same way that you apply formatting in Microsoft Word, Excel, and PowerPoint.

The type of formatting available depends on the data type you set in your database. If you have set a field's data type as Date/Time, you may choose from predefined formats or customize a setting based on the predefinitions. Memo and Text fields have no predefined formats. For an explanation of some formatting rules, see the "Understanding Formatting Rules" QuickFacts elsewhere in this chapter.

You can turn on rich text formatting on any Memo field in your table. Some text can be bold or italicized, and you can change the text colors. In the background, Access 2007 uses *HTML* (Hypertext Markup Language) to make this happen.

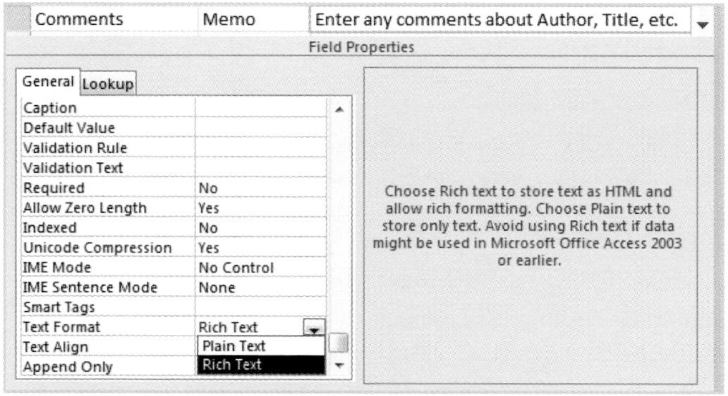

ENABLE RICH TEXT FORMATTING

1. Open the table in Design View.

2. Add a new field with the Memo data type.

   –Or–

   Click an existing **Memo** field.

3. In the Field Properties section of the Design View grid, click the **General** tab.

4. Click the **Text Format** down arrow, and click **Rich Text**. A message box appears. If you want to convert the column to rich text, click **Yes**.

5. Save your table.

APPLY RICH TEXT

When a Memo data type field is highlighted on a datasheet, the Rich Text tools become available on the Home tab Rich Text group.

1. Open a form in Form View or a table/datasheet in Datasheet View.

2. Select text in a field that has been enabled for rich text See "Enable Rich Text Formatting" above.

3. In the Home tab Rich Text group, apply one of the alignment, text direction, numbered or bulleted lists, or color attributes. Figure 8-13 shows some examples of how rich text can spice up your data.

Alignment buttons | Text direction buttons
Set bullets or numbering | Font color buttons
Rich Text

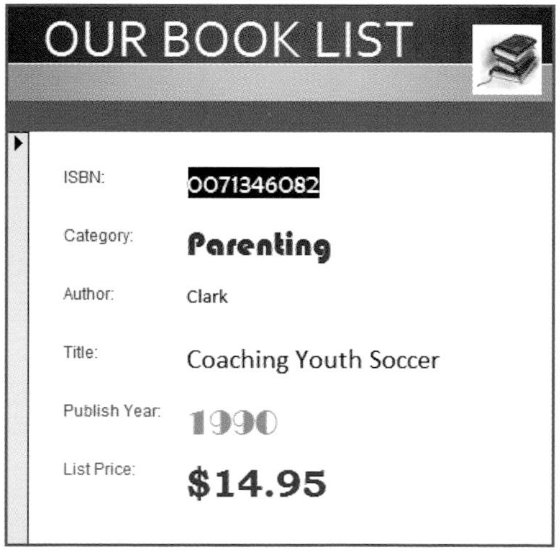

Figure 8-13: **Rich text formatting allows you to create colorful reports.**

Print Your Data

Access provides a broad array of printing options, many tailored to the object you are interested in printing.

Set Up the Print Job

You can print an object directly, modify several printing features in the Print dialog box that affect the printed page, and review and make changes to the page in Print Preview prior to printing. Some features are not available for all objects you want to print (for example, tables/datasheets and queries don't let you change columnar settings) and only affect printing of the current object (although the settings are retained for the next time you print the same object).

USE QUICK PRINT

If you want to print an Access 2007 object without making any changes, you can send it directly to the default printer.

1. Ensure that the object you want to print is the active object in your database.
2. Click the **Office Button** in the upper-left corner of the Access window.
3. Point to **Print** and click **Quick Print**. You may see a message that the object is printing to the default printer.

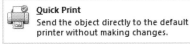

> **Quick Print**
> Send the object directly to the default printer without making changes.

CHANGE PAPER LAYOUT, SIZE, AND SOURCE

1. Click the **Office Button**, and click **Print**. The Print dialog box appears. Click **Properties**. The Document Properties dialog box for your printer appears, as seen in Figure 8-14. (The steps to perform these actions and the locations of the options vary according to each printer/printer manufacturer. The following steps are typical, though you may find the options are located in different tabs within the Document Properties dialog box.)

   - In the Layout tab, in the Orientation area, select the layout—**Portrait** (tall) or **Landscape** (wide)—that works best for how your data is arranged.

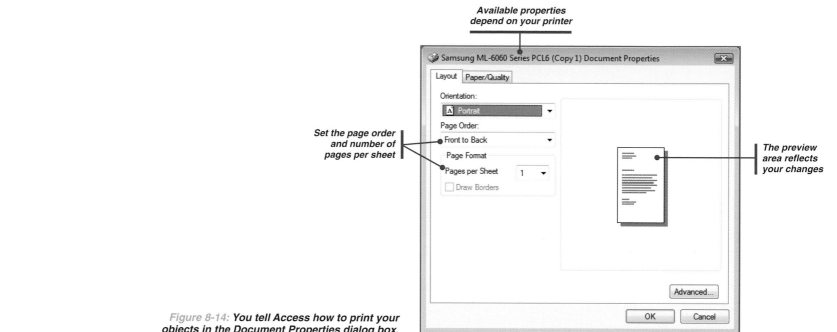

**Available properties
depend on your printer**

Set the page order
and number of
pages per sheet

**The preview
area reflects
your changes**

Figure 8-14: **You tell Access how to print your
objects in the Document Properties dialog box.**

- In the Page Order area, click **Front To Back** or **Back To Front**, depending on how you want your object to print.

- Choose the number of pages you want printed per sheet.

- Click the **Paper/Quality** tab to open the relevant dialog box. Click the **Paper Source** down arrow to choose the location from which you want the printer to obtain the paper.

- Click the **Media** down arrow to tell the printer what type of media to print on.

- From either the Layout or Paper/Quality tab, click **Advanced** to open the Advanced Options dialog box for your printer.

- Click the **Paper Size** down arrow to select the paper size you want.

- Depending on your printer, make any other selections you require.

- Click **OK** twice to return to the Print dialog box.

ADJUST MARGINS

You can adjust the distance between edges of the printed page and where text and pictures are printed for the current object.

1. Click the **Office Button**, and click **Print**.

2. Click **Setup** 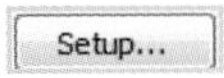 Setup... to open the Page Setup dialog box.

3. Adjust the settings in the Top, Bottom, Left, and Right text boxes to the respective margins you want by typing new values. As you make changes, the Sample area shows the new location of the margins.

4. Click **Print Data Only** if you want to print just the information from a form or report. (If printing a datasheet, you can select whether to print headings. When printing a table, this option is "Print Heading.") In the case of *split forms* (a form in which you see both the Datasheet and Form View at the same time):

   ● Click **Print Form Only** to print just the form.

   –Or–

   ● Click **Print Datasheet Only** to print just the datasheet.

   If neither option is selected, both will print.

5. Click **OK** when finished making all changes in the Page Setup dialog box.

CHANGE COLUMNAR PRINT SETTINGS

The output from a report, or the labels and fields in Form View, are printed together as a column. You can make more efficient use of paper by aligning the printed data into more than one column.

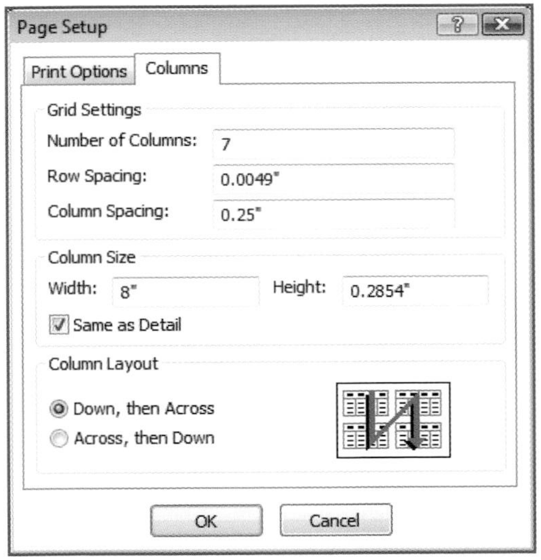

1. In the Page Setup dialog box, click the **Columns** tab, shown in Figure 8-15:

   ● In the Grid Setting area, type how many columns you want (your paper width and column width will be determining factors), and determine the sizing between rows and columns.

   ● In the Column Size area, click the **Same As Detail** check box to print the column the same size as you set up in the form or report in Design View. To adjust the column width and row height, clear the check box, and type new values.

   ● In the Column Layout area (multiple columns only), select the direction in which you want the columns printed.

2. Click **OK** when finished making all changes in the Page Setup dialog box.

*Figure 8-15: **The Columns tab lets you determine how your object will print.***

Review Data Before Printing

Print Preview provides an accurate picture of your data and layout so that you can make changes before committing to expending ink/toner and paper.

The Print Preview window, shown in Figure 8-16, allows you to toggle between two magnifications (100 percent and what will fit on a single page) by clicking your mouse, and you can navigate through the pages to be printed using a navigation bar. Print Preview's other features are available from the Print Preview tab.

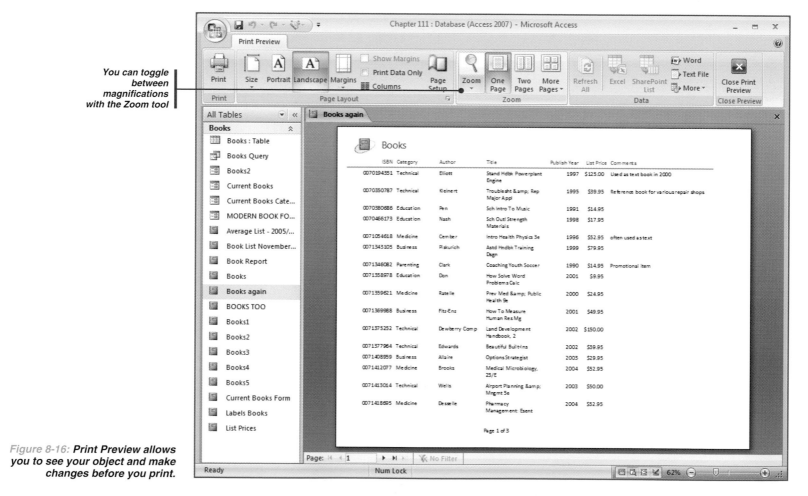

You can toggle between magnifications with the Zoom tool

Figure 8-16: **Print Preview allows you to see your object and make changes before you print.**

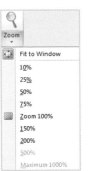

Print Preview

Size

Letter 8.5" x 11"	
Legal 8.5" x 14"	
Executive 7.25" x 10.5"	
A4 8.27" x 11.69"	
A5 5.83" x 8.27"	

B5 (JIS) 7.17" x 10.12"

Folio 8.5" x 13"

Envelope #10 4.12" x 9.5"

Envelope DL 4.33" x 8.66"

Envelope C5 6.38" x 9.02"

Envelope B5 6.93" x 9.84"

Envelope Monarch 3.87" x 7.5"

1. To open Print Preview, click the **Office Button**, point to **Print**, and click **Print Preview**.

2. In the Print Preview tab Print group, click **Print** to open the Print dialog box.

3. In the Print Preview tab Page Layout group:

- Click **Size** to set the paper size on which to print.
- Click **Portrait** or **Landscape** to set the orientation of your printed object.
- Click **Margins** to choose from three pre-defined settings or to choose the last custom setting.

Margins

Last Custom Setting
Top:	0.25"	Bottom: 0.33"
Left:	0.25"	Right: 0.25"

Normal
Top:	0.75"	Bottom: 0.75"
Left:	0.35"	Right: 0.35"

Wide
Top:	1"	Bottom: 1"
Left:	0.75"	Right: 0.75"

Narrow
Top:	0.25"	Bottom: 0.25"
Left:	0.25"	Right: 0.25"

- Click **Page Setup** to open the Page Setup dialog box and change the margins, orientation, and set columns.
- Click **Print Data Only** to print the data without the form labels.
- Click **Columns** to open the Page Setup dialog box for the Columns tab.

4. In the Print Preview tab Zoom group:

- Click **Zoom** to choose from several magnifications.
- Click **One Page**, **Two Pages**, or **More Pages** to see pages in those respective configurations.

5. In the Print Preview tab Data group, you may export Access data to other Office programs. For more information on exporting Access data, see Chapter 10.

6. Click **Close Print Preview** to return to your object.

Zoom

Fit to Window
10%
25%
50%
75%
Zoom 100%
150%
200%
500%
Maximum 1000%

TIP

You can also use the Zoom tools in the Access window status bar to change the magnification in Print Preview.

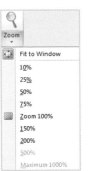

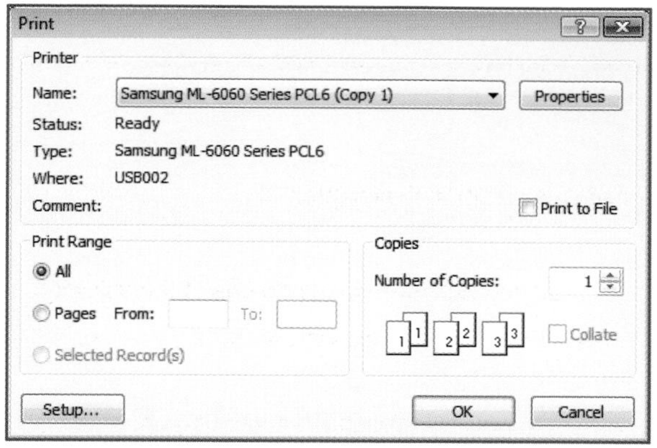

Figure 8-17: *The Print dialog box lets you set many printing options.*

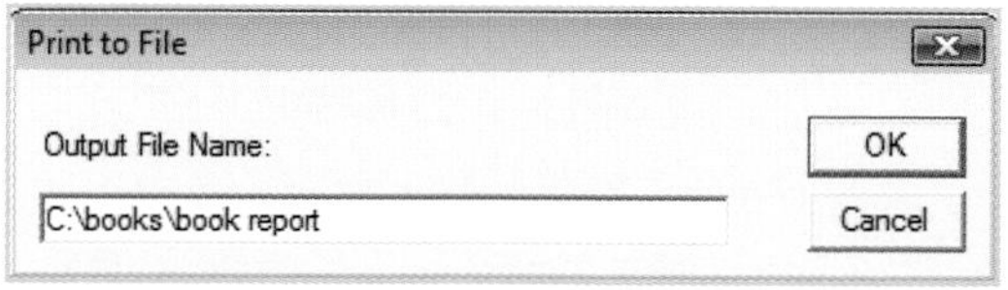

Output the Print Job

You can print to printers attached to your computer or to printers on your network. You can also print to a file instead of a printer and choose features provided by your printer manufacturer. All this is accomplished from the Print dialog box, as shown in Figure 8-17.

To open the Print dialog box, press **CTRL+P**.

–Or–

Click the **Office Button**, and click **Print**.

CHOOSE A PRINTER

In the Printer dialog box, click the **Name** down arrow, and select a printer that is installed on your computer from the drop-down list. The printer name is displayed in the Name drop-down list box, and information about the printer is listed below (see Figure 8-17).

PRINT MULTIPLE COPIES

1. In the Copies area, click the **Number Of Copies** spinner to the number of copies you want.

2. Click the **Collate** check box to print each copy from start to finish before starting to print the next copy.

   –Or–

   Clear the **Collate** check box to print each page the number of times set in the Number Of Copies spinner before printing the next page.

PRINT TO A FILE

You can print your printer information to a file instead of directly to a physical device.

1. Click the **Print To File** ☑ Print to File check box.

2. Select any other print options you want, and click **OK**.

3. In the Print To File dialog box, type the path and file name of where you want the print file located.

4. Click **OK**.

PRINT ALL PAGES

- Open the object (or run the object, in the case of queries) that you want to print. In the Print dialog box, under Print Range, click **All**. Click **OK**.

  –Or–

- Use a Quick Print technique described earlier in the chapter.

PRINT SPECIFIC PAGES

1. In the Print dialog box, under Print Range, click **Pages**, and do one of the following:

   - To print a range of pages, use the **From** and **To** fields to set starting and ending pages.

   - To print one page, set both the **From** and **To** fields to the same page number.

   - To print from a page to the last page, set only the **From** field.

```
Print Range
○ All
◉ Pages  From:    8  To:    14
```

2. Click **OK**.

PRINT SPECIFIC RECORDS

1. Select the records in Datasheet View that you want to print.

2. In the Print dialog box, under Print Range, click **Selected Record(s)**.

```
○ Pages  From:        To:
◉ Selected Record(s)
```

3. Click **OK**.

NOTE

When you use the Navigation Pane to select the object you want to print and then click **Print** on the Quick Access toolbar or from the Office Button menu, some objects might print differently from what you'd expect. For example, when you print a query, the query is run first, then printed.

How to...

- *Understanding Access 2007 Security*
- Create a Trusted Location
- Create and Use Certificates to Trust Databases
- *Creating Passwords*
- Encrypt a Database
- Remove Database Objects from View
- Keeping Data Safe
- Secure the Database with the User-Level Security Wizard
- *Understanding the User-Level Security Model*
- Document a Database
- Compact and Repair a Database
- *Troubleshooting the Compact And Repair Database Utility*
- Back Up a Database

Chapter 9

Securing and Administrating Access

This chapter addresses the issue of database security. The overriding purpose of database security is to prevent both inadvertent and intentional damage to the data and the database objects. Proper security measures prevent anyone who might view or edit the information from gaining unauthorized access. They also prevent anyone from making design changes without express permission to do so. You can protect both the data and the design elements with a variety of approaches. In addition, there are administrative measures you can take, such as creating database backups, that supplement the security precautions you have in place.

9

UNDERSTANDING ACCESS 2007 SECURITY

Access 2007 borrows from former President Reagan's philosophy of détente, that is, "trust but verify," in its pursuit to simplify database security and avoid most of the repetitious and annoying dialog boxes you had to deal with in earlier versions of Access to open a database.

Security Warning ✕

Opening "C:\Matthews\QuickSteps\Access2007\Books-97 Format.mdb"

This file may not be safe if it contains code that was intended to harm your computer.
Do you want to open this file or cancel the operation?

| Cancel | Open | More Info |

Access 2007 believes that it's better to let you open a database and view its data and disable any potential malicious code or actions that could cause security risks, unless it's verified that:

- The database is stored in a trusted location.

–Or–

- The database is digitally signed and you trust the originator of the certificate.

Chapter 1 described the security warning that appears in the message bar below the ribbon and the steps to take to enable content or not.

Continued . . .

Microsoft Office Trusted Location ？✕

Warning: This location will be treated as a trusted source for opening files. If you change or add a location, make sure that the new location is secure.

Path:

C:\Program Files (x86)\Microsoft Office\Office12\ACCWIZ\

Browse...

☑ Subfolders of this location are also trusted

Description:

Main trusted location|

Date and Time Created: 11/15/2006 3:15 PM

| OK | Cancel |

Apply Security to an Access Database

Access offers several comprehensive methods of securing a database and its objects, including digitally signing databases, encrypting database files, and applying user-level security. Several security measures are unique to Access 2007 files, although provisions are made for security models in earlier Access versions. In addition, there are less comprehensive actions you can take to prevent users from inadvertently making changes to data.

Create a Trusted Location

The easiest way to let Access know that you trust the content in a database is to store the database file in a folder that you let Access know you trust. Your local computer is the recommended place to locate a trusted folder, although you can use a folder on your network. When you open a database stored in a trusted location, content will be enabled and you will no longer see the security warning advising you of that.

🛡 **Security Warning**   Certain content in the database has been disabled | Options... |

1. Click the **Office Button**, click **Access Options**, and click the **Trust Center** option. Under Microsoft Office Access Trust Center, click **Trust Center Settings**. | Trust Center Settings... |

2. In the Trust Center, click the **Trusted Locations** option. The Trusted Locations page appears, with at least one default secure location for databases created by Access wizards, as shown in Figure 9-1.

3. To add a secure location on your network, first click the **Allow Trusted Location On My Network** check box. Then, to add a secure location on your local computer or on the network, click **Add New Location**.

4. In the Microsoft Office Trust Location dialog box, click **Browse** and navigate to the folder you want to secure. Click **OK**.

5. Click the **Subfolders Of This Location Are Also Trusted** check box if you want to include them. Add a description if you want to add amplifying information in addition

UNDERSTANDING ACCESS 2007 SECURITY (Continued)

Users familiar with earlier versions of Access are probably wondering what happened to user-level security, where you could grant access to various components of the database based on the permissions you granted to others. Good news and bad news. For databases saved in the earlier Access file formats, such as .mdb, user-level security is supported within Access 2007. If you open a database in Access 2007's .accdb format, user-level security will not be available.

Another layer of database protection Access provides is the file encryption feature common to other Office 2007 programs. By password-protecting a database, you can sleep well at night, knowing that if your data falls into nefarious hands, the database cannot be opened and your private information will appear as gobbledygook if attempts are made to use it.

Finally, for a more casual sense of security, you can keep others from viewing certain aspects of the database by simply removing those objects from view.

All of these security precautions are described in this chapter.

---

to the time and date the folder is secured that Access provides. Click **OK** to add the location to the User Locations list.

6. To remove or change an existing trusted location, select the location and click **Remove** or **Modify**, respectively (see Figure 9-1).

7. Click **OK** twice when finished to close the Trust Center And Access Options window.

Create and Use Certificates to Trust Databases

A certificate provides a digital signature to a file and lets others know that a database came from a trusted source (if you trust the certificate originator, you trust the files that are digitally signed by the originator and are assured the files have not been altered). You can create your own certificate and apply it to Access 2007 databases you provide to others as part of a *package*.

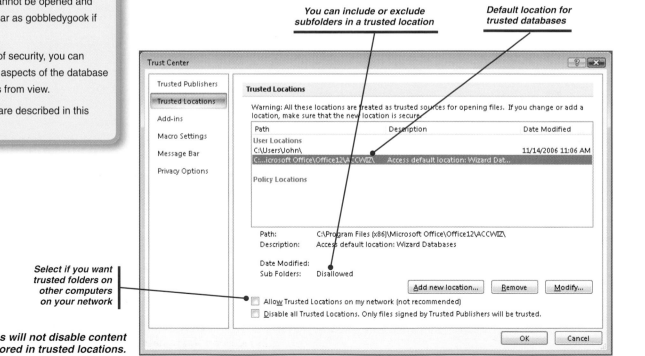

You can include or exclude subfolders in a trusted location

Default location for trusted databases

Select if you want trusted folders on other computers on your network

Figure 9-1: Access will not disable content for databases stored in trusted locations.

NOTE

You can create a *self-signed* certificate, which provides a limited measure of confidence to recipients of your databases that the data really came from a trusted source. To be fully confident that a database containing executable code (that is, code that can perform actions on your system or data) is from a trusted source, you can provide a certificate from a commercial certificate authority that attests you are who you profess to be. VeriSign (www.verisign.com) is an example of one of the larger certificate authorities.

NOTE

You cannot digitally sign a database in a pre-Access 2007 file format (.accdb) using the Publish feature on the Office Button menu. However, you can use a technique from earlier versions to digitally sign a database. Open the pre-Access 2007 database, and, in the Database Tools tab Macro group, click **Visual Basic**. In the Visual Basic window, select the database in the Project Explorer in the left pane, click the **Tools** menu, and click **Digital Signature**. In the Digital Signature dialog box, click **Choose**, select the certificate you want to assign to the database, and click **OK** twice. Close the Visual Basic window.

Microsoft Visual Basic - Books-2003 Format [design]

File   Edit   View   Insert   Debug   Run   Tools   Add-Ins   Window   Help

Project - books97

acwztool (ACWZTOOL)
books97 (Books-2003 Format)

Packaging encapsulates the database in an Access Deployment file (.accdc) and signs the package with a certificate. For databases you receive from others, Access will alert you to the presence of an untrusted certificate, and you can decide whether or not to trust the content.

CREATE A CERTIFICATE

You need a certificate before you can digitally sign a database and publish it to others.

1. Click the Start menu button.
2. Click **All Programs**, click **Microsoft Office**, click **Microsoft Office Tools**, and click **Digital Certificate For VBA Projects**. The Create Digital Certificate dialog box appears, shown in Figure 9-2.
3. Type a name for the certificate (this is the name others will see when they open a signed database from you), and click **OK**. You are notified that your self-certificate is created. Click **OK**.

SelfCert Success

Successfully created a new certificate for CBTS.

OK

PUBLISH A DIGITALLY SIGNED DATABASE

1. Open an Access 2007 database.
2. Click the **Office Button**, click **Publish**, and click **Package And Sign**.
3. In the Select Certificate dialog box, select the certificate you want to use to sign the database, and click **OK**.

Publish the database for others

Document Management Server
Share the database by saving it to a document management server.

Package and Sign
Package the database and apply a digital signature.

Select Certificate

Select the certificate you want to use.

Issued to	Issued by	Intended P...	Friendly name	Expiration ...
CBTS	CBTS	Code Signing	None	1/1/2012

OK   Cancel   View Certificate

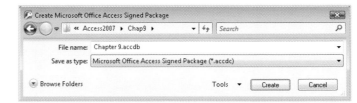

4. In the Create Microsoft Office Access Signed Package dialog box, navigate to the folder where you want the database/package located. Name the package and click **Create**. (Note that the package is saved in the .accdc file format.)

USE A DIGITALLY SIGNED PRE-ACCESS 2007 DATABASE

1. Open the database.

2. If the certificate is validated and trusted by Access (typically, this is a certificate issued by a commercial certificate authority), there is no action needed on your part. The database will open with enabled content, and the security warning in the message bar will be omitted.

3. If the signed database is from a self-certificate, Access will not typically trust it. Click the security warning **Options** button in the message bar. You should see the Microsoft Office Security Options dialog box, similar to that shown in Figure 9-3. Access will display the particulars of the certificate. Review them and when satisfied they are trusted, click **OK** to enable the content.

EXTRACT AN ACCESS 2007 DATABASE FROM A PACKAGE

When you open a package sent to you by another Access 2007 user, you open it as you would any other database file.

1. If the publisher is trusted (that is, you've previously trusted content from them and they are listed in the Trusted Publishers list of your Trust Center), the database file can be extracted from the package.

–Or–

If the package comes from an untrusted publisher (even if the digital signature is valid), a Security Notice dialog box appears, where you can both choose to open the database and add the publisher to your Trusted Publishers list.

2. In either case, in the Extract Database To dialog box that appears, select where you want the extracted database file stored, and rename it if desired. Click **OK**.

Figure 9-2: *You can provide some assurance to others that databases they receive from you are really from you and have not been changed.*

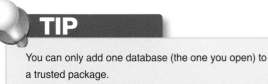

TIP

You can only add one database (the one you open) to a trusted package.

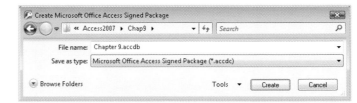

QUICK**FACTS**

CREATING PASSWORDS

Some basic guidelines for creating a password include:

- Create a strong password that combines uppercase and lowercase letters with numbers and symbols. For example, "67TrCg!89sdJ" is a strong password, while "MyFavoriteCat" is not.
- Passwords should be eight or more characters.
- Never use a word that appears in the dictionary.
- Do not use characters that have a special meaning in Access: " \ [ ] : | < > + = ; , . ? *.

TIP

When you encrypt a database, you are using one of the Microsoft Office 2007 128-bit encryption algorithms. These provide greater security than the encryption algorithms used in previous versions of Access.

NOTE

By default, databases are opened in *shared* open mode, which allows others to concurrently open the database and access the data. You can change this behavior so that only one user has exclusive use of the data. To change the default open mode behavior, click the **Office Button**, click **Access Options**, and click the **Advanced** option. Under Advanced, click the behavior you want, and click **OK** when finished.

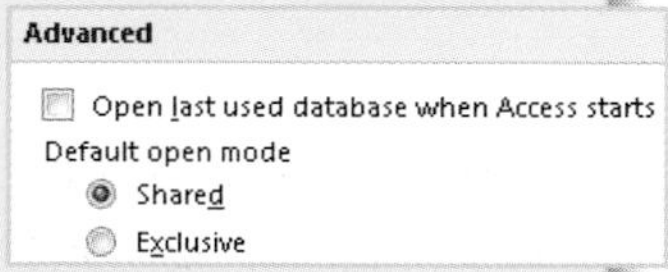

Advanced

☐ Open last used database when Access starts

Default open mode
- ◉ Share*d*
- ○ E*x*clusive

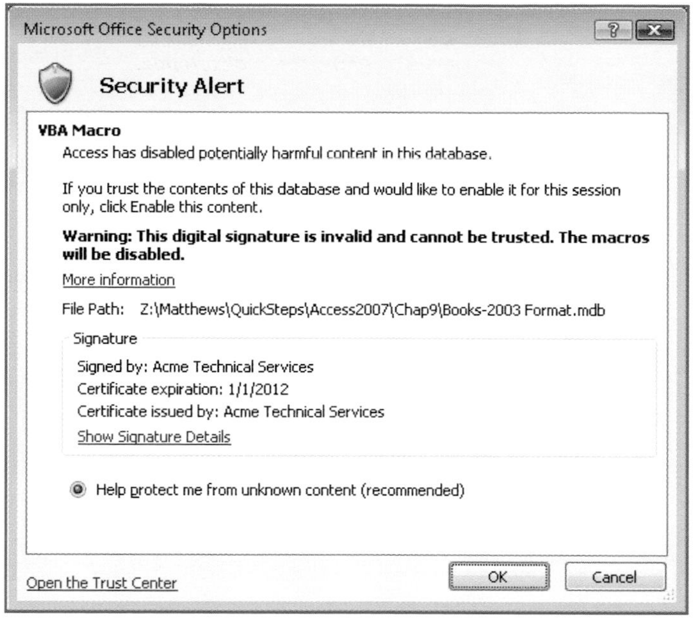

Microsoft Office Security Options

🛡 **Security Alert**

VBA Macro

Access has disabled potentially harmful content in this database.

If you trust the contents of this database and would like to enable it for this session only, click Enable this content.

Warning: This digital signature is invalid and cannot be trusted. The macros will be disabled.

More information

File Path: Z:\Matthews\QuickSteps\Access2007\Chap9\Books-2003 Format.mdb

Signature

Signed by: Acme Technical Services
Certificate expiration: 1/1/2012
Certificate issued by: Acme Technical Services

Show Signature Details

◉ Help protect me from unknown content (recommended)

Open the Trust Center   OK   Cancel

Figure 9-3: *Access will notify you of self-certificates, but will not enable content without your approval.*

Encrypt a Database

A database password only protects a database from being opened by someone who doesn't know the password. Anyone who knows the password can open the database. Once the database is open, the user can do anything with it.

ASSIGN A PASSWORD

You must have exclusive use of the database to assign a password.

1. Make sure all users have closed the database.

2. Click the **Office Button**, and click **Open**. In the Open dialog box, shown in Figure 9-4, select the database you want to protect with a password, click the **Open** down arrow, and click **Open Exclusive**.

3. In the Database Tools tab Database Tools group, click **Encrypt With Password**.

Switchboard Manager
Linked Table Manager   Encrypt with Password
Add-ins ▾   Make ACCDE

Database Tools

Figure 9-4: *You can select how to share a database using options in the Open dialog box.*

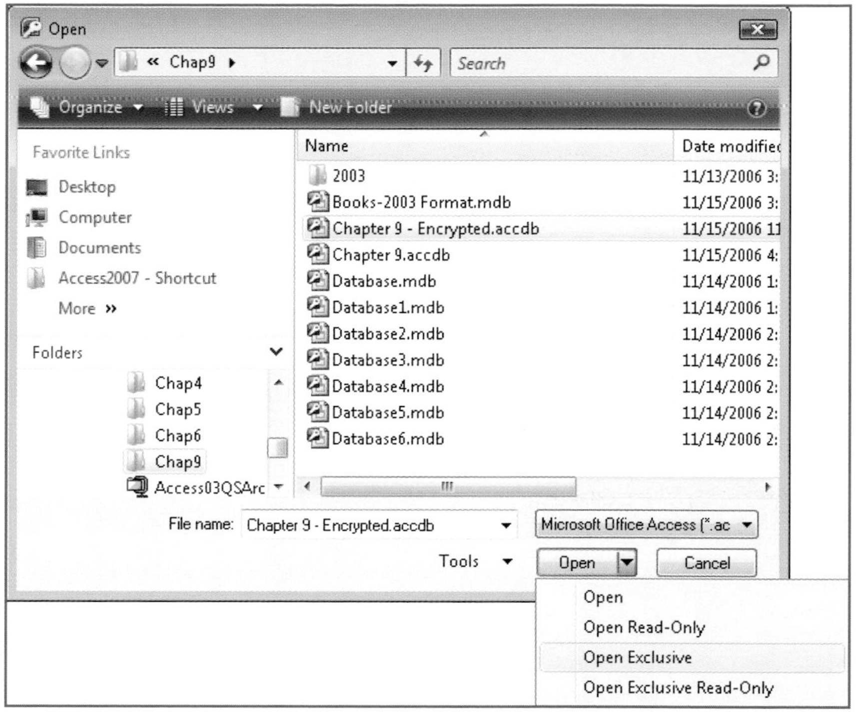

CAUTION

Don't forget your password. You won't be able to open the database without it. Write it down and store it in a safe place.

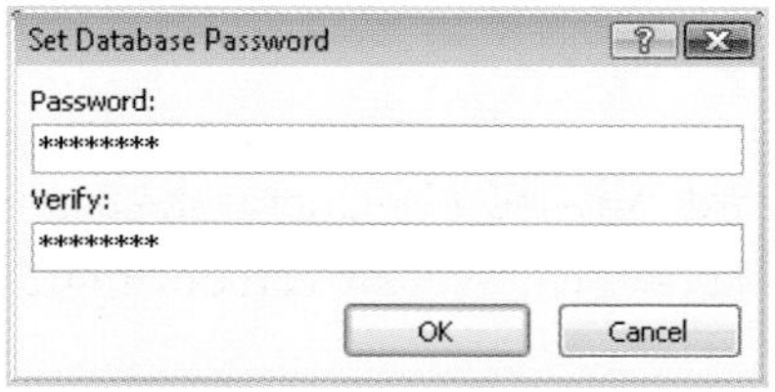

4. In the Set Database Password dialog box, type the password. Repeat the password in the Verify text box, and then click **OK**.

5. The next time you try to open the database, you will be asked for the password.

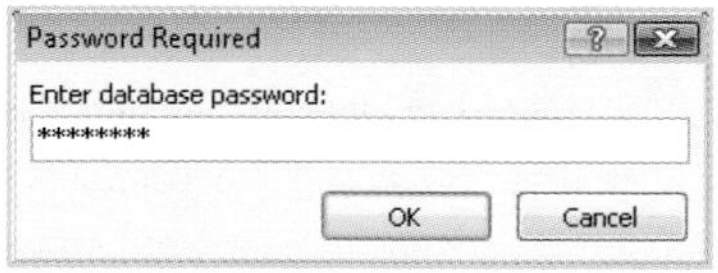

REMOVE A PASSWORD

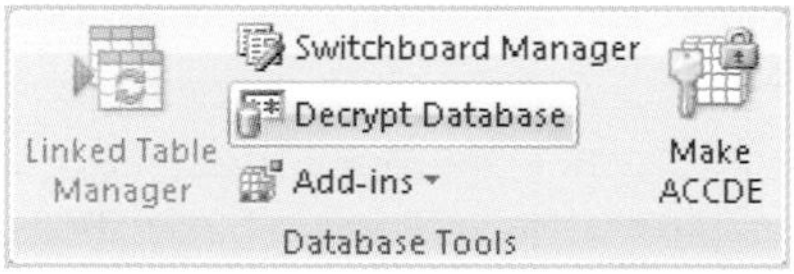

1. Open the database in Exclusive mode.

2. In the Database Tools tab Database Tools group, click **Decrypt Database**.

3. In the Unset Database dialog box, type the password and click **OK**.

Remove Database Objects from View

Hiding database objects does not really tighten security, per se; although it does keep certain objects from appearing in the Navigation Pane and out of sight/out of harm's way to casual users.

KEEPING DATA SAFE

There are several actions you can take to keep data safe from unintended changes that supplement any security measures you are implementing.

PREVENT EDITING TO RECORDS

You can lock all records, or just the record you are editing, from changes in the open form or datasheet (and also lock records in underlying tables). This feature is useful when a database is shared. Chapter 10 described how to share a database.

1. Open the database whose records you want to prevent against editing.

2. Click the **Office Button**, click **Access Options**, and click the **Advanced** option.

3. Under Advanced, click the default record-locking behavior you want.

   Default record locking
   - ⦿ No locks
   - ○ All records
   - ○ Edited record

4. Click **OK** when finished.

LIMIT VALUES IN A LOOKUP FIELD

A lookup field can appear in a form as a combo box or as a list box from which the user chooses a value. Users may also enter a value not already on the list. If you don't want other values in the field:

1. Open the table in Design View.

2. Select the lookup field in the upper pane.

3. Click the **Lookup** tab in the lower pane.

4. Click the **Limit To List** property text box, click its down arrow, and click **Yes**.

5. Save the table design.

Continued . . .

HIDE DATABASE OBJECTS

- To hide a group of objects in the Navigation Pane, right-click the group title bar, and click **Hide**.

- To hide an object within a group in the Navigation Pane, right-click the object and click **Hide In This Group**.

VIEW HIDDEN DATABASE OBJECTS

In order to view objects or groups that are hidden, you will need to see them in order to change their status.

1. Right-click a blank area of the Navigation Pane, and click **Navigation Options**.

2. Click the **Show Hidden Objects** check box, and click **OK**. Any hidden objects or groups appear dimmed in the Navigation Pane.

   Display Options
   - ☑ Show Hidden Objects   ☐ Show System Objects
   - ☐ Show Search Bar

3. Right-click the hidden object or group you want to return to full view, and click **Unhide In This Group** or **Unhide**, respectively. Figure 9-5 shows the command for revealing a table.

4. To return remaining hidden objects to a fully hidden status, right-click a blank area of the Navigation Pane, click **Navigation Options**, and clear the **Show Hidden Objects** check box. Click **OK**.

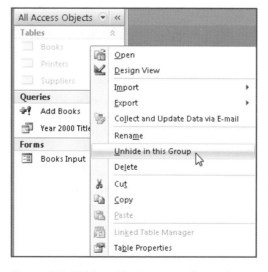

*Figure 9-5: **Hidden objects appear dimmed so that you can "view" them and select which ones to reveal.***

Secure the Database with the User-Level Security Wizard

The User-Level Security Wizard can secure any or all of the objects in your database. All the relationships and linked tables are kept intact when you secure the database with the User-Level Security Wizard. It also makes a backup copy of the original database in case you have forgotten to do so. The backup file has the same name as the original database, but with the *.bak* file extension.

KEEPING DATA SAFE (Continued)

REQUIRE VALID DATA

To make that sure newly entered data is correct, include data validation rules in a table or form design. See Chapter 3 for more information on using data validation.

PREVENT DATA CHANGES IN A FORM

To keep a user from entering, deleting, or editing data in a form:

1. Open the form in Design View, and double-click the form selector.

2. In the Property Sheet, click the **Data** tab.

3. Click the **Allow Edits** property text box, click its down arrow, and click **No**.

4. Repeat step 3 to set the Allow Deletions and Allow Additions properties.

5. Save the form design.

NOTE

In some pre-Access 2007 versions, you could assign user-level security in a multiuser environment. The security model operated on the principle that not all users need to have access to all the data or all the design elements in the database. Users were organized into groups, each of which has specific responsibilities. This information was stored in a workgroup information file (WIF). Access 2007 supports this security model for databases created in Access 2003 and earlier versions that supported it. See the "Understanding the User-Level Security Model!" QuickFacts and "Secure the Database with the User-Level Security Wizard" for information on how to implement user-level security.

With the User-Level Security Wizard, you can be specific about which users enjoy which permissions. You can also decide who belongs to which groups and also edit user passwords and personal IDs (PIDs). A PID is similar to a password and is used in combination with the user name to identify an account.

START THE USER-LEVEL SECURITY WIZARD

The database must be open before you can work with the User-Level Security Wizard.

1. Open the pre-Access 2007 database whose objects you want to secure.

2. In the Database Tools tab Administer group, click **Users And Permissions**, and click **User-Level Security Wizard**.

3. In the first page of the wizard, click **Create A New Workgroup Information File** if one doesn't exist.

    –Or–

    Select **Modify My Current Workgroup Information File** to make changes in an existing WIF.

    In either case, click **Next**.

Do you want to create a new workgroup information file or modify the current one?

- ◉ Create a new workgroup information file.
- ○ Modify my current workgroup information file.

4. In the next page, shown in Figure 9-6, browse to where you want to locate the workgroup information file, name the file, and accept the workgroup ID (WID) the User-Level Security Wizard offers, or enter a unique string in the WID box. (The WID is a case-sensitive string of between 4 and 20 alphabetic and numeric characters.) Optionally, add your name and your company's name.

5. Click the **I Want To Create A Shortcut To Open My Security-Enhanced Database** check box, and click **Next**.

SECURE INDIVIDUAL OBJECTS

The third page of the User-Level Security Wizard, shown in Figure 9-7, shows tabs for each of the objects in the current database. By default, all objects are

UNDERSTANDING THE USER-LEVEL SECURITY MODEL

The user-level security model is based on the idea of workgroups whose members share the data and privileges. The group and user accounts list the members of the workgroup. A *group account* is a collection of user accounts. Each member of the group is permitted some degree of freedom in dealing with data and objects. A *user account* belongs to a single user and includes the user name and personal ID (PID).

The four pieces of a user-level security model are:

- A **user** is a person who uses the database.

- A **group** is a set of users, all of whom operate at the same security level and need access to the same parts of the database.

- A **permission** gives a user or group the right to carry out a specific action. For example, Read Data permission allows opening a table or query for viewing but not for entering new data or editing existing data.

- An **object** refers to any of the Access tables, queries, forms, reports, macros, or modules—as well as to the database itself.

Depending on what the user needs to do with the database, you can assign her to any of the groups provided by the User-Level Security Wizard. To give a user more permissions than one group has, you can assign that user to more than one group:

- **Backup Operators** can open the database exclusively for backup and compacting, but are not permitted to see any of the database objects.

- **Full Data Users** have full permission to edit data, but are not allowed to make any design changes.

Continued . . .

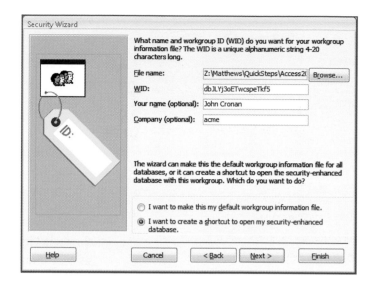

Figure 9-6: **You can select a name and location for the workgroup information file and create your own ID (creating your own ID is not recommended).**

Figure 9-7: **You can easily remove security attributes from objects that don't need them.**

QUICKFACTS

UNDERSTANDING THE USER-LEVEL SECURITY MODEL (Continued)

- **Full Permission Users** have full permissions on all database objects, but are not allowed to assign permissions to others.

- **New Data Users** can read and insert data, but are not allowed to delete or update existing data. They are also not allowed to alter any object designs.

- **Project Designers** have full permission to edit data and all objects, but are not allowed to alter any tables or relationships.

- **Read-Only Users** can read all the data, but are not allowed to change data or any design object.

- **Update Data Users** can read and update all data, but are not allowed to insert or delete data. They are also not allowed to make any design changes.

CAUTION

Applying user-level security to a database can prevent opening the file if you lose or forget required information to access the database, or if you are otherwise unfamiliar with working with users, groups, and setting permissions. We recommended that you use this feature only to change existing settings to a workgroup information file, unless you are comfortable working in a multiuser environment.

CAUTION

If you choose to make the WIF identified in Figure 9-6 the default, every Access database you open will use it, unless you specify that it be opened with a different WIF.

secured by the wizard, but you can exclude some and keep the existing security measures in the others.

1. Clear the check box next to the object that you want to leave as is.

2. Click the tab (such as Queries, Forms, or Reports) for any other object whose security selections you want to change.

3. When finished, click **Next**. If you have secured your Visual Basic code with a password, the User-Level Security Wizard asks for the password in the next page. If not, you move on to setting up group accounts.

SET UP GROUP ACCOUNTS

Setting up group accounts involves choosing the appropriate groups for your application based on the tasks assigned to the users. In the next page of the wizard, shown in Figure 9-8, you can view which permissions are assigned to specific security groups, and then decide how to assign the users to the different groups. A unique group ID is assigned to each group by the User-Level Security Wizard.

1. Select a group in the group list to read the description of the permissions in the Group Permissions area. Figure 9-8 shows the permissions granted to the New Data Users group.

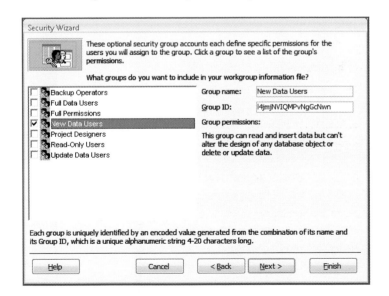

Figure 9-8: *The security group accounts provide specific permissions to their members.*

2. Click the check boxes for the groups you want to include in the security model, and click **Next**.

3. The next page of the wizard allows you to assign some permissions to the Users group, but strongly recommends against that. Click **No, The Users Group Should Not Have Any Permissions**. Click **Next**.

ADD, EDIT, AND REMOVE USERS

In the next page of the wizard, shown in Figure 9-9, you can get specific about which users to add to the workgroup. You can also delete a user from the workgroup and edit a user's password or PID.

1. Click **Add New User** in the left pane.

2. Type a name in the User Name text box, and type a password in the Password text box. The user's PID is automatically entered, but you can change it if you want to.

3. Click **Add This User To The List**.

4. Repeat steps 1–3 to add other users to the workgroup.

5. To remove a user from the workgroup, select the name and click **Delete User From The List**.

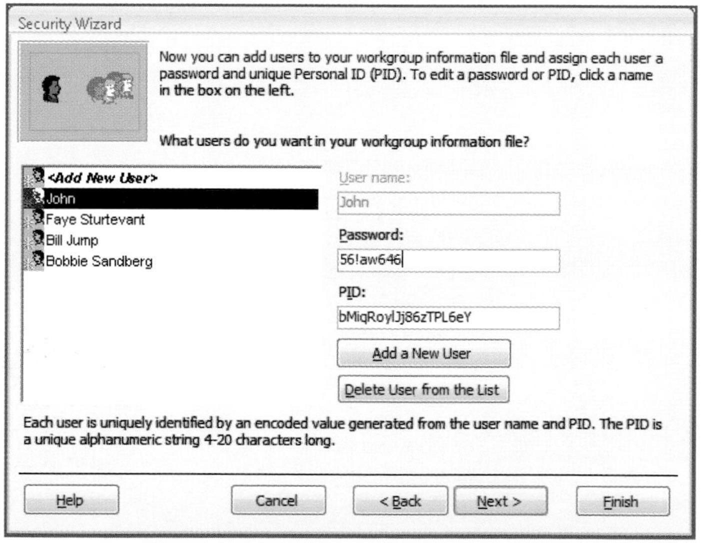

Figure 9-9: **You can manage which users will have access to the objects you previously identified.**

> **NOTE**
>
> You can assign a user to more than one group. The user then has all the permissions associated with all the groups she belongs to.

6. To edit user information, select the name and change the password or PID.
7. Click **Next** when finished with the users in the workgroup.

ASSIGN USERS TO GROUPS

The final step in defining user-level security is to assign each user to one of the groups that you have selected. You have two ways to carry this out in the next page of the User-Level Security Wizard. You may start with a user and add the user to groups, or start with a group and assign users to it.

1. In the next page, click **Select A User And Assign The User To Groups**. The user names you added to the workgroup appear in the Group Or User Name drop-down list. The group names you included appear in the pane below the list.

   –Or–

   Click **Select A Group And Assign Users To The Group** to assign users to a group.
2. Assign a user to groups or select a group and assign users, depending on your selection in step 1.
3. Repeat steps 1 and 2 to make additional assignments. Click **Next** when finished.
4. In the final page of the wizard, enter a name and path for the unsecured backup database, and click **Finish**.

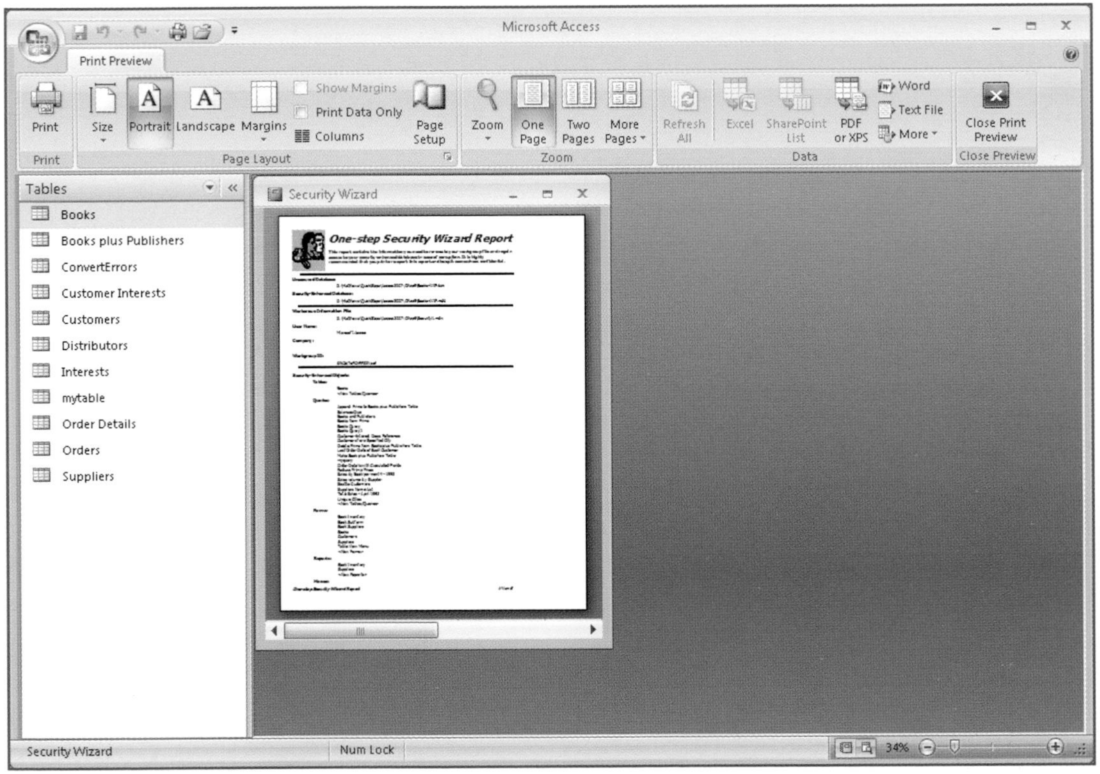

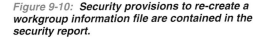

Figure 9-10: ***Security provisions to re-create a workgroup information file are contained in the security report.***

SAVE OR PRINT THE SECURITY REPORT

It is extremely important to document and save all the security provisions you have set. When the User-Level Security Wizard is finished, a security report is displayed in Print Preview, as shown in Figure 9-10. You will need all this information if you have to rebuild the WIF.

You have three ways to save the document:

- Click **Print** on the Print Preview tab to print a hard copy of the report. Store the printout in a safe place.

- In the Print Preview tab Data group, click one of the export options. The More button provides other options, including saving the report as a Snapshot. Figure 9-11 shows the report saved as a Microsoft Word .rtf file.

- When you close Print Preview, you are asked if you want to save the report as a Snapshot (.snp). Click **Yes**.

Administer a Database

Access provides tools to assist you in managing the size of your database, as well as to repair a database that may have become corrupted. You can also create a printout of your database relationships, database properties, and definitions of your database objects.

Document a Database

If you are working alone on your own database, you probably don't need extensive documentation of the database objects. In a group setting, however, where there is a large information management team, documentation is extremely important. With up-to-date object definitions, errors can be quickly isolated and fixed.

The documentation can include all or a select group of objects in the database.

1. Open the database you want to document.

Figure 9-11: *Saving the security report in an easy-to-retrieve format might save some headaches if you ever need to re-create the workgroup information file.*

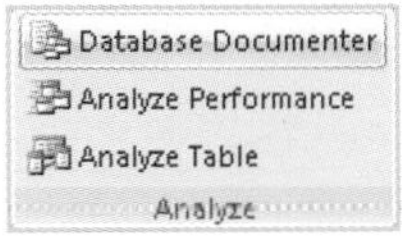

Database Documenter

Analyze Performance

Analyze Table

Analyze

2. In the Database Tools tab Analyze group, click **Database Documenter**. The Documenter opens, as shown in Figure 9-12.

3. Click each object tab, and click the objects you want documented; or click **Select All**.

–Or–

Click the **All Objects Types** tab, and click **Select All**. This includes relationships and the database properties, as well as the definitions of all the database objects.

NOTE

You can export the Documenter's report as a Snapshot, as a Word RTF file, or in another format, such as HTML or PDF (with the optional add-in). Select the relevant option in the Print Preview tab Data group.

4. If you don't need all the information about an object, you can click **Options** and choose how much you want to see. Figure 9-13 shows the choices you have with table documentation. Click **OK**.

5. Click **OK** in the Documenter when you have finished making your selections. The results appear in Print Preview, as shown in Figure 9-14.

6. In the Print Preview tab, click **Print**, or press **CTRL+P**, to open the Print dialog box.

–Or–

TIP

Some definitions can cover many pages. Be sure to check how many before you start to print.

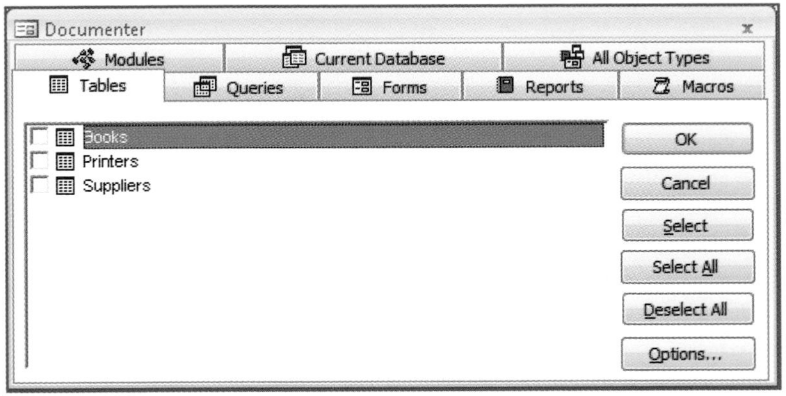

Click **Print** on the Quick Access toolbar to print all pages to your default printer.

See Chapter 8 for more information on printing database objects.

Documenter

| Modules | Current Database | All Object Types |
| Tables | Queries | Forms | Reports | Macros |

- ☐ Books
- ☐ Printers
- ☐ Suppliers

OK
Cancel
Select
Select All
Deselect All
Options...

*Figure 9-12: **You can select just those objects you want documented.***

Print Table Definition

Include for Table
- ☑ Properties
- ☑ Relationships
- ☑ Permissions by User and Group

Include for Fields
- ○ Nothing
- ○ Names, Data Types, and Sizes
- ● Names, Data Types, Sizes, and Properties

Include for Indexes
- ○ Nothing
- ○ Names and Fields
- ● Names, Fields, and Properties

OK
Cancel

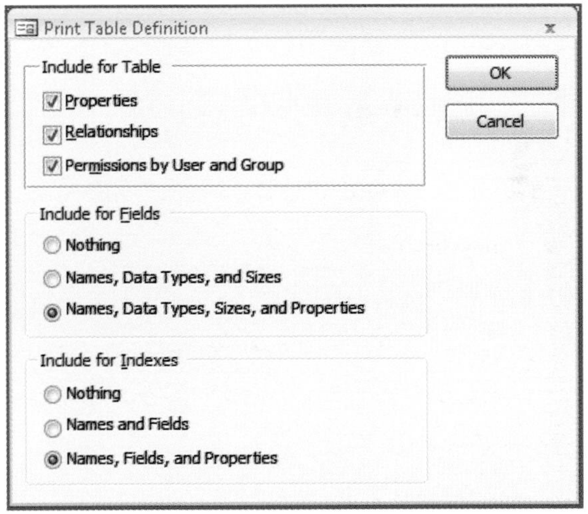

*Figure 9-13: **Choose the table definition items to include in the Documenter's data.***

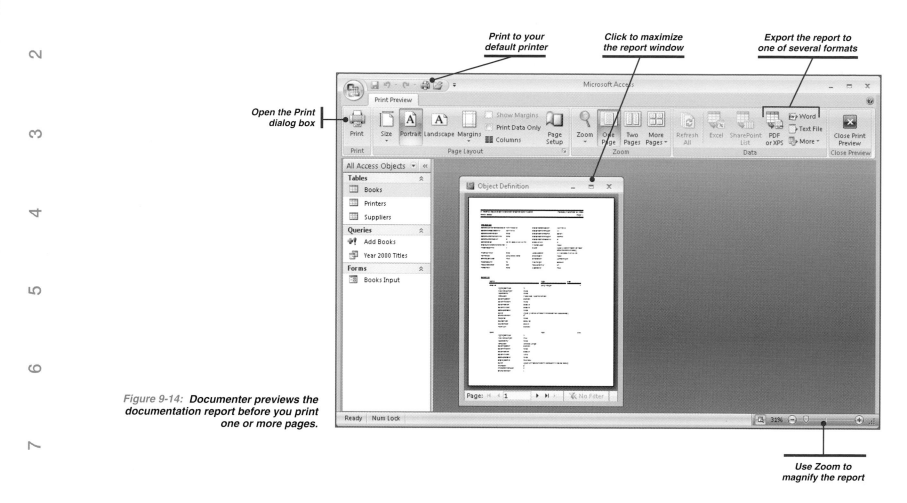

Print to your default printer

Click to maximize the report window

Export the report to one of several formats

Open the Print dialog box

Use Zoom to magnify the report

Figure 9-14: *Documenter previews the documentation report before you print one or more pages.*

Compact and Repair a Database

As you improve and modify your database, the file can become scattered on your hard disk, with empty blocks of space in between. The *Compact And Repair Database* utility removes the empty spaces and rearranges the file more efficiently to improve performance. If there has been some damage, this utility can find the problems and offer to repair them.

QUICK**FACTS**

TROUBLESHOOTING THE COMPACT AND REPAIR DATABASE UTILITY

If the Compact And Repair Database utility doesn't work, one of the following problems may exist:

- The database may be open by another user. Wait for the other user to close the database, and try again.

- There is not enough free space for both the original and the repaired database on the disk. Go back and delete any unnecessary files, and try again.

- You may not have the required Open/Run and Open Exclusive permissions (in a user-level security model).

- The name of the database from an earlier version of Access may include a character that is no longer permitted, such as the grave accent (`). Return to the earlier version of Access, change the name, and then try again.

- The database file may be set to Read Only.

You can start the compact and repair process with the database open or closed.

- Open the database you want to compact and/or repair. Click the **Office Button**, and click **Compact And Repair Database**. No other actions are required.

  –Or–

- If the database is closed, you can compact and repair it to the same file or with a different name in another location by using the Database To Compact From dialog box. From the Getting Started page, click the **Office Button**, and click **Compact And Repair Database**.

Back Up a Database

When working with an important database, it is a good idea to have a backup copy on hand. Creating a backup database on a regular basis can help reduce the risk of losing important data.

Before making a backup copy, make sure that all users have closed their databases so that all changes in the data have been saved.

BACK UP A DATABASE FROM ACCESS

You can use Access to create a regular copy to keep as a backup copy. No compression or other reformatting takes place—you just create a regular database file.

1. Open the database you want to back up.

2. Click the **Office Button**, click **Manage**, and click **Back Up Database**.

3. In the Save As dialog box, if desired, choose the location for the copy, and type a name for it. Click **Save**.

TIP

If yours is a multiuser environment, be sure to back up the workgroup information file, too. See "Secure the Database with the User-Level Security Wizard" earlier in the chapter.

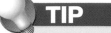

BACK UP INDIVIDUAL DATABASE OBJECTS

If you want to back up only a few objects instead of the whole database:

1. Create a new, empty database.
2. In the External Data tab Import group, click **Access**.

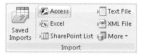

3. Locate and select the database in the Get External Data – Access Database dialog box. Accept the first option, and click **OK**.
4. Click each tab in the Import Objects dialog box, as shown in Figure 9-15, and select the objects you want. See Chapter 4 for more information about importing. Click **OK** to import the objects.
5. Save the new database.

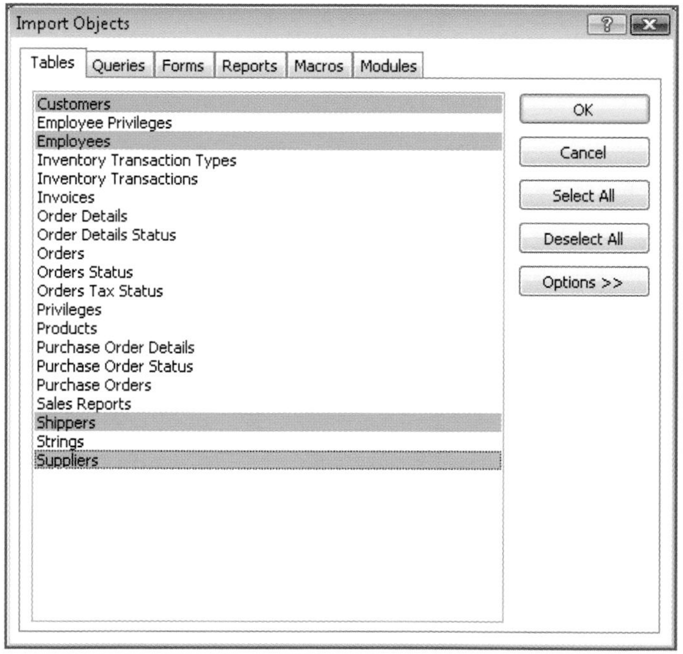

Figure 9-15: ***Back up individual objects by importing them into a new database.***

How to...

- Create a Crosstab Query with a Wizard
- Sorting and Filtering a Crosstab Query
- Create a PivotTable
- Create a PivotChart
- Understanding Drop Zones in PivotTables
- Analyze Database Performance and Design
- Understanding SharePoint
- Merging Data with Microsoft Word
- Export Access Data
- Link Tables
- Add a Hyperlink Field to an Existing Table
- Creating a Hyperlink to a File or Web Page
- Create a Welcome Form

Chapter 10
Extending Access

The final chapter of this book will take you one step deeper into some of the more advanced features of Access. By "extending Access," we mean to extend subjectively features and tools beyond setting up a database, as well as to objectively extend your Access data by sharing it with others. You will analyze data using a Crosstab query, PivotTables, and by letting Access provide a second opinion on your database and table design. In addition, you will learn how to share Access data by merging it with Microsoft Word to create various documents, exporting data to several formats, creating linked tables in your database from tables in other databases, working with hyperlinks, and finally, creating a custom switchboard to guide users when they first open a database you provide to them.

Use Advanced Data Analysis Tools

Access provides both basic and advanced tools to be used when analyzing and presenting data. This chapter will take you through a few of the advanced features, from using a Crosstab query to creating a data access page.

Create a Crosstab Query with a Wizard

A Crosstab query presents information in a slightly different way than do the other queries. (See Chapter 5 for more information on queries.) Rather than displaying the information in a standard datasheet format, the Crosstab query looks more like a spreadsheet, as shown in Figure 10-1. Calculated data and the fields from a table or query that supply the values that, in turn, make up the calculation reside in the grid of the query.

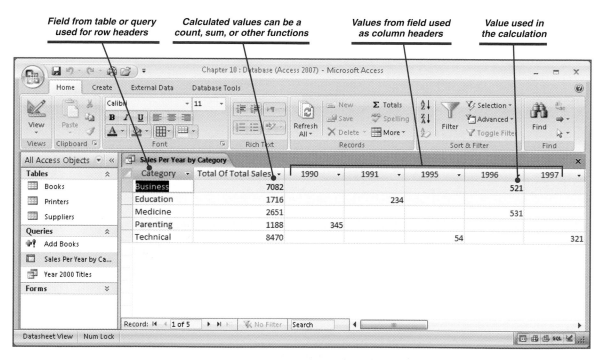

Field from table or query used for row headers

Calculated values can be a count, sum, or other functions

Values from field used as column headers

Value used in the calculation

Figure 10-1: The Crosstab query displays data based on the calculation of values at intersections of rows and fields you select.

TIP

If you use more than one field as a row header, add them to the Selected Fields list in the order you want the data sorted. For example, if you want more detail than shown in Figure 10-1, you would first add the Category field and then the Author field to see a breakdown of sales by author within each category.

Sample:			
Category	Publish Year1	Publish Year2	Publish Year3
Category1	Count(Total Sales)		
Category2			
Category3			
Category4			

NOTE

To include field names from more than one table in a Crosstab query, create a query combining all the field names you need, and then use that query to create a Crosstab query.

1. Open the Navigation Pane in the database in which you want to create the query.

2. In the Create tab Other group, click **Query Wizard**. In the New Query dialog box, click **Crosstab Query Wizard**, and click **OK**.

3. In the first page of the Crosstab Query Wizard, click **Tables**, **Queries**, or **Both** to display the tables and/or queries in the database. Click the table or query where you first want to select the fields that will appear in your query results, and click **Next**.

4. In the next page, shown in Figure 10-2, choose the field(s) you want as row headings (maximum of three fields). Move the field(s) from the Available Fields list to the Selected Fields list. Double-click the fields you want or use the select/remove buttons between the two list boxes to add or remove fields. Click **Next**.

5. On the third page in the Crosstab Query Wizard, you select the field whose values you would like displayed as column headers (see Figure 10-1). Click the field you want, and it's added to the Sample area. Click **Next**.

6. Click the field that you would like to make a calculated value. Click the function with which you would like to calculate the value. Click the **Yes, Include Row Sums** check box to display the row calculations. The Sample area shows your selections. Click **Next**.

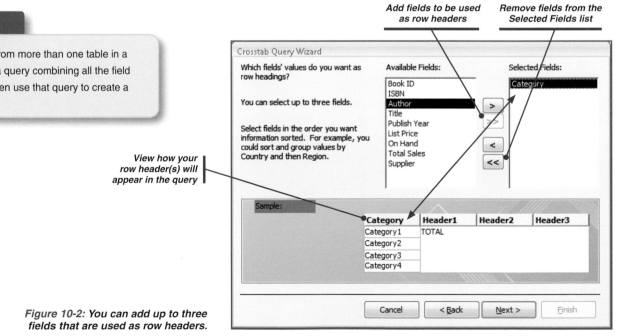

Add fields to be used as row headers

Remove fields from the Selected Fields list

View how your row header(s) will appear in the query

Figure 10-2: You can add up to three fields that are used as row headers.

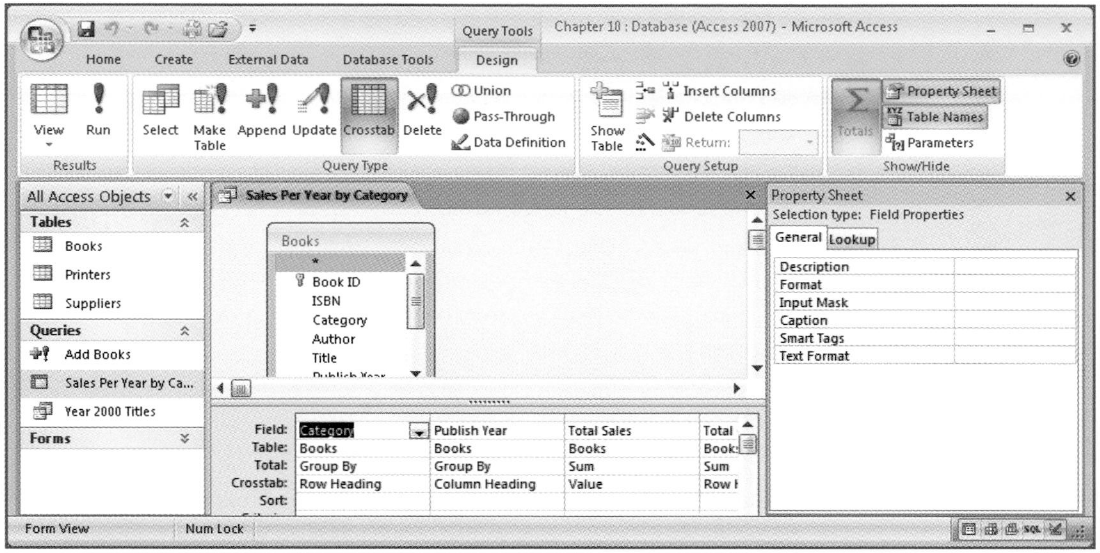

Figure 10-3: *Design View of a Crosstab query looks and behaves similar to the queries described in early chapters.*

7. In the final page of the wizard, accept the default query name or type a title/name for the query. Choose whether to view (run) the query as is or to modify its design. Click **Finish** when done. Depending on your choice, the new Crosstab query will be displayed as a datasheet with the fields you selected earlier in the wizard, shown in Figure 10-1.

–Or–

The Crosstab query will open in Design View, ready for adding criteria and other changes, shown in Figure 10-3.

In either case, the new query will be listed under Queries in the Navigation Pane.

Create a PivotTable

PivotTables allow you to present your data in an easily understood format. You can dynamically change the layout of a PivotTable to analyze data in different ways. You can move row headings, column headings, and page fields until you achieve the desired layout. Each time you change the layout, the PivotTable immediately recalculates the data based on the new design.

1. Open the database that contains the table or query for which you want to create the PivotTable.

2. In the Navigation Pane, open the table or query you want to use as the basis for the PivotTable.

3. In the Home tab Views group, click the **View** down arrow, and click **PivotTable View**.

–Or–

To save the PivotTable as a form, in the Create tab Forms group, click **More Forms** and click **PivotTable**.

QUICKSTEPS

SORTING AND FILTERING A CROSSTAB QUERY

Setting up the Crosstab query is only the beginning of what you can do to retrieve information from the query. You can apply filters and sort columns by using the AutoFilter down arrows in column headers and/or a column's context menu (see Chapter 5 for more information on retrieving information from a datasheet by sorting and filtering).

SORT CROSSTAB QUERY COLUMNS

1. Click the **AutoFilter** down arrow ▾ in the column header whose column contains the values by which you want to sort the query.

Continued . . .

QUICKSTEPS

SORTING AND FILTERING A CROSSTAB QUERY *(Continued)*

–Or–

Right-click a cell in the column that contains the values by which you want to sort the query.

2. Click the ascending ↑↓ or descending ↓↑ sort buttons at the top of the menu. The sort options are tuned to the data type of the column. For example, Number data type columns are sorted between smallest and largest. Text data type columns are sorted alphabetically between A and Z.

FILTER A CROSSTAB QUERY USING AUTOFILTER

Filters allow you to temporarily display only records that contain one or more values you select in a column.

1. Click the **AutoFilter** down arrow in the column header whose column contains the values by which you want to filter the query.

2. Click the check boxes for the values that are contained in the records you want to display, and click **OK**.

–Or–

Click *Data Type* **Filters** (where *Data Type* is the data type of the column), click a pre-built criteria, type the value(s) and any operators (such as AND or OR) you want, and click **OK**.

Continued . . .

In either case, a new object is created and displays a PivotTable layout area with *drop zones* and a supporting Design tab (PivotTable Tools), as shown in Figure 10-4.

4. Display the PivotTable Field list, if it is not shown (in the Design tab Show/Hide group, click **Field List**).

5. Drag a field from the PivotTable Field list to one of the drop zones (see the "Understanding Drop Zones in PivotTables" QuickFacts).

–Or–

Fields are added to drop zones according to what you want them to do

Contextual Design tab provides supporting PivotTable tools

Move fields from the Field list to a drop zone

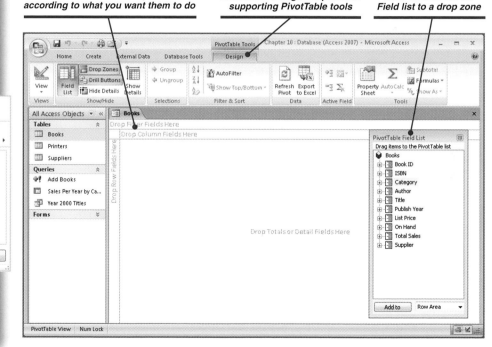

Figure 10-4: Data within the PivotTable can be pivoted to provide new analysis opportunities.

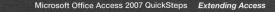

QUICKSTEPS

SORTING AND FILTERING A CROSSTAB QUERY *(Continued)*

FILTER A CROSSTAB QUERY USING A CONTEXT MENU

- Right-click a value in the column you want to filter by, and click one of the criteria listed at the bottom of the menu.

  –Or–

- Click *Data Type* **Filters** (where *Data Type* is the data type of the column), click a pre-built criteria, type the value(s) and any operators (such as AND or OR) you want, and click **OK**.

REMOVE AND REAPPLY FILTERS

Filtered Crosstab queries are identified by a filtering icon in the column header and on the navigation bar:

- To temporarily remove a filter, click the **Filtered** button ▼ Filtered on the navigation bar. The button is renamed "Unfiltered."

- To reapply the filter, click the **Unfiltered** button on the navigation bar. The button is renamed "Filtered."

- To permanently remove a filter, click the **AutoFilter** down arrow of the filtered column, and click **Clear Filter From** *Field Name*.

TIP

Don't hesitate to experiment with the PivotTable layout. You are not affecting any underlying data. Also, you can easily remove any fields you place in a drop zone. To remove a field from the PivotTable layout area, drag the field header from the drop zone it is currently in to an area outside the layout area.

Select the field in the Field list, click the down arrow in the lower-right corner of the Field list, click where you want the field added, and click **Add To** (see Figure 10-5).

6. To move a field from one drop zone to another, drag its header into the new drop zone.

   –Or–

   Select the new drop zone in the Field list, and click **Add To**.

7. Repeat steps 5 and 6 to create the layout that displays the information you want. You can drop more than one field in a drop zone and easily reverse any action you take. Figure 10-6 shows an example of how you can quickly view several key aspects of data (in this case, sales by year, sales by category, and sales by author are sorted, filtered, and subtotaled).

Create a PivotChart

PivotCharts provide the same ability to dynamically change data as do PivotTables, but in a chart format. The creation method is just as simple as for PivotTables.

1. Open the table or query in the database for which you want to create the PivotChart.

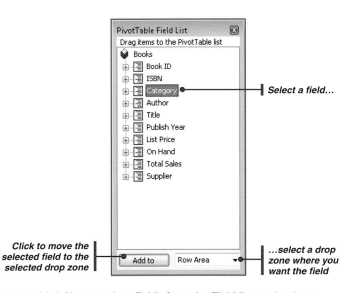

Select a field...

Click to move the selected field to the selected drop zone

...select a drop zone where you want the field

Figure 10-5: You can drag fields from the Field list to the drop zones, or select fields and use the controls to place them.

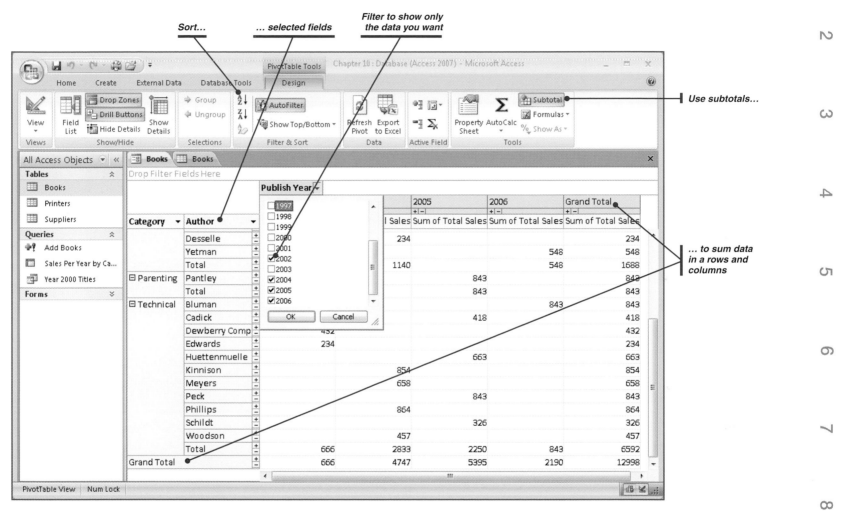

Figure 10-6: *You can quickly glean information from your data by pivoting fields and sorting and filtering the results.*

2. In the Home tab Views group, click the **View** down arrow, and click **PivotChart View**.

–Or–

Click **PivotTable View** in the Views area of the status bar.

In either case, the PivotChart layout area will be displayed, as shown in Figure 10-7, with a Field list containing all the fields from the chosen table or query.

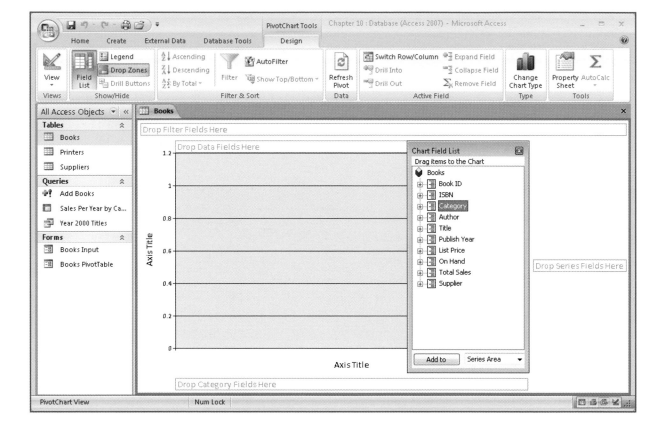

Figure 10-7: PivotCharts utilize a similar Design tab to provide associated tools and a methodology to move fields from the Field list to drop zones on the layout.

3. Drag items from the PivotChart Field list to the applicable chart areas on the PivotChart layout to build the chart. Use the chart tools to filter data, add a legend, remove PivotChart elements, and add titles, as shown in Figure 10-8. Pivot the different values to analyze your data from a visual standpoint.

4. Right-click the **PivotTable** tab, and click **Close**. In the dialog box, click **Yes** to save the layout. To view the PivotChart again, select the table or query it's based on, and switch to PivotChart View.

QUICKFACTS

UNDERSTANDING DROP ZONES IN PIVOTTABLES

A PivotTable layout consists of several drop zones, where you place fields to give alternate views of your data. You "pivot" the data by moving fields from one zone to another:

- **Drop Row Fields Here** allows you to display each category of that item in its own row. Typically, these items are descriptive and identifying, not numerical—for example, Country, Salesperson, and Title.

- **Drop Column Fields Here** allows you to display each category of the item in its own column. Typically, these items are descriptive and identifying, not numerical—for example, Category or Product Name.

- **Drop Totals Or Detail Fields Here** allows you to sum or otherwise perform calculations and display the results. Typically, these items are numerical and capable of being counted, summed, and calculated.

- **Drop Filter Fields Here** allows you to filter the view to a particular part of the data. For example, if your PivotTable displays information regarding your product line, you can place the field named Categories in the Drop Filter Fields Here area to display only the product line within selected categories.

NOTE

More information on PivotCharts and on charting in general is offered in *Microsoft Office Excel 2007 QuickSteps*, published by McGraw-Hill/Osborne.

Analyze Database Performance and Design

After you create a database and set up tables and other objects, you're probably wondering if there weren't things you could have done differently to be more efficient. One solution is to hire a database administrator to look over your design. A faster and cheaper method is to let Access take a crack at it. There are two tools you can use: one will take a look at any objects in your database that you select; the other is specific to tables.

USE THE PERFORMANCE ANALYZER

1. Open the database whose performance you want Access to check.

2. In the Database Tools tab Analyze group, click **Analyze Performance**.

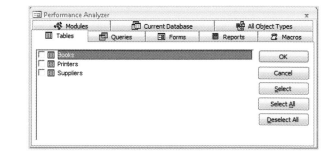

3. In the Performance Analyzer, use the object tabs to select the objects you want Access to check.

   –Or–

   Click **Select All** to check all objects in the database.

   In either case, click **OK** when finished. If Access detects any issues, it returns a report, similar to that shown in Figure 10-9, with varying degrees of recommendations.

4. If the recommendations won't affect underlying data, select the ones you want to change, and click **Optimize**. If the recommendations might cause potential loss of data, you will have to manually employ it. Click **Close** when finished.

Hide drop zones and the Field list
to better display your PivotChart

Add a legend to label
your data series

Change the chart type to something
more suited to your audience

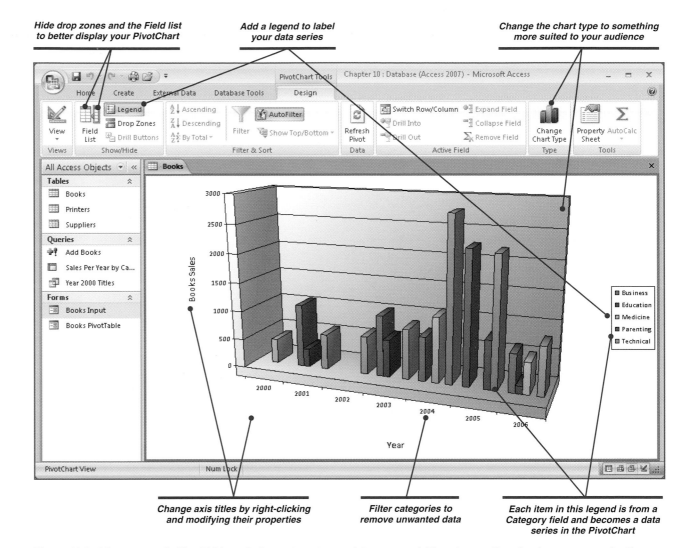

Change axis titles by right-clicking
and modifying their properties

Filter categories to
remove unwanted data

Each item in this legend is from a
Category field and becomes a data
series in the PivotChart

Figure 10-8: After you apply PivotTable techniques to get your data arranged, it's only a matter of using common charting tools to bring a PivotChart to life.

Figure 10-9: *Access provides a "second opinion" on your design for the database objects you select.*

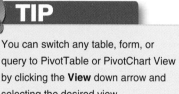
CHECK TABLES FOR DUPLICATE DATA

The Table Analyzer Wizard looks at a table and determines whether your table can be divided into two or more related tables and your data parsed to avoid repeating data (and thereby making searches and other database actions more efficient). For example, if you have a table that stores ordering and customer information, you wind up repeating information for each customer, such as name, address, and phone numbers, in repeat orders. The Table Analyzer Wizard might recommend that you create a Customer table and an Order table and then relate the two based on a generated unique primary key (and assist you along the way to perform the actions).

1. Open the database whose data you want Access to check.

2. In the Database Tools tab Analyze group, click **Analyze Table**. The first two pages in the wizard explain the problem created by duplicated data and provide examples (Figure 10-10 shows the first one). Click **Next** after reading through each page.

QUICKFACTS

UNDERSTANDING SHAREPOINT

Access 2007 integrates tightly with Office SharePoint Server 2007 (the server-based product on which the latest version of SharePoint sites are created) to promote data sharing and linking. SharePoint sites provide an interactive way for users to use Access data and objects using a Web browser, as well as to connect through Access 2007.

While setting up a SharePoint site is beyond the scope of this book, if you have access to such a site, you can use Access 2007 to great advantage, including:

- Move a database to SharePoint, creating lists from your tables where users can work with the lists on SharePoint or create linked tables on their local version of Access.

- Import data from a SharePoint list into an Access 2007 database.

- Export Access 2007 tables and queries to a SharePoint list.

- Export tables and queries to SharePoint lists.

The External Data tab SharePoint Lists group contains the first step in the process of moving data to a SharePoint site and the tools to keep the data up-to-date.

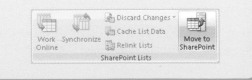

Figure 10-10: *The Table Analyzer Wizard starts by informing you of the problem duplicate data creates and lets you know how it will try and fix your table.*

3. In the third page, click the table you want to Access to split into additional tables, and click **Next**.

4. In the fourth, and subsequent, pages, let Access decide how to split the table (you will have final decision-making authority). You will have the opportunity to rename proposed tables (see Figure 10-11), select primary keys, correct any errors Access finds, and have Access create a query for you based on the new related tables.

Share Data

Sharing data is an essential element of any workplace environment. This section will take you through exporting and linking Access data to a variety of applications. In addition, the Internet has done a great job of connecting people and information. Access taps into Web technology in a variety of ways.

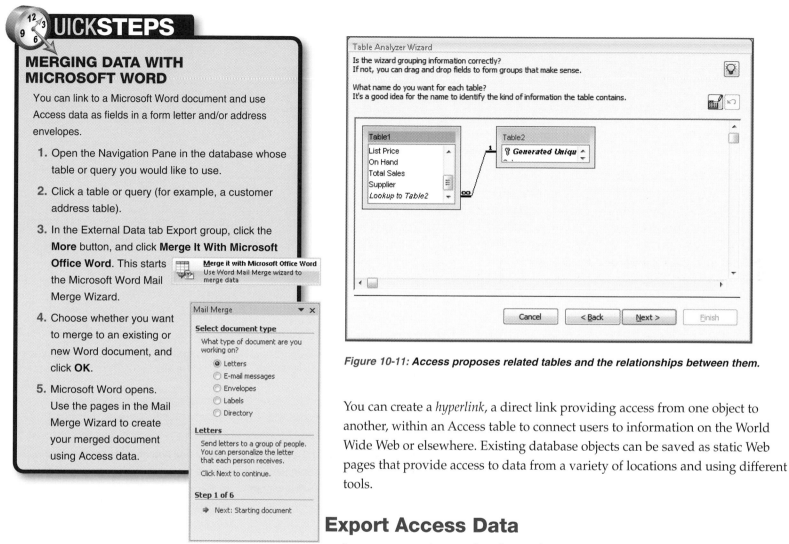

QUICKSTEPS

MERGING DATA WITH MICROSOFT WORD

You can link to a Microsoft Word document and use Access data as fields in a form letter and/or address envelopes.

1. Open the Navigation Pane in the database whose table or query you would like to use.

2. Click a table or query (for example, a customer address table).

3. In the External Data tab Export group, click the **More** button, and click **Merge It With Microsoft Office Word**. This starts the Microsoft Word Mail Merge Wizard.

> **Merge it with Microsoft Office Word**
> Use Word Mail Merge wizard to merge data

4. Choose whether you want to merge to an existing or new Word document, and click **OK**.

5. Microsoft Word opens. Use the pages in the Mail Merge Wizard to create your merged document using Access data.

Mail Merge

Select document type

What type of document are you working on?

- ● Letters
- ○ E-mail messages
- ○ Envelopes
- ○ Labels
- ○ Directory

Letters

Send letters to a group of people. You can personalize the letter that each person receives.

Click Next to continue.

Step 1 of 6

➡ Next: Starting document

Figure 10-11: Access proposes related tables and the relationships between them.

You can create a *hyperlink*, a direct link providing access from one object to another, within an Access table to connect users to information on the World Wide Web or elsewhere. Existing database objects can be saved as static Web pages that provide access to data from a variety of locations and using different tools.

Export Access Data

Just as you can import data from other programs (see Chapter 4), you can export Access objects to a variety of other data formats.

1. Open the Navigation Pane in the database whose objects you would like to export.

2. Click the table, query, form, or report you would like to export. If you want to export specific records, open the object and select the records you want to export.

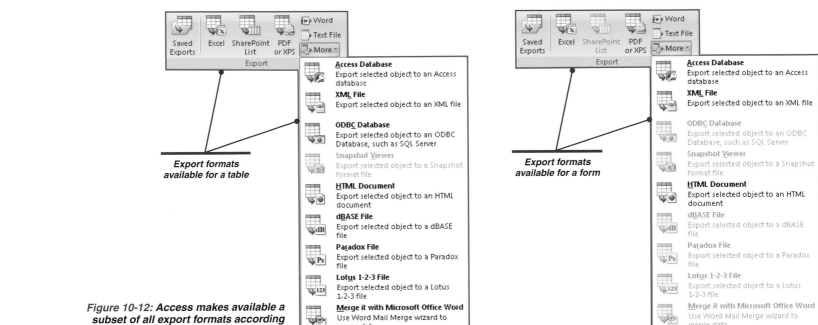

Export formats
available for a table

Export formats
available for a form

Figure 10-12: Access makes available a
subset of all export formats according
to the object that is selected or opened.

TIP

The quickest way to publish some or all of your database objects to a Web page is to export your data as an *HTML* (Hypertext Markup Language) file. While this type of file presents a static view of your data, it can be easily posted to a Web site. To provide enhanced functionality to your data, export your data to a SharePoint list. See the "Understanding SharePoint" QuickFacts later in the chapter.

3. In the External Data tab Export group, the export options that are available for the object you selected will be available. Click the **More** button to see additional options. Figure 10-12 shows the export formats that are available for tables.

4. Click the export format you want. An Export dialog box appears, similar to that shown in Figure 10-13, that's tuned to the particular export format you have selected. Locate and name the files, and select any of the available options. Click **OK**.

5. When the export is finished, you can save the steps you used for a quick way to repeat the export and create an Outlook task to remind you to repeat the export. Click the **Save Export Steps** check box, name the export, and click **Create Outlook Task**. Click **Save Export** when finished. If you chose to create a task, a new task is created, as shown in Figure 10-14.

6. To view the exported file, go to the location where you saved the file, and open it in the format's corresponding application.

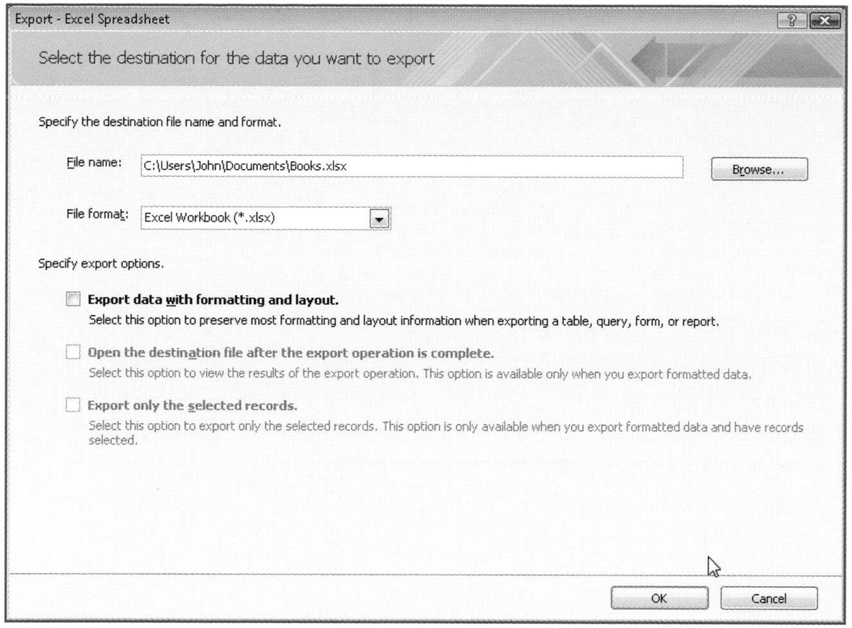

Export - Excel Spreadsheet

Select the destination for the data you want to export

Specify the destination file name and format.

File name: C:\Users\John\Documents\Books.xlsx [Browse...]

File format: Excel Workbook (*.xlsx)

Specify export options.

☐ **Export data with formatting and layout.**
Select this option to preserve most formatting and layout information when exporting a table, query, form, or report.

☐ Open the destination file after the export operation is complete.
Select this option to view the results of the export operation. This option is available only when you export formatted data.

☐ Export only the selected records.
Select this option to export only the selected records. This option is only available when you export formatted data and have records selected.

[OK] [Cancel]

*Figure 10-13: **Exporting an object is simply a matter of telling Access where you want the new file located and then selecting options specific to the export format.***

Link Tables

Access can *link*, or connect, data in multiple Access databases, as well as between Access databases and other applications. It doesn't matter whether that data resides on your computer or on a network.

1. Open the database in which you would like to import one or more linked tables.

2. In the External Data tab Import group, click **Access** (or another database format). In the Get External Data dialog box, browse to the location of the database file (not applicable if you're connected to an Open Database

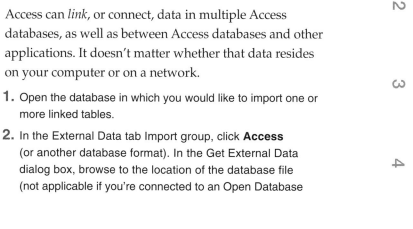

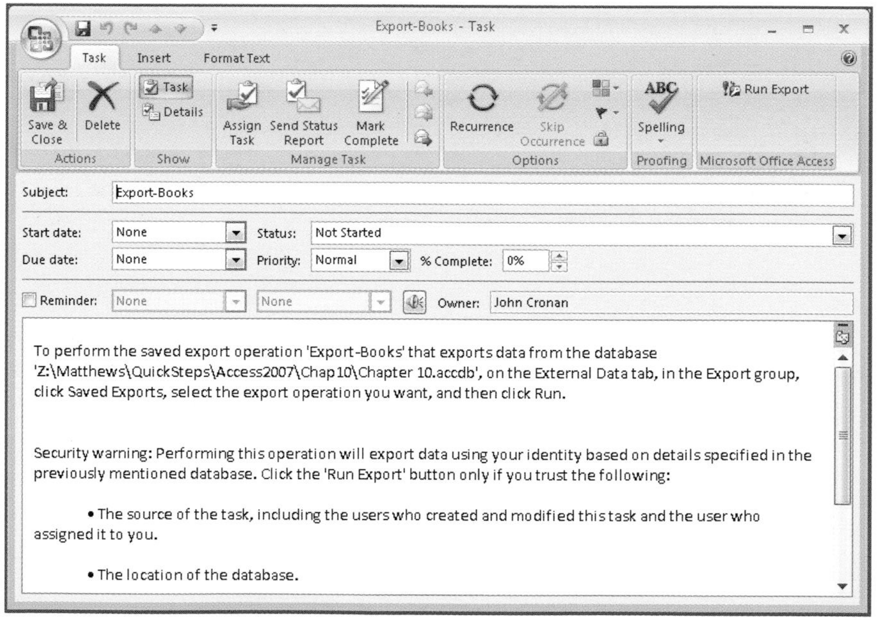

*Figure 10-14: **An Outlook task is created to remind you of the particulars of a saved export.***

10

Connectivity—ODBC—database), and click **Link To The Data Source By Creating A Linked Table**. Click **OK**.

> Specify the source of the data.
>
> File name: C:\Users\John\Documents\Issues.accdb   [Browse...]
>
> Specify how and where you want to store the data in the current database.
>
> ○ **Import tables, queries, forms, reports, macros, and modules into the current database.**
> If the specified object does not exist, Access will create it. If the specified object already exists, Access will append a number to the name of the imported object. Changes made to source objects (including data in tables) will not be reflected in the current database.
>
> ⦿ **Link to the data source by creating a linked table.**
> Access will create a table that will maintain a link to the source data. Changes made to the data in Access will be reflected in the source and vice versa. NOTE: If the source database requires a password, the password will be stored with the linked table.

3. In the Link Tables dialog box, select the table(s) you want to link to, and click **OK**. Each table is listed in the Navigation Pane and identified with a cross icon.

> All Access Objects ▼ «
> **Tables** ⌃
>   Books
>   Printers
>   Suppliers
>   Switchboard Items
> ⁺ **Customers**
> **Queries** ⌄
> **Forms** ⌄

Add a Hyperlink Field to an Existing Table

To create a hyperlink within a table, you need to establish the field data type as a hyperlink. A hyperlink data type lets you store simple or complex links to files or documents outside your database. The "pointer" can contain a Uniform Resource Locator (URL) that points to a location on the World Wide Web or to a place on a local intranet. It can also use a file address to provide access to a file on your computer or on a server in your network.

1. In the database that will hold your newly created hyperlink(s), open the table in Datasheet View.

CREATING A HYPERLINK TO A FILE OR WEB PAGE

Placing a hyperlink in a form or report is a great way to connect data from files or the Internet to the information displayed in your form or report.

1. Open your form or report in Design View.

2. In the Design tab Controls group, click **Insert Hyperlink** 🖳. The Insert Hyperlink dialog box appears, as shown in Figure 10-15.

3. In the Link To column, click **Existing File** or **Web Page**. Click either the **Browse Web** or the **Browse File** button to find the web page or file, respectively, to which you would like to link.

4. Type the text you would like displayed to represent the hyperlink in the Text To Display text box. Click **OK**. You will return to Design View. Drag your new hyperlink control to the appropriate location within the form or report.

2. Double-click the **Add New Field** column header at the rightmost end of the table, type a name for your new hyperlink field name, and press ENTER.

3. In the Datasheet tab (Table Tools) Data Type & Formatting group, click the **Data Type** down arrow, and click **Hyperlink**. Right-click the table name tab, and click **Save**. Data typed into the new field will be underlined and ready to search for the hyperlinked location.

Create a Welcome Form

When you create a database intended to be used by less experienced Access users, you can create a Welcome form (or *switchboard*) that opens first when the database is opened and clearly offers a choice of activities. The user can click a button to open a form, preview a report, or perform nearly any action. Figure 10-16 shows an example of a Welcome form.

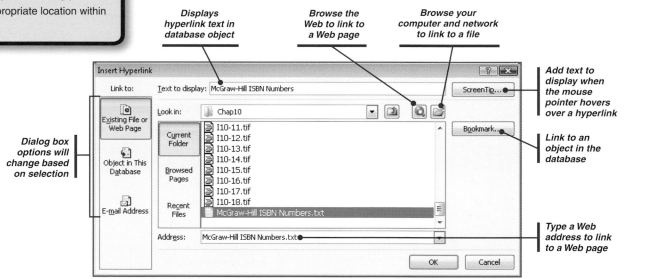

Figure 10-15: *The Insert Hyperlink dialog box provides a means to link to data residing at various locations.*

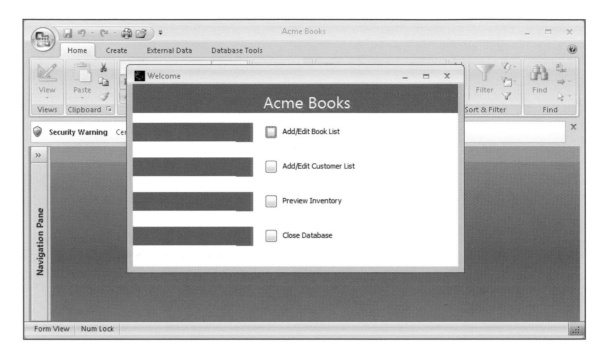

*Figure 10-16: **The Switchboard Manager, with the help of a few property changes, lets you greet users with a professional Welcome form.***

SET UP THE SWITCHBOARD

1. Open the database in which you want a Welcome form.

2. In the Database Tools tab Database Tools group, click **Switchboard Manager**. If you haven't created a switchboard yet, click **Yes** to create one.

3. In the Switchboard Manager, click **Edit** to create your first items on the default switchboard page.

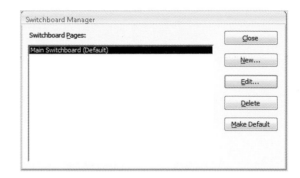

4. In the Edit Switchboard Page dialog box, type a name for the form title, and click **New** to add an item.

5. In the Edit Switchboard Item dialog box, click the **Command** down arrow, and click the action for the item. (Depending on your choice, you might need to select additional information, such as the form or report you want to open.) In the Text box, type the text that will appear to the user. Click **OK**.

Edit Switchboard Item		
Text:	Add/Edit Book List	OK
Command:	Open Form in Add Mode ▾	Cancel
Form:	Books Input ▾	

6. Repeat steps 4 and 5 to add additional items to the switchboard. Click the **Move Up** and **Move Down** buttons in the Edit Switchboard Page dialog box to place the items in the order you want. Click **Close** when finished. Click **Close** a second time to close the Switchboard Manager.

SET FORM PROPERTIES

In order for the switchboard to behave as a pop-up form, you need to set the properties.

1. In the Navigation Pane, right-click **Switchboard** (listed under Forms), and click **Design View**.

2. Display the Property Sheet (in the Design tab Tools group, click **Property Sheet**), ensure that **Form** is the selection type, and click the **Format** tab.

3. Click in the **Caption** text box, and type <u>Welcome</u>.

4. Click the **Other** tab, click the **Pop Up** down arrow, and click **Yes**.

5. Set any other properties you want to change. Right-click the form name tab, and click **Save**.

6. Click the **Office Button**, click **Access Options**, and click the **Current Database** option. Under Application Options:

- Click the **Application Title** text box, and type the name you want users to see.

- Click **Browse** next to the Application Icon text box, and locate an icon file (.ico) or bitmap (.bmp) to display on your switchboard.

- Click the **Use As Form And Report Icon** check box.

- Click the **Display Form** down arrow, and click **Switchboard**.

7. Click **OK** when finished. Click **OK** again to acknowledge that you must close and reopen the database. The form will appear on top of the Access window (see Figure 10-16).

10

A

.accdb file extension, 2, 12
Access 95, 11–13
Access 97, 11–13
Acquiring data, 78–88
Administration, 183–200
  of databases, 196–200
Advanced filters, 105–106
ALT+F4, 18
Arithmetic operators, 103–104
Attachments
  as data type, 37
  data type restrictions on, 51
AutoCorrect, 78
AutoFilter, 206
AutoFormat, 172–173
AutoNumber
  as changed data type, 51
  as data type, 37

B

Back and Forward, in Help search, 24
Backup, of databases, 199–200
Backup operators, security for, 192
Blank columns, 89
Blank Form tool, 123–124
Blank Report tool, 149
Bottom values, 114
Bound controls, 130
Bound objects, 163
Browse
  of folders, 29
  in Help, 22

C

Calculated controls, 130,
  132–133
Calculating data, 74
Calculating values, 157

Caption field property, 58
Cascade, 21
Cells, 33
Certificates, 185–188
Change Font Size, 24
Characters
  copy of, 72
  moving, 72
Chart Wizard, 164, 167
Charts. See also PivotChart
  from Excel, 164–168
Clipboard, 71
Closing
  of databases, 23, 32
  of queries, 111–112
  of tables, 34
Colors, in Datasheet View, 93–94
Column(s)
  deletion of, 73–74
  insertion of, 89–90
  locking and unlocking, 93
  moving, 91–93
  renaming, 91–93
  sorting in, 66
Column width, 90–91
  defaults for, 91
Columnar printing settings, 176
Combo Box Wizard, 130–132
Command buttons, 135
Compact And Repair Database
  utility, 198–199
Compacting, of databases, 198–199
Comparison operators, 103–104
Compatibility, of files, 12–13
Conditional formatting, 163–164
Context menu, 205
  to switch views, 49
Contextual tabs, 8
Control layouts, 139
Controls, 115–142
  copy of, 136
  deletion of, 137

list of, 131
rearranging, 138–139
selection of, 137–138
types of, 130
Conversion
  of Access versions, 11
  errors during, 13
  of open older databases, 14
  Save As with, 13
  security with, 14
Copy
  of characters, 72
  of controls, 136
  of data, 70–73
  of fields, 72
  of records, 73
Crosstab queries, 202–204
  filtering of, 204–206
  sorting of, 204–206
CTRL+C, 18
CTRL+F4, 18
CTRL+O, 18
Currency
  as changed data type, 51
  as data type, 37
Custom dictionaries, 77

D

Data
  acquiring, 78–88
  calculation of, 74
  copy of, 70–73
  duplication of, 34, 211–212
  editing, 67–78
  entering, 67–78
  export of, 213–215
  filtering of, 98–106
  import of, 79–84
  indexing of, 59
  moving, 70–73
  presentation of, 161–181

printing, 175–181
  in reports, 153
  required entry of, 57–58
  sharing, 212–213
  shortcut editing of, 69
  sorting, 95–98
  in tables, 67–88
Data entry form, 142
Data types, 36–37
  attachments as, 37, 51
  AutoNumber as, 37, 51
  changing, 49–50
  currency as, 37, 51
  date/time as, 37, 51
  filter for, 101
  hyperlink as, 37, 51
  import and, 84
  input masks and, 55
  Lookup Wizard as, 37
  memo as, 37, 51
  number as, 37, 51
  OLE object as, 37, 51
  restrictions on, 51
  Yes/No as, 37, 51
Databases
  administration of, 196–200
  backup of, 199–200
  building, 32
  closing, 32
  compacting of, 198–199
  creation of, 25–44
  design of, 26–32
  documentation of, 196–198
  extracting, 187
  identifying information for,
    40–41
  performance analysis of,
    209–212
  planning of, 26–27
  relational, 41
  renaming of, 47
  repair of, 198–199

Databases (*cont.*)
  security for, 184–196
  templates for, 26–31
Datasheet View, 33
  changing data type in, 49
  colors in, 93–94
  defaults for, 92
  filter in, 99
  find data in, 74
  fine-tuning fields in, 48
  multivalue lookup fields and, 64
  switching to, 48–49
  tables and, 66
Date, as Smart Tag, 59
Date/time
  as changed data type, 51
  as data type, 37
  defaults for, 129
  on forms, 127, 129
  in reports, 159
dBase, 80
Defaults
  for column width, 91
  for Datasheet View, 92
  for date/time, 129
  in field values, 57
  in file formats, 14
  with Help window, 22
  for opened databases, 188
  with templates, 29
  text as, 36, 38
Deletion
  of columns, 73–74
  of controls, 137
  of records, 73
  of tables, 46–47
Design, of databases, 26–32
Design area, 110
Design View, 33, 170
  changing data type in, 50
  of crosstab query, 204
  fine-tuning fields in, 48

for forms, 120, 124–126
Lookup Wizard and, 60
Navigation Pane in, 50
for queries, 109
queries in, 108–111
for reports, 144–145, 146,
  149–151
switching to, 48–49
tables in, 35–37
Dictionaries, 77
Digital signature, 186–187
Documentation, of databases,
  196–198
Documents
  recent, 8
  tabs for, 8, 18–20
Documents folder, 29
Drop zones, 209
Duplication, of data,
  34, 211–212

E

E-mail
  forms with, 13
  import from, 85–88
  management of, 88–89
Empty cells, filter by, 101
Empty tables, 35
Encryption, 185, 188–189
Enforce Referential Integrity,
  43–44
Errors, during conversion, 13
Excel, 6
  charts from, 164–167
  import from, 80
Exclusion, filter by, 102
Exit Access, 24
Export, 213–215
Expression Builder, 103, 107,
  112–113

Expressions
  in groups, 156
  in validation rules, 56
Extend mode, 68
Extracting databases, 187

F

F1, for Help, 22
Field(s), 33
  captions for, 58
  copy of, 72
  defaults in, 55–56
  field list and, 126
  fine-tuning of, 48–64
  indexing of, 59
  limited values in, 56–57
  modifying, 45–64
  moving, 72
  multivalued, 63–64
  selecting records, fields, and
    columns with, 72–73
Field list, 126
Field names
  changing, 48
  in tables, 34
Field Properties, 51, 52
File(s)
  compatibility of, 12–13
  hyperlinks to, 217
  text, 80–82
  XML, 80
File formats, defaults in, 14
File types, 7
Filters
  advanced, 105–106
  clearing, 104–105
  of crosstab queries,
    204–206
  of data, 98–106
  for data types, 101
  by empty cells, 101

by exclusion, 102
by forms, 102
in help search, 22
for input, 101
operators in, 102–104
as queries, 98
reapplying, 104–105, 206
removing, 104–105, 206
by selection, 99–101
wildcards in, 102–104
Financial symbol, as Smart Tag, 60
Find, for databases, 14–15
Find and replace, 74–75
Font group commands, 152
Foreign keys, 41
Form(s)
  creation of, 115–142
  data entry, 142
  date/time on, 127, 129
  with e-mail, 13
  filter by, 102
  with multiple records, 119–120
  multiple-table, 123
  as objects, 10
  for outgoing Outlook messages, 87
  page numbers on, 127, 129
  preventing data changes in, 191
  sorting in, 97–98
  title on, 127–128
Form properties, 170–171
Form tool, 116, 117
Form View, 116, 123
  filter in, 99
Form Wizard, 120–122
Format symbols, 51–52
Formatting
  automatic, 172
  conditional, 163–164
  predefined, 172–173
  of reports, 151–152
  rich text, 173–174
  rules for, 171

Formatting reports, 151–152
Forward-compatibility, 12
Framework, of tables, 33–41
Freeze Columns, 93
Full data users, security for, 192
Full permission users, 193

G

Gallery, 6
Get External dialog box, 79
Getting Started page, templates
   and, 28
Graphics, 168–170
Grid, 110–111
Gridlines, 94
Group(s), 10
Group accounts, 192, 193–194
   users in, 195–196
Group headers and footers, 158
Group levels, 147–148
   sort in, 156
Group, Sort, And Total pane, 153–156

H

Headers and footers, for
   groups, 158
Help, 8, 21–23
   browse in, 22
   F1 for, 22
   Icon for, 22
   with internet, 21
   opening, 22
   Search in, 22
   Tools in, 23
Help search
   Back and Forward in, 23
   filters in, 22
   Home in, 23
   Keep On Top in, 23

Print in, 23
Refresh in, 23
Show/Hide Table of Contents in, 23
Stop in, 23
Help window, 23
   defaults with, 22
Hide, columns, 92–93
Home, in Help search, 23
HTML. See Hypertext Markup
   Language
Hyperlinks, 213, 216–217
   as changed data type, 51
   as data type, 37
Hypertext Markup Language
   (HTML), 174, 214

I

Icons
   for Help, 22
   for Print, 175
   for shortcuts, 19
   for templates, 29
Identifying information
   for databases, 40–41
   search using, 41
Image(s), modifying, 162
Image controls, 135–136
Image formats, 162
Image properties, 162
Import
   of data, 79–84
   data types and, 84
   from e-mail, 85–88
   from Excel, 80
   of objects, 83–84
   from Outlook, 80, 85–88
   from Paradox, 80
   from SharePoint, 80
   from spreadsheets, 82–83
   of tables, 83–84

from text files, 80–82
from web pages, 80
from XML files, 80
Import Spreadsheet Wizard, 82
Indexing, of data fields, 59
Innermost field, 96
Input, filter for, 101
Input Mask Wizard, 55–56
Input masks
   customized, 55–56
   data entry in, 54–55
   data types and, 55
   placeholders in, 55
   symbols for, 54
Insertion
   of columns, 89–90
   with shortcuts, 69
Internet
   help with, 21

J

Junction tables, 42

K

Keep On Top, 23
   in Help search, 23
Keyboard, 18
   navigation with, 68
   opening with, 3
   for selecting data, 69–70

L

Label Wizard, 159–160
Labels, 159–160
Landscape, 175
Language options, 77
Layout View, 122

Limited field values, 56–57
   for security, 190
Lines, 168–169
Link tables, 215–216
Live Search, 30
Locking columns, 93
Logical operators, 103–104
Lookup columns, 89–90
Lookup fields, 13
Lookup list, 62–63
Lookup values, 61
Lookup Wizard, 60–64, 90
   as data type, 37
Lotus 1-2-3, 80

M

Macros, as objects, 10
Many-to-many relationship, 42
Margins, 176
.mdb file extension, 2, 12
Memo
   as changed data type, 51
   as data type, 37
Microsoft Office Online, 30
   Smart Tags on, 59
Microsoft Word, 213
Modifying controls, 140–142
Modifying reports, 151–160
Modules, as objects, 10
Mouse
   and ribbon, 48
   selection with, 72–73
Moving characters, 72
Moving columns, 91–93
Moving data, 70–73
Moving fields, 72
Moving records, 73
Multiple fields, sorting in, 96–98
Multiple-table forms, 120
Multivalued fields, 63–64

N

Navigation, with keyboard, 68
Navigation Pane, 9–11
  in Design View, 50
  table changes with, 45
Number
  as changed data type, 51
  as data type, 37
  data type restrictions on, 51

O

Object windows, 21
Objects, 10, 192
  bound, 163
  closing, 18
  forms as, 10
  hiding, 190
  import of, 83–84
  macros as, 10
  modules as, 10
  pages as, 10
  queries as, 10
  removal of, 189–190
  reports as, 10
  security for, 191–193
  tables as, 10
  unbound, 163
Office Button, 5, 6
  renaming with, 47
Office Clipboard, 71
OLE object
  as data type, 37
  data type restrictions on, 51
One-to-many relationship, 44
Open
  of Access, 2–5
  of database, 6–9
  of tables, 33
Open dialog box, 6, 7

Operators, in filters, 102–104
Option Group Wizard, 134
Orientation, 175
Orphans, 43
Outermost, 96
Outlook, 13
  import from, 80, 85–88
Overlapping object windows,
  18–20
  arranging, 20–21

P

Page breaks, in reports, 158
Page numbers
  on forms, 127, 129
  in reports, 158
Paper, 175
Paradox, 6
  import from, 80
Passwords
  creation of, 188
  protection of, 185
Paste, into table, 84
PDF. *See* Portable Document Format
Performance analysis, of databases,
  209–212
Permissions, 192
Person name, as Smart Tag, 60
Personal ID (PID), 192
Personalization, 15–21
PID. *See* Personal ID
PivotChart, 206–208, 210
PivotTable, 204–206, 210
  drop zones in, 209
Placeholders, in input masks, 55
Portable Document Format
  (PDF), 216
Portrait, 175
Preview Chart, 168
Primary key

assignment of, 38–40
  characteristics of, 40
  problem with, 72
Print
  of data, 175–181
  in Help search, 23
Print icon, 175
Print Preview, 178–179
Project designers, 193
Property Sheet, 113, 140, 171
Property Update Options, 53
Publishing, 214

Q

Queries, 107–112
  closing, 111–112
  creation of, 108–111
  crosstab, 202–206
  in design area, 110
  filters as, 98
  lookup values in, 61
  modification of, 108–111
  as objects, 10
  properties of, 113–114
  relationships in, 109
  saving, 111–112
  stopping, 111
  totals in, 110
Query Design View, 109
Query Wizard, 107–108
Quick Access toolbar, 5, 6
  customization of, 15–18
  relocating, 17
  tools on, 15–16
Quick Launch, 4

R

Read-only users, 193
Rearranging controls, 138–139

Recent documents, 8
Records, 33
  copy of, 73
  deletion of, 73
  moving, 73
  multiple, 119–120
  preventing editing to, 190
  sort of, 96–98
Rectangles, 168–169
Referential integrity, 43–44
Refresh, in Help search, 23
Relational database, 41, 48
Relationships
  defining, 42
  identification of, 41–44
  many-to-many, 42
  one-to-many, 44
  in queries, 109
  tab for, 42–43
Renaming
  columns, 91–93
  of databases, 47
  with Office Button, 47
  of tables, 47–48
Repair, of databases, 198–199
Replace. *See* Find and replace
Replies, management of,
  88–89
Report(s), 143–160
  calculations in, 157
  data in, 153
  date/time in, 159
  formatting of, 151–152
  grouping levels in, 147–148
  modifying, 151–160
  as objects, 10
  properties of, 170–171
  sections of, 150
  summary values in, 147
Report tool, 145
Report Wizard, 145–148

Required data entry, 57–58
Resizing Access window, 8
Retrieving information, 95–114
Ribbon, 4, 5–6
  mouse and, 48
Rich text formatting, 173–174
Rows, height of, 94

S

Save As, with conversion, 13
Saving queries, 111–112
Search
  in Help, 22
  using identifying information, 41
Sections, in reports, 150
Security, 5, 183–200
  with conversion, 14
  for user classes, 192
Security report, 195–196
Selecting controls, 137–138
Selection
  of controls, 137–138
  filter by, 99–101
  with mouse, 72–73
SharePoint, 13, 212
  import from, 80
Sharing data, 212–213
Shortcuts, 7
  display and use of, 18
  for editing data, 69
  icons for, 19
  insertion with, 69
  to open database, 9
  opening with, 3
  in tables, 68–70
Show/Hide Table of Contents,
  in Help search, 23
Shutter bar, 10
Simple Query Wizard, 107–108
Smart Tags, 59–60

Sort
  ascending, 97
  in columns, 66
  crosstab queries, 204–206
  of data, 95–98
  descending, 97
  in group levels, 156
  with lookup values, 62
  in multiple fields, 96–98
  of records, 96–98
  in tables, 96–97
Spelling, verification of,
  76–77
Split Form tool, 116–119, 121
Splitter Bar, 119
Spreadsheets. *See also* Excel;
  Lotus 1-2-3
  import from, 82–83
  tables and, 34
SQL databases, 58
Stacked control layout, 139
Start Menu, 3
Status bar, 8
  to switch views, 49
  switching views with, 36
Stop, in Help search, 23
Summary reports, 158
Summary values, 147
Super tooltips, 21
Switchboard Manager,
  217–220

T

Tab
  contextual, 8
  for documents, 8, 18–20
  for relationships, 42–43
Table(s)
  arranging, 89–94
  closing of, 34

creation of, 25–44
data in, 67–88
Datasheet View and, 66
deletion of, 46–47
in design area, 110
empty, 35
field names in, 34
framework of, 33–41
hyperlinks to, 216–217
import of, 83–84
junction, 42
linking, 215–216
lookup values in, 61
modifying, 45–64
naming of, 32
as objects, 10
opening of, 33
pasting into, 84
renaming of, 47–48
shortcuts in, 68–70
sorting in, 96–97
spreadsheets and, 34
structure of, 27
from templates, 38
working in, 65–94
Table Analyzer Wizard, 211–212
Table of Contents pane, 22
Tabular control layout, 139
Tabular style, 125
Telephone number, as Smart
  Tag, 59
Templates
  customization of, 31
  for databases, 26–31
  defaults with, 29
  downloading, 29–31
  Getting Started page and, 28
  tables from, 38
Text
  as default, 36, 38
  find and replace, 74–75

Text files, import from, 80–82
Tile Horizontally, 21
Tile Vertically, 21
Title
  on forms, 127–128
  in reports, 148, 158
Title bar, 10
Tools
  adding, 17
  in Help, 23
  hiding, 17
  on Quick Access toolbar,
    15–16
  rearranging, 18
  removing, 17
Top values, 114
Totals, in queries, 110
Trusted locations, 184–185

U

Unbound controls, 130,
  134–136
Unbound objects, 163
Undo, with table deletion, 47
Unfreeze All Columns, 93
Unhide. *See* Hide
Uniform Resource Locator
  (URL), 216
Unlocking columns, 93
Update data users, 193
Uppercase letters, 52–53
URL. *See* Uniform Resource
  Locator
User-Level Security Wizard,
  190–196
Users, 192
  adding, 194–195
  editing, 194–195
  in group accounts, 195–196
  removing, 194–195

V

Validation rules, 56–57
  for security, 191
Validation text, 57
Values
  bottom, 114
  top, 114
Views toolbar, 8
Visual Basic, 10

W

Web pages
  hyperlinks to, 217
  import from, 80
  publishing to, 214
Welcome form, 217–220
WIF. *See* Workgroup information file
Wildcards, in filter, 102–104
Windows Explorer, 6, 7, 9
Windows flag key, 18

Windows themes, 141, 173
Word, 213
Workgroup information file
  (WIF), 191

X

XML files, import from, 80
XML Paper Specification (XPS), 216
XPS. *See* XML Paper Specification

Y

Yes/No
  as changed data type, 51
  as control, 134
  as data type, 37

Z

Zero-length string, 57–58
Zoom, 179